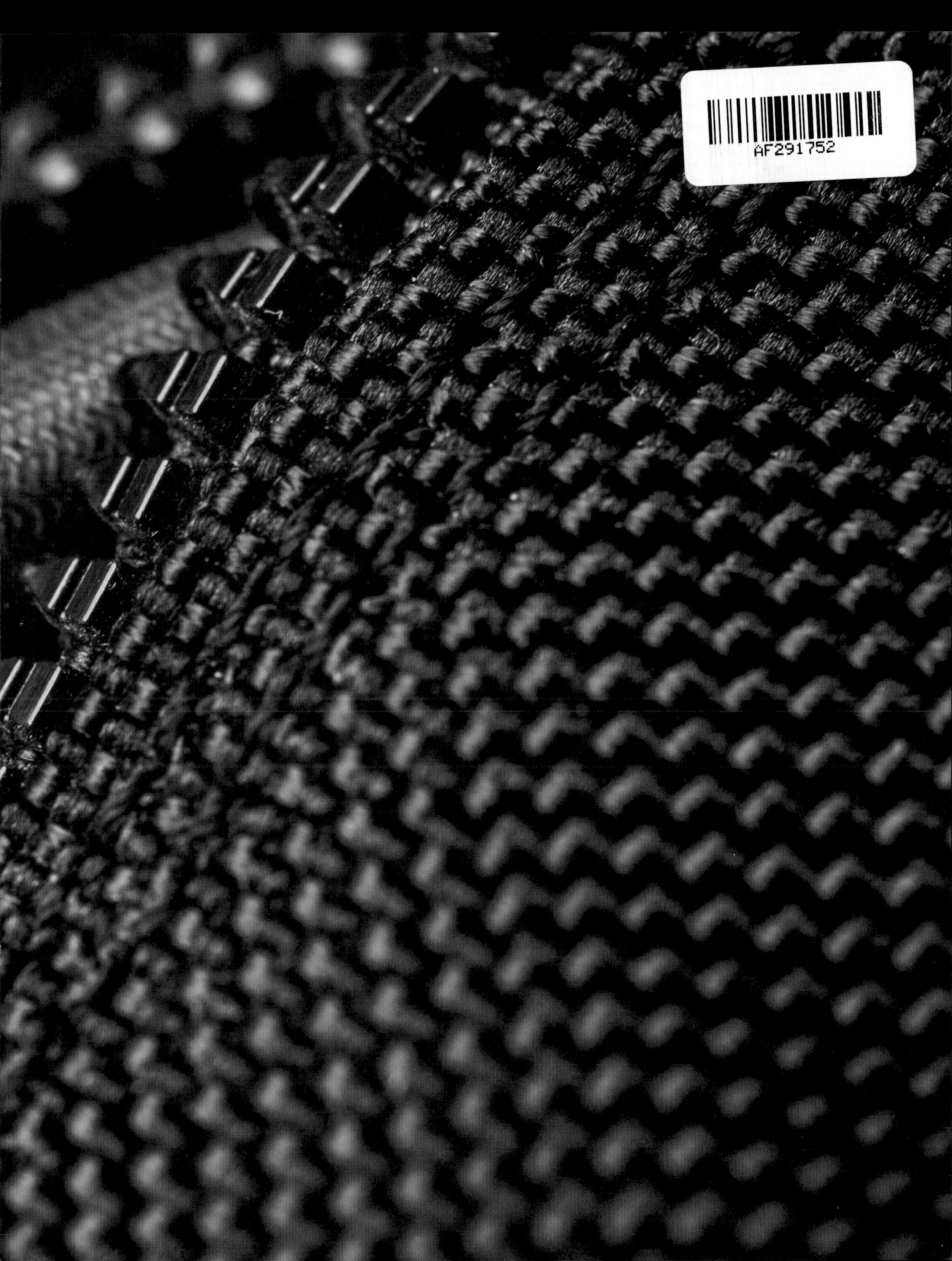
AF291752

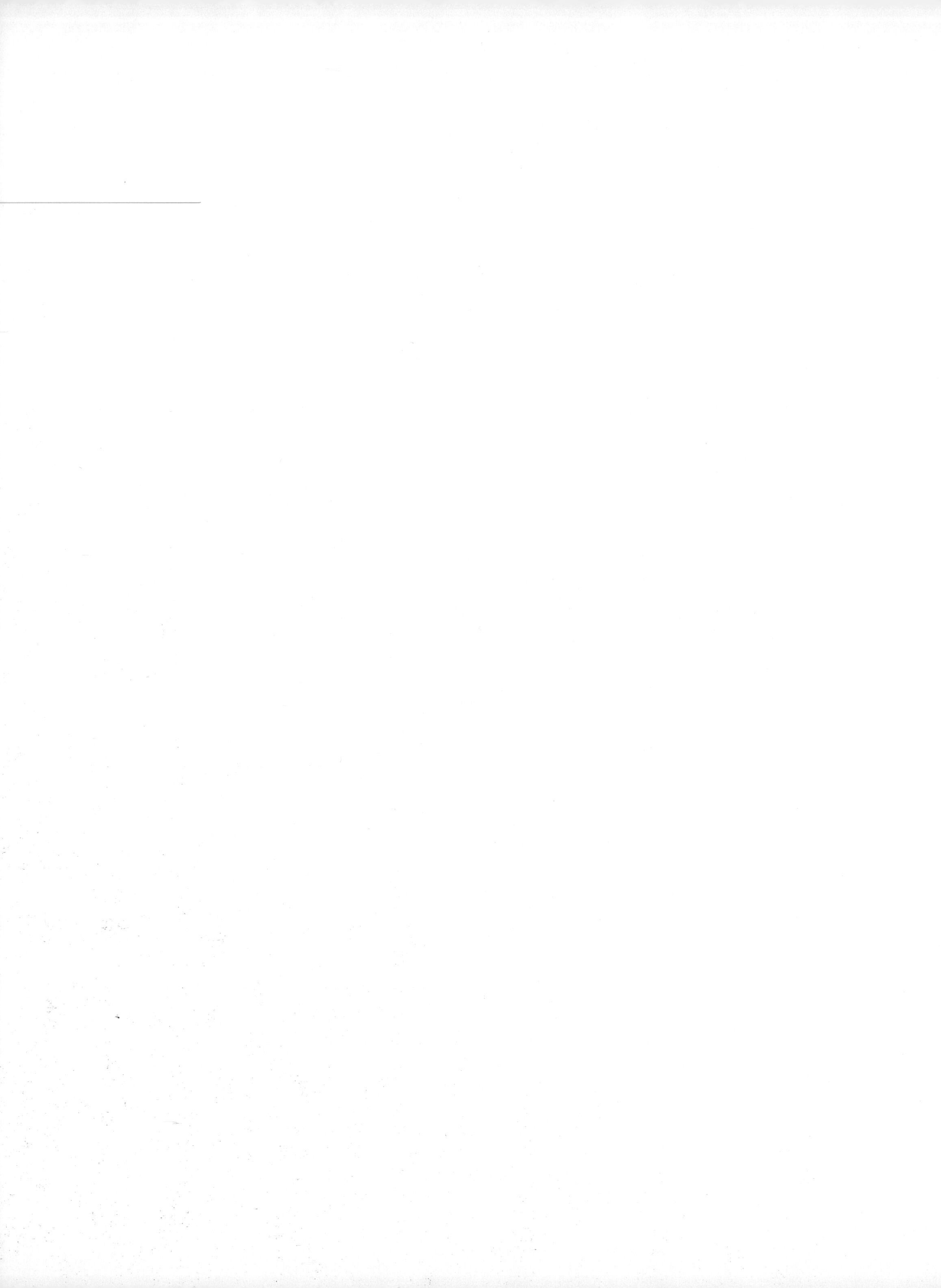

THE FASHION ICONS

NIKE

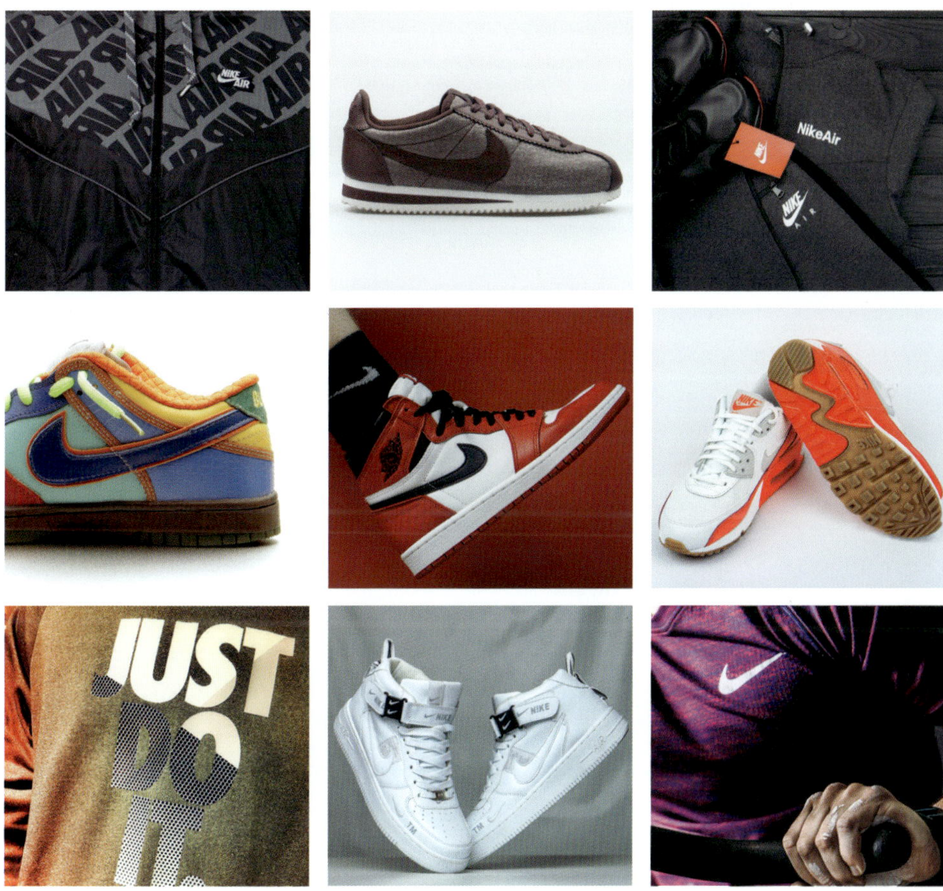

Emilie Murray

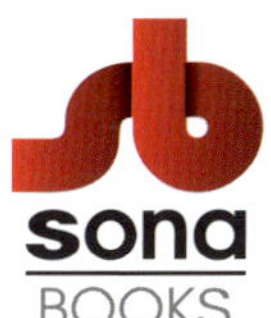

sona BOOKS

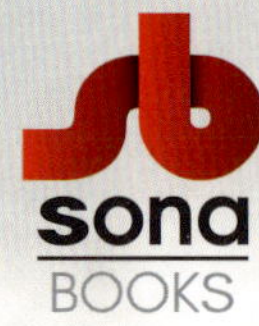

© Danann Media Publishing Limited 2025

First published in the UK 2025 by Sona Books an imprint of Danann Media Publishing Ltd.

WARNING: For private domestic use only, any unauthorised copying, hiring,
lending or public performance of this book is illegal.

CAT NO: SON0633

Photography courtesy of

Getty images:

Najlah Feanny	The Asahi Shimbun	Bloomberg	Michael Ochs Archives	Jemal Countess
Sopa Images	Popperfoto	Maja Hitij	Phil Sheldon	Fireshot
Patrick Smith	Ed Lacey	Keystone / Stringer	Cindy Ord	
J.D. Cuban	Adek Berry	Richard Baker	Robert Stiggins	
Vladimir Zakharov	Bettmann	Fairfax Media Archives	Icon Sportswire	

Alamy images:

xMarshall	Stockimo	Jessica Girvan	imageBROKER.com /	PA Images
Anastasiia Yanishevska	Donka Zheleva	Stephen Chung	GmbH & Co. KG	xMarshall
Mykhailo Polenok	BFA / Amazon Studios	Associated Press	Mark Peterson	Bincidaphoto
Wirestock, Inc.	Retro AdArchives	Science History Images	WoodysPhotos	Heorshe
JBsports	UPI	PCN Photography	Retro AdArchives	Postmodern Studio
Steve Hellerstein	Wirestock, Inc.	Old-Time Images	adsR	
Patti McConville /	Newscom	Hera Vintage Ads	Adam Stoltman	

Other images Wiki Commons

Book cover design Darren Grice at Ctrl-d
Layout design Alex Young at Cre81ve
Proof reader Juliette O'Neill
Editor Sofia Della Valle

All rights reserved. No Part of this title may be reproduced or transmitted in any material
form (including photocopying or storing it in any medium by electronic means and
whether or not transiently or incidentally to some other use of this publication) without
the written permission of the copyright owner, except in accordance with the provisions of
the Copyright, Designs and Patents Act 1988.Applications for the copyright owner's written
permission should be addressed to the publisher.

This is an independent publication and it is unofficial and unauthorised and as such has no
connection with Nike or any other organisation connected in any way whatsoever with Nike
featured in the book.

Made in EU.
ISBN: 978-1-917259-11-8

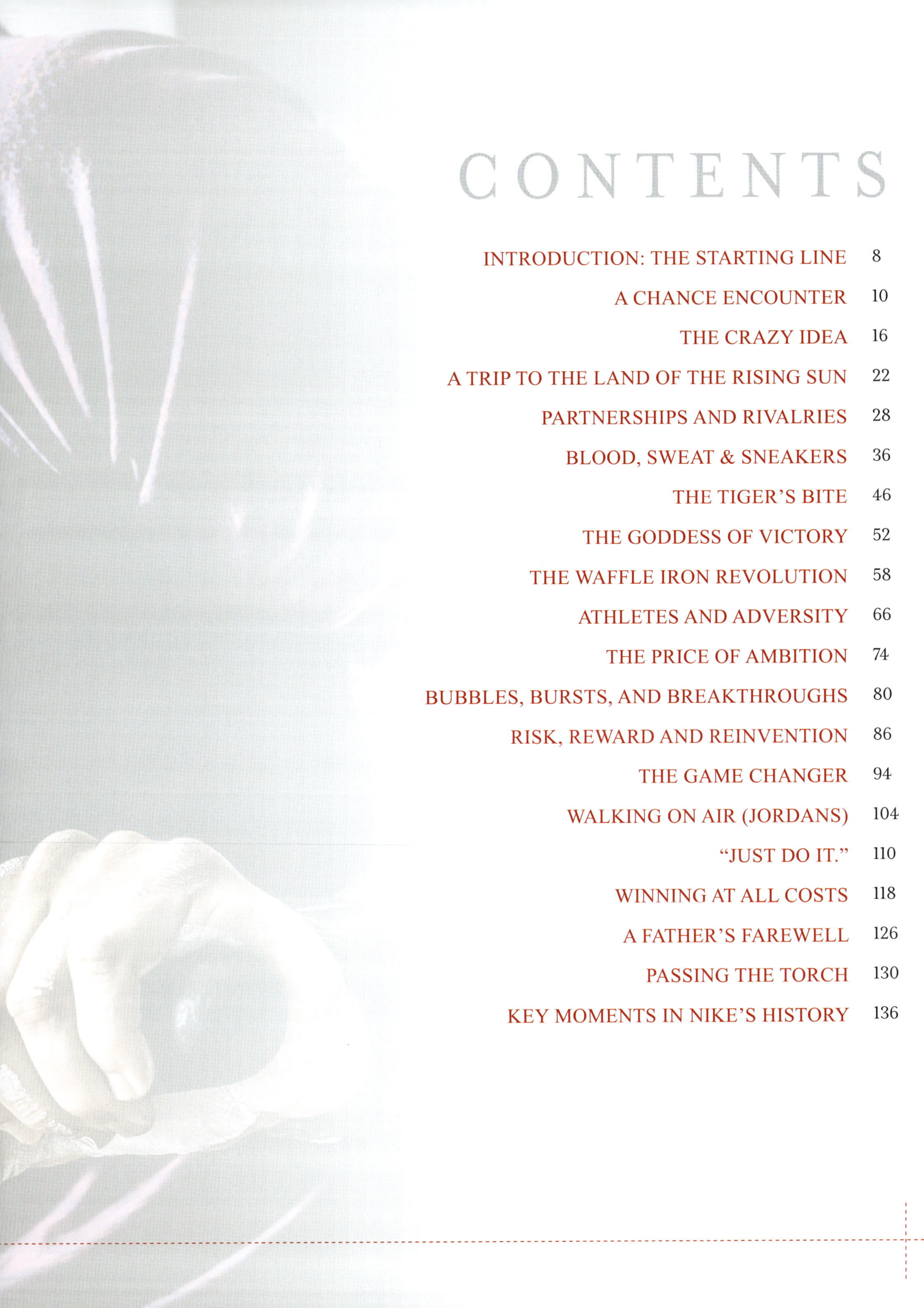

CONTENTS

INTRODUCTION:
THE STARTING LINE

Last year Nike celebrated its 50th anniversary. This impressive milestone marks the perfect opportunity to revisit the extraordinary, sometimes rocky and always thrilling journey of a company that started as a grassroots operation run from the trunk of an old Plymouth Valiant. A company that quickly grew into one of the most successful, recognisable, and influential brands on the planet.

At the heart of this remarkable transformation stood Phil Knight, a self-described shy kid from Oregon, who dared to challenge the norms of athletic performance with his unrelenting vision, boundless ambition and commitment to bold innovation. His "crazy idea" was initially dismissed as outlandish, but the budding entrepreneur saw merit in his idea even when nobody else did. It was that precise self-assuredness that allowed Phil to forge a global empire out of a few pairs of imported running shoes and turn his scrappy company into multi-billion-dollar enterprise in its first half century.

Nike has always been a proponent of fresh ideas—lightweight, breathable materials and boundary-breaking designs are what got the company started. But what took Nike from a modest start-up into a household name was the brand's ability to adapt to the rapidly changing world around them. In the mid-80s, when Phil and his team realised that their sales were starting to plateau and that creating a superior product was not the be-all and end-all of market dominance, they quickly understood that the most important thing was to market their products. More than anything, it was their revolutionary marketing campaigns, linking everyday runners and budding professionals to a community of dreamers, that elevated the status of the brand to that of a global icon. Additionally, Nike dared to speak the language of change. As the decades passed, the company used its platform to spark dialogues about social justice, athletic empowerment, gender equality, and body positivity. By embracing the "unpopular ideas", Nike cemented itself as a trend setter rather than follower.

In its first half-century, Phil's company had become the most valuable apparel brand in the world—worth more than twice as much as Adidas, its closest sportswear rival, and ahead of heritage brands like Louis Vuitton, Gucci, and Chanel—but, more importantly, Nike has become part of the movies we watch, the songs we hear, the museums we frequent, the business we do. It has become part of how we think about who we are and how we got here. Nike is "an emblem of individuality, in an age where individuality has become rampant".

This is the story of how one man, one idea, and one Swoosh changed the world—one step, one leap, and one revolution at a time.

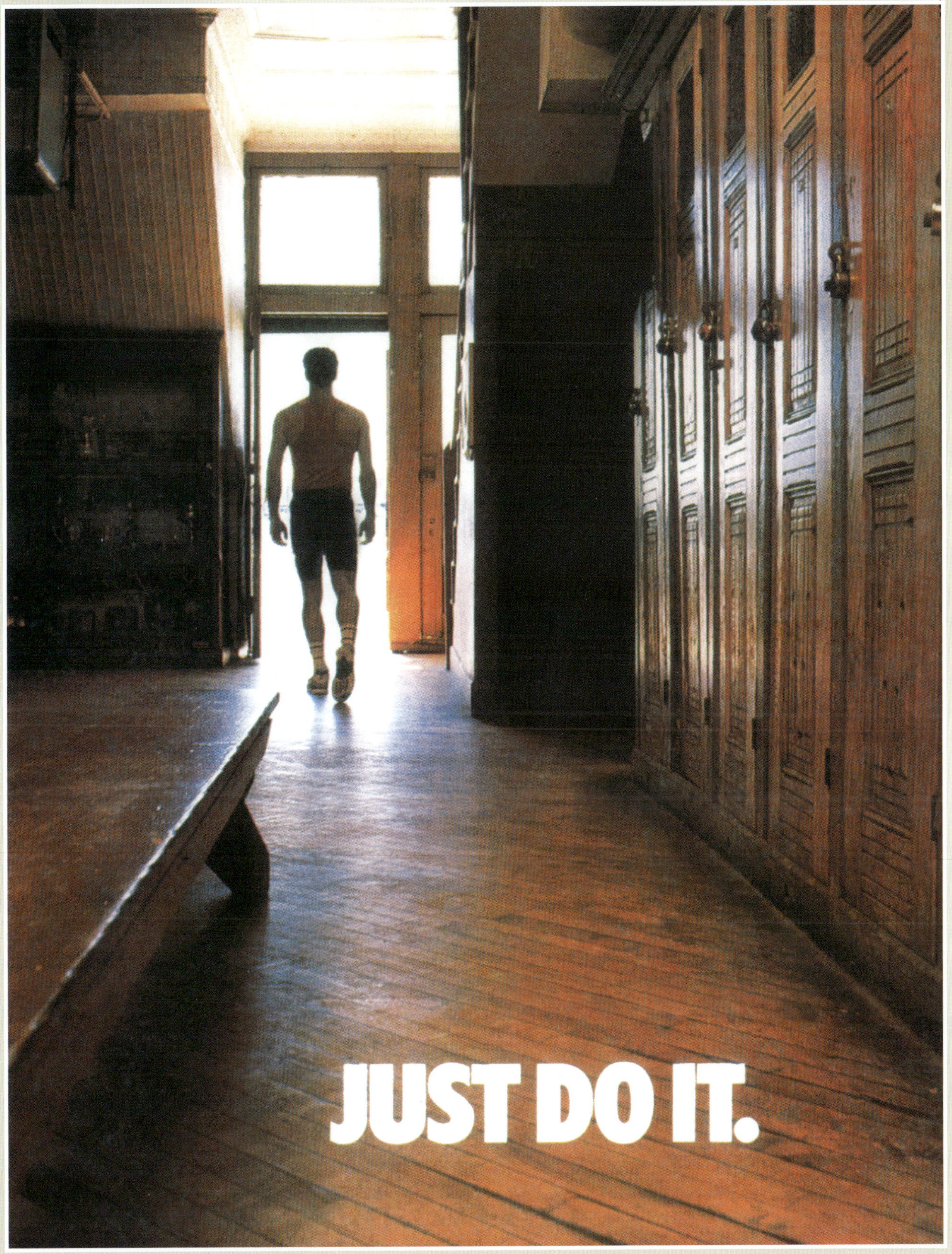

ABOVE: 1985 Nike magazine advert

A CHANCE ENCOUNTER

1938 - 1962

"If there was no Bill Bowerman, there would have been no me. He had about as much of an impact on my life as any one person could have. He taught me about competition and ingrained it in me. He taught me not to praise ordinary performances."

Phil Knight

Philip Hampson Knight, better known to the world as Phil Knight, was born on February 24, 1938, in Portland, Oregon to William "Bill" Knight, a lawyer turned newspaper publisher, and his wife, Lota Cloy Knight, née Hatfield.

Phil grew up in a residential neighbourhood in Southeast Portland called Eastmoreland, in a comfortable but disciplined household.

His father was a prominent figure in Portland as the publisher of The Oregon Journal, one of the city's leading newspapers. Bill was known for his hard-nosed, no-nonsense approach to life and business, a quality that left a lasting impression on his son. He believed in the value of hard work and personal

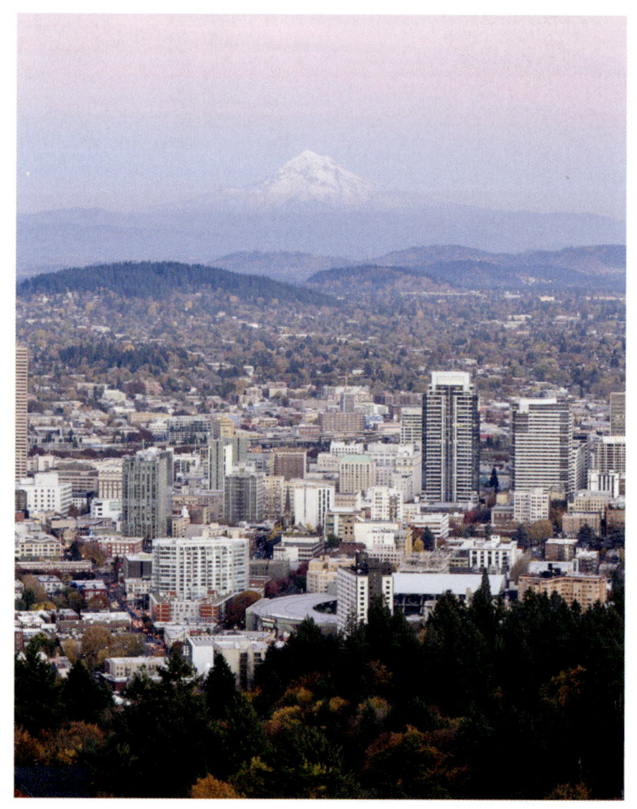

RIGHT: Portland, Oregon skyline
OPP PAGE: Phil Knight in 1995

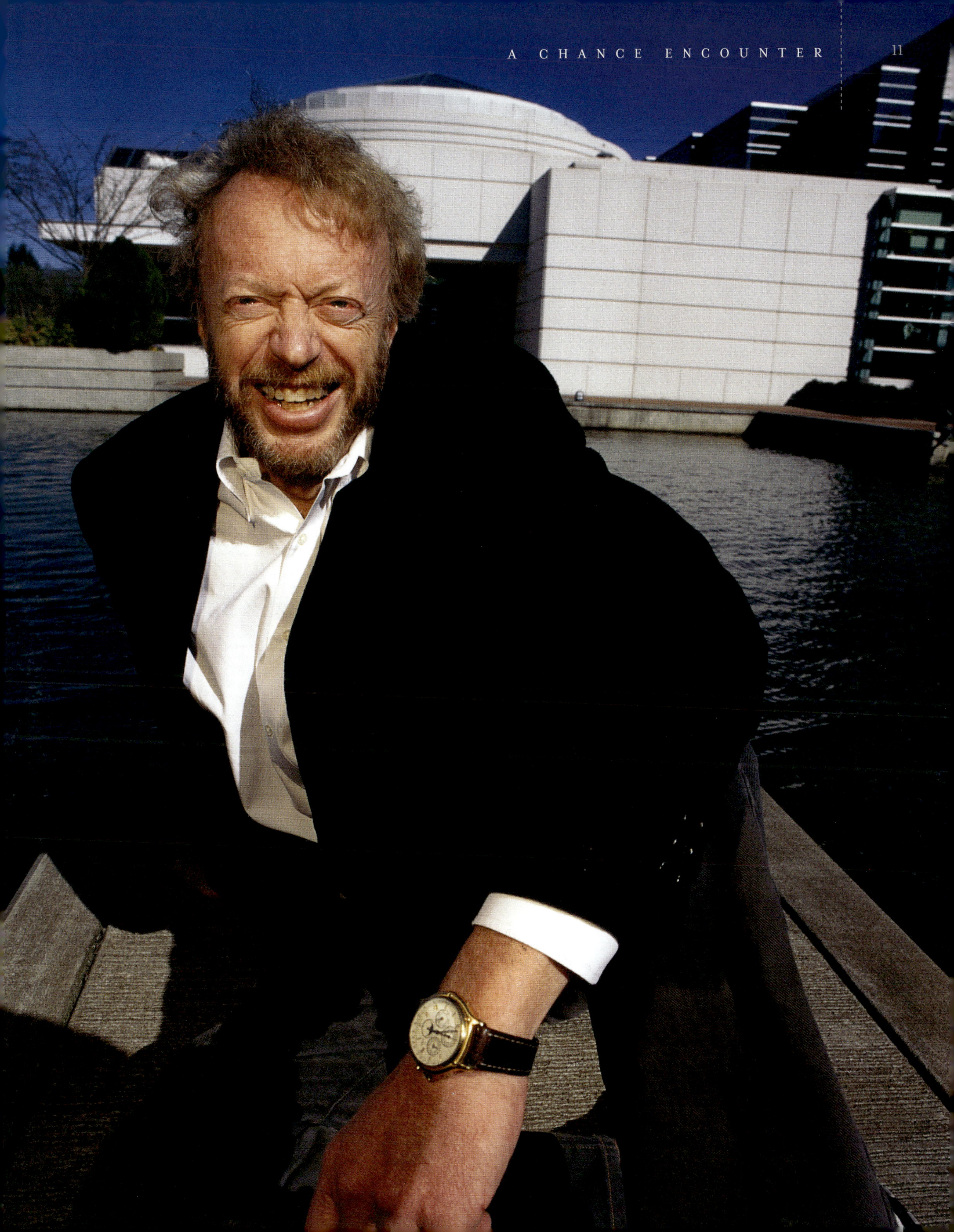

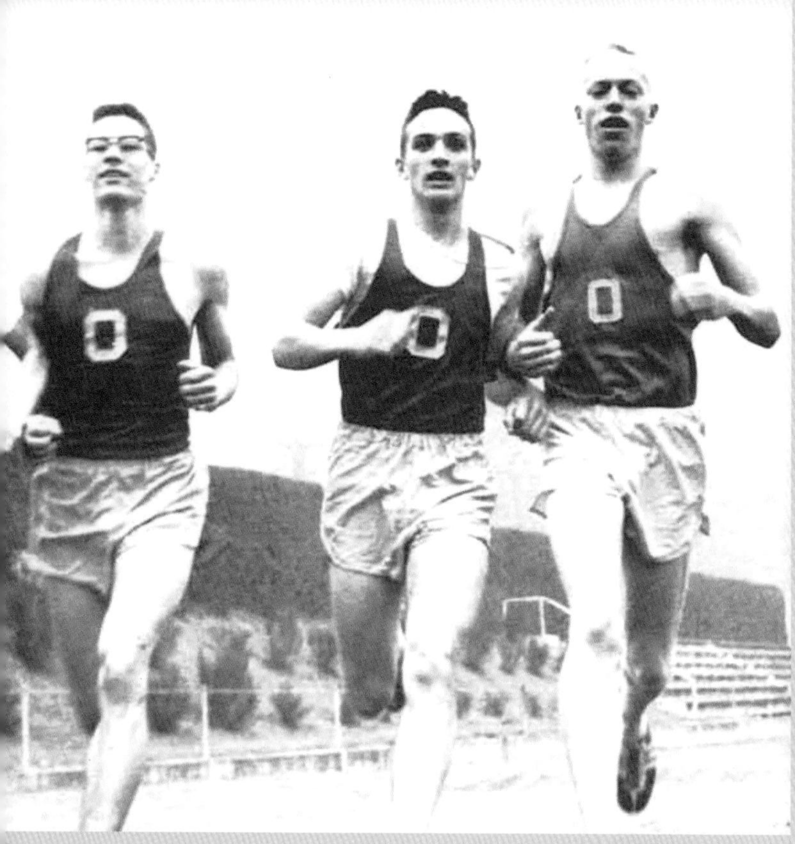

responsibility, frequently preaching that nothing in life should be handed to anyone on a silver platter, not even to his own son. In high school, when Phil asked for a job at The Oregon Journal, Bill straight up refused to hire him. He wanted his son to make his own way, find his own identity, and earn his success without any advantages that could be attributed to family connections. After his father denied to offer him a job at the paper, Knight sought work elsewhere and even managed to get hired as a sports scores tabulator for the rival newspaper *Oregonian*.

Phil's childhood was shaped by his father's high expectations, but it wasn't always an easy relationship. He later recalled their strained bond stating, "My father, though good and kind, suffered some deep and inexplicable shame because he was the son of a butcher. His affect, therefore, was an elaborate overcompensation, a stylized emulation of *respectability*, which precluded any "vulgar" displays of emotion. In all my life I can't recall him once paying me a direct compliment. Nor did he ever bestow his unconditional approval. So I looked elsewhere".

From an early age, Phil showed a rebellious streak and a desire to forge his own path. He took an avid interest in sports but due to his relatively small size, was unable to compete in any contact sports in high school and instead became a runner. Phil ran for Cleveland High School's track team, but his performance was modest at best. Despite his lack of standout athletic talent, his passion for the sport was clear. Running would eventually become a defining feature of his identity, both personally and professionally, but in his youth, it served primarily as a metaphor for his life—a constant, steady pursuit of self-improvement.

Knight continued his education at the University of Oregon in Eugene, where he studied business and worked as a sports reporter for the Oregon Daily Emerald. His interest in running continued during his undergraduate years as he became a middle-distance runner for the university's track team. Here, Phil became part of a world-class track program, but more importantly, he would make the acquaintance of someone that would profoundly change the course of his life: the legendary coach Bill Bowerman.

ABOVE: Knight (right) running track at the University of Oregon in 1958

OPP PAGE: Bill Bowerman (left), Dyrol Burleson (center), and George Larson (right) discuss Burleson's new U.S. record for the mile run, 25 May, 1961

BILL BOWERMAN

Bill Bowerman was born on February 19, 1911, in Portland, Oregon, to Jay Bowerman, a former governor of Oregon, and Elizabeth Hoover Bowerman. Following the divorce of his parents in 1913, Bill moved to the rural town of Fossil, Oregon, where he was raised by his mother and maternal grandparents.

Bowerman attended Medford High School, where his interest in athletics began to take shape. He participated in multiple sports, including football and track. After high school, Bill enrolled at the University of Oregon in 1929, where he initially went to study journalism and play football, earning a reputation for his toughness and determination. However, it was track and field that would ultimately capture his interest, despite not initially competing in the sport.

After graduating in 1934, Bill moved to Portland to teach biology and coach football at Franklin High School, before returning to Medford the following year. There, he married Barbara Young in 1936 and welcomed three boys. Bowerman had been an Army Reserve and following the attacks on Pearl Harbor in 1941, he spent a few years in the 86th Mountain Infantry Regiment.

After his stint in the military, Bill moved his family to Eugene, where he became head track and field coach

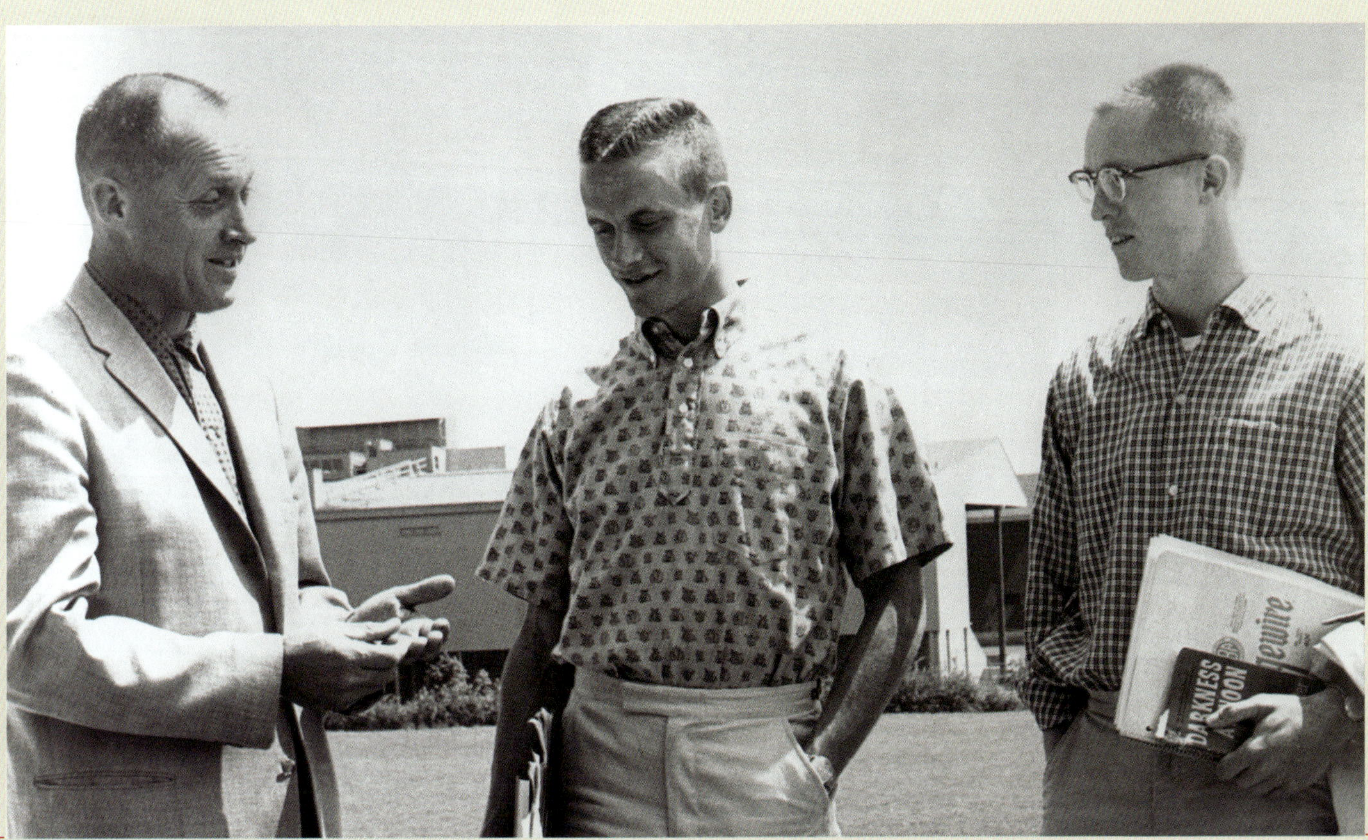

at his Alma Mater, a position he would hold for the next 24 years. During his tenure, Bowerman transformed Oregon into a powerhouse of collegiate athletics. His teams won four National Collegiate Athletic Association (NCAA) track and field championships (1962, 1964, 1965, and 1970) and produced 33 Olympians. Under his leadership, the University of Oregon's track program became one of the most respected in the country.

Bill's coaching philosophy was grounded in discipline, precision, and an emphasis on scientific training methods. He believed in adapting training regimens to each athlete's unique physiology, tailoring workouts to prevent injuries and optimize performance. This individualized approach to coaching was groundbreaking at the time, when many coaches employed a one-size-fits-all strategy.

His contributions to the world of sports came through his relentless pursuit of athletic innovation, particularly in the realm of footwear. Bowerman was constantly tinkering with ways to improve the performance of his athletes, and he became obsessed with the idea of designing a lighter, more functional running shoe. Bill's experiments with shoes began in the 1950s. He would often take apart existing shoes, strip them down, and reconstruct them with different materials to reduce weight without sacrificing support. His persistent tinkering would eventually pay off when he met Phil Knight, and the pair would go on to shape the future of the sports footwear industry.

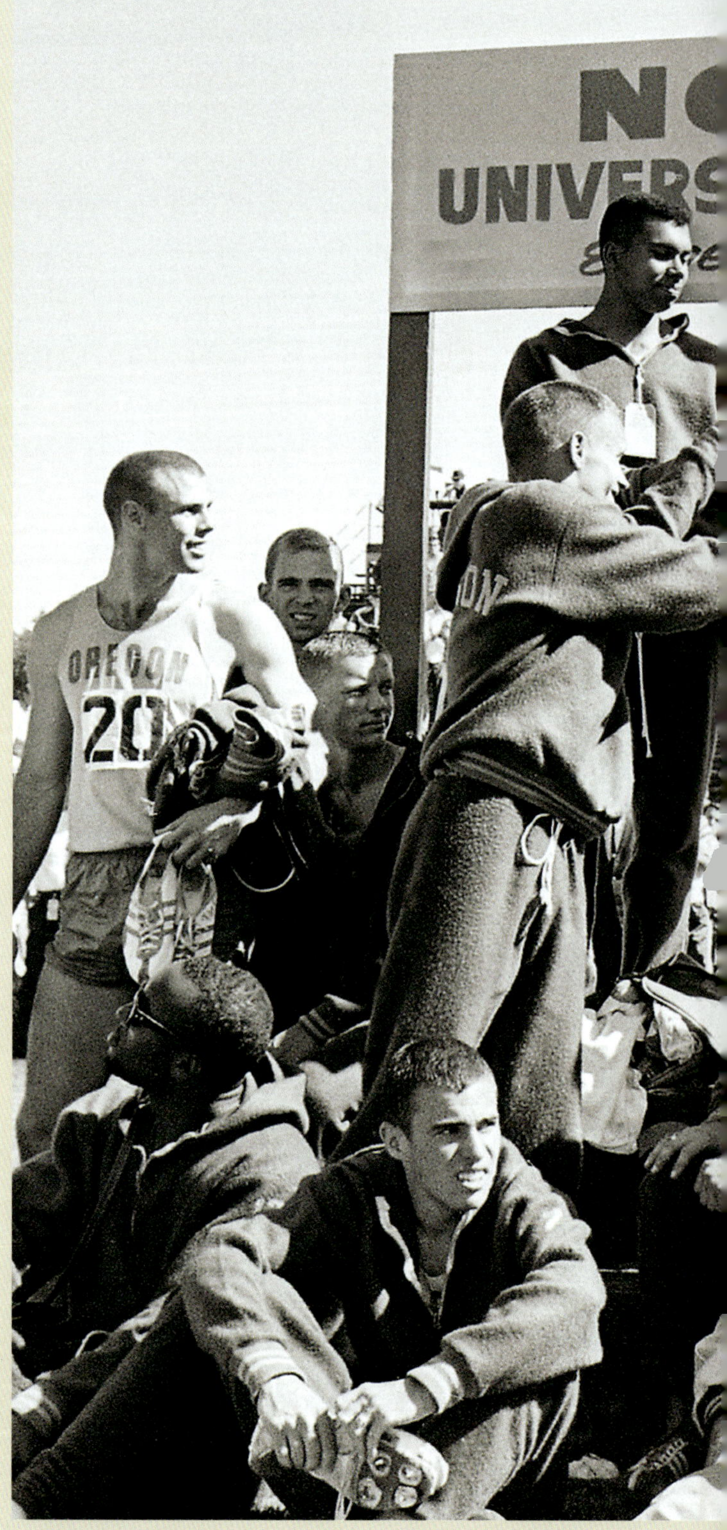

RIGHT: Oregon University coach Bill Bowerman, with hat, and his team after their NCAA team championship win on June 16, 1962
OPP PAGE: Coach Bill Bowerman gives last minute advice to Phil Knight, Mark Robbins, and Steve Schell

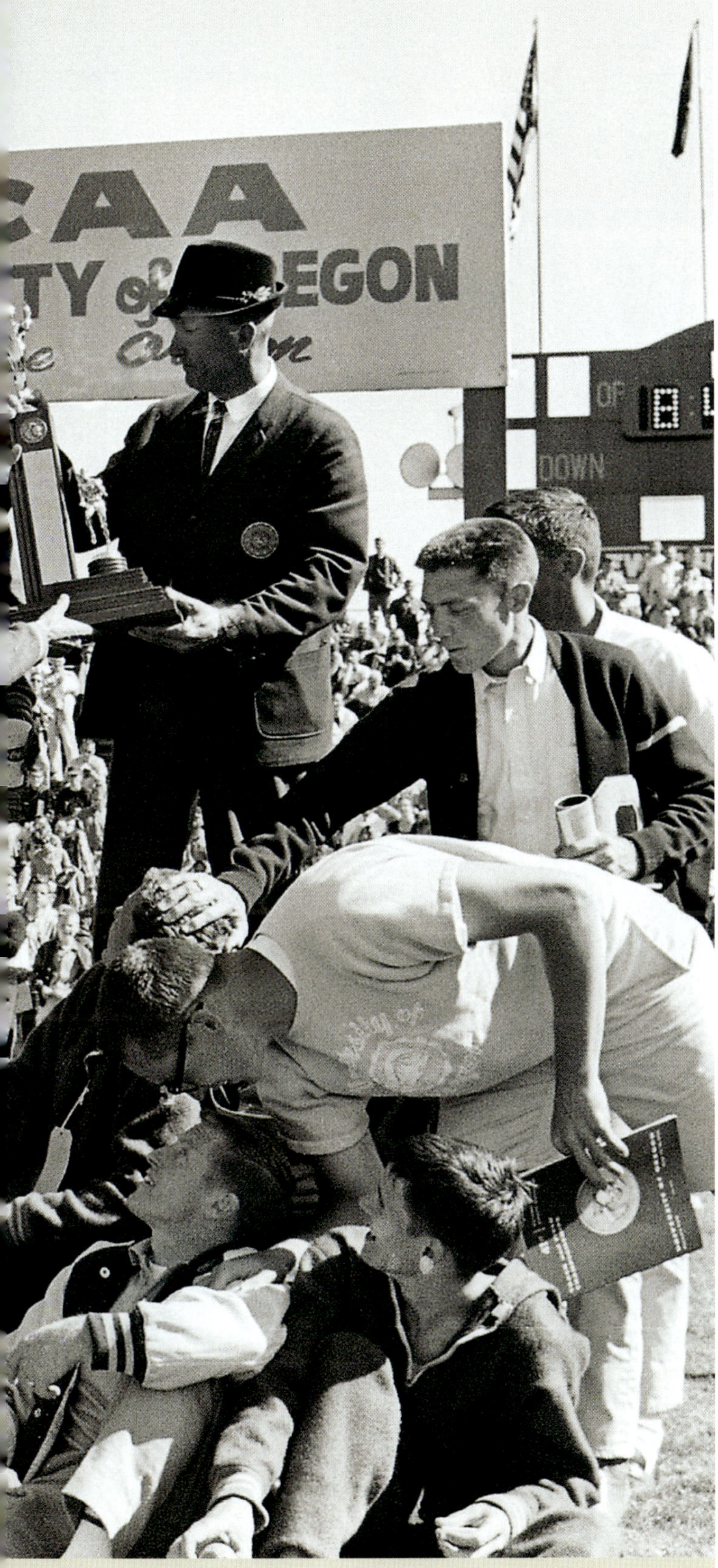

Bill Bowerman wasn't simply a track coach or a business partner, he was also a father figure and guiding source for Knight.

"Of course, I couldn't have told you any of this in August 1955, when I arrived at the University of Oregon", Phil later commented on his relationship with Bowerman, "I couldn't have explained that I was operating at a severe father deficit, that I urgently needed supplemental support and guidance from an older man I respected, even (ideally) revered. I had no such self-awareness".

In 1959 Phil graduated from the University of Oregon with a business degree. He immediately enlisted in the Army and served one year on active duty. Following his stint in the military, Knight decided to further his education and enrolled at Stanford Graduate School of Business.

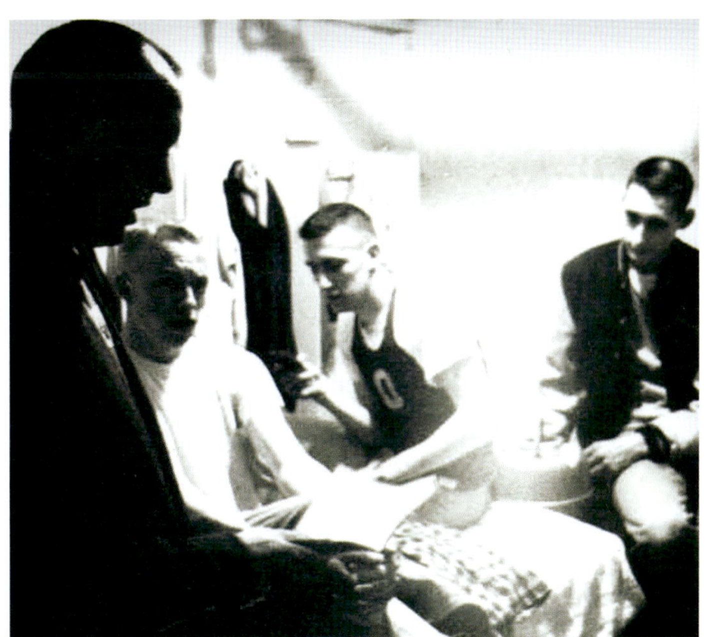

THE CRAZY IDEA
1962

"History is one long processional of crazy ideas. The things I loved most—books, sports, democracy, free enterprise—started as crazy ideas... Let everyone else call your idea crazy... just keep going. Don't stop. Don't even think about stopping until you get there, and don't give much thought to where "there" is. Whatever comes, just don't stop."

Phil Knight

Phil Knight's journey towards creating Nike began with a pivotal moment during his time at Stanford University. While pursuing his MBA in the early 1960s, Phil produced a paper for a small-business class, "Can Japanese Sports Shoes Do to German Sports Shoes What Japanese Cameras Did to German Cameras?", that essentially laid out the foundation for his entrepreneurial vision. In the essay, Knight proposed a bold idea: importing high-quality, low-cost athletic shoes from Japan to compete with the dominant German brands, like Adidas and Puma, that were monopolizing the American sports shoe market. He was inspired by Japan's impressive post-war manufacturing process and believed that Japanese companies could produce shoes that were not only more affordable but also technologically superior.

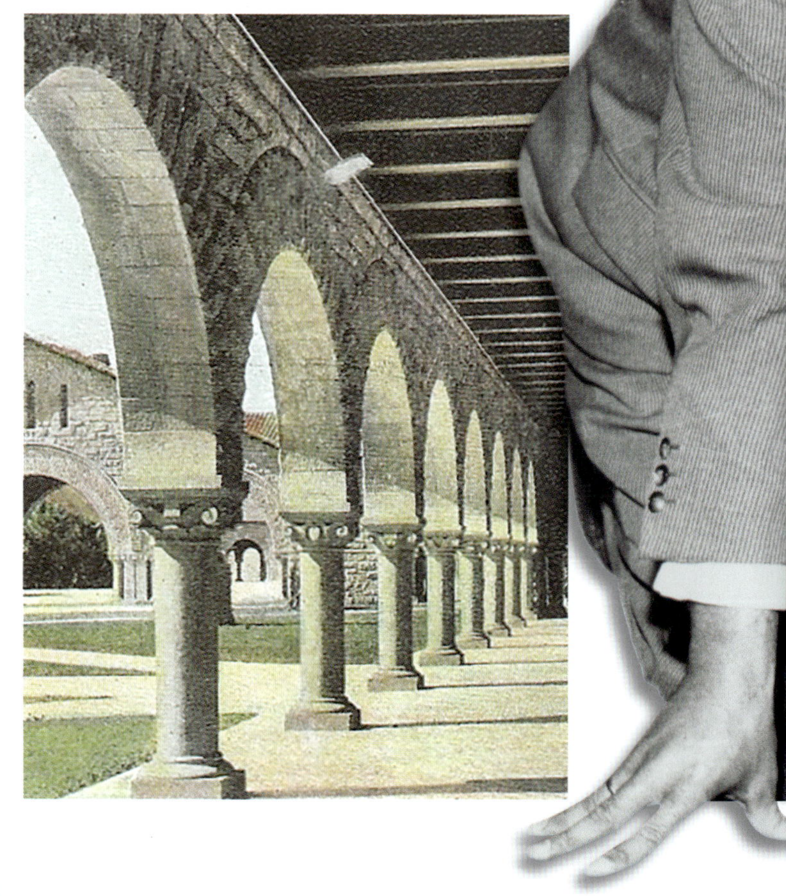

RIGHT: Arcade at Stanford University
OPP PAGE: German sprinters Heinz Futterer (left) and Armin Hary do publicity work for Puma, 17th April 1962

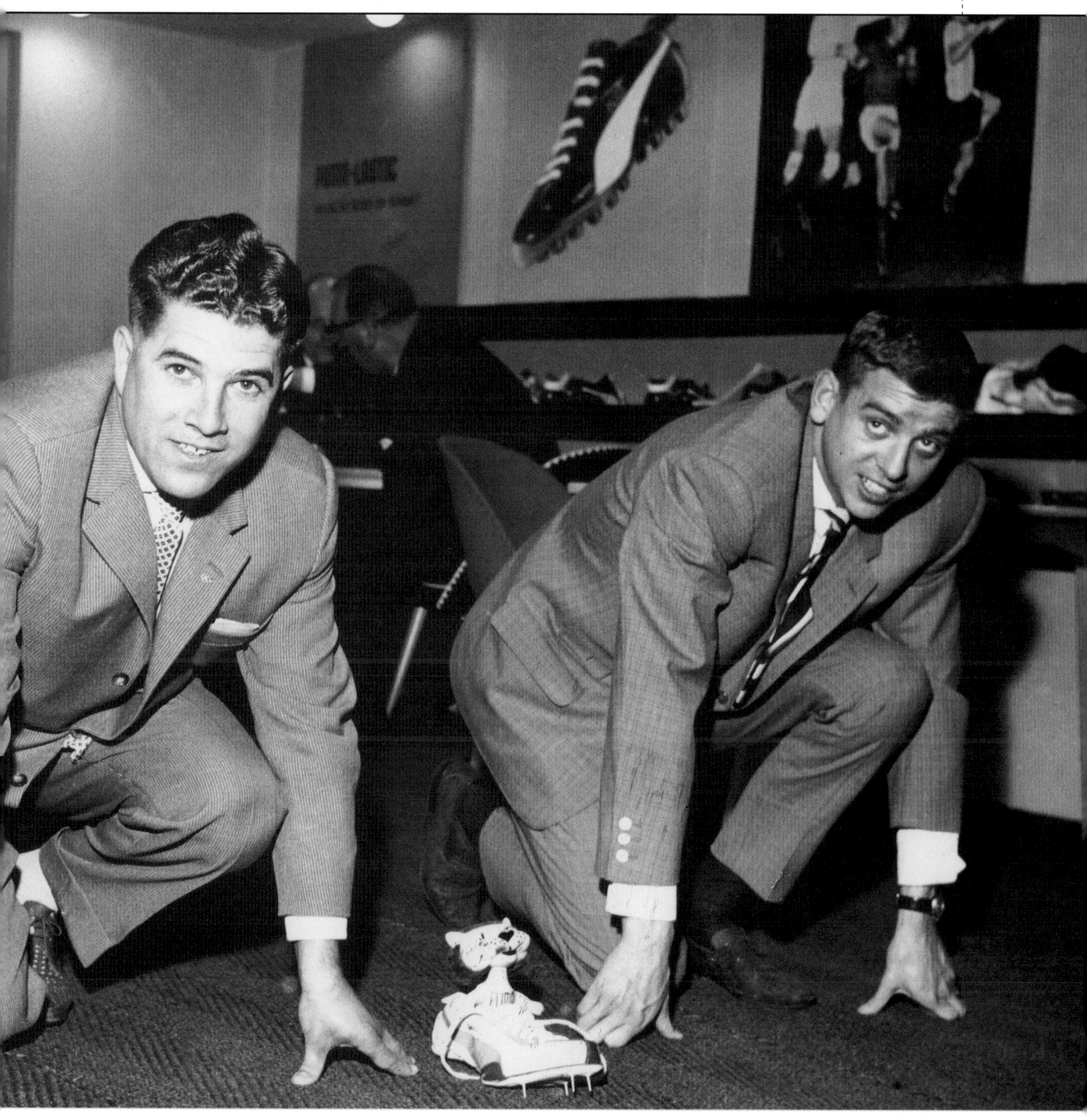

"CAN JAPANESE SPORTS SHOES DO TO GERMAN SPORTS SHOES WHAT JAPANESE CAMERAS DID TO GERMAN CAMERAS?"

After World War II, Japanese manufacturers quickly gained a reputation for their exceptional craftsmanship and innovation, qualities that would help transform the country's economy and global standing. In the aftermath of the war, Japan's infrastructure was devastated, but this challenge became an opportunity for renewal.

Initially, Japanese manufacturers focused on producing low-cost goods, but they soon distinguished themselves through superior quality, efficiency, and precision.

One key factor in their success was the adoption of new manufacturing principles, notably influenced by figures like W. Edwards Deming, an American statistician who introduced methods of quality control. Japanese manufacturers soon became masters of lean production, eliminating waste and streamlining processes to enhance both quality and cost-effectiveness. This allowed them to produce

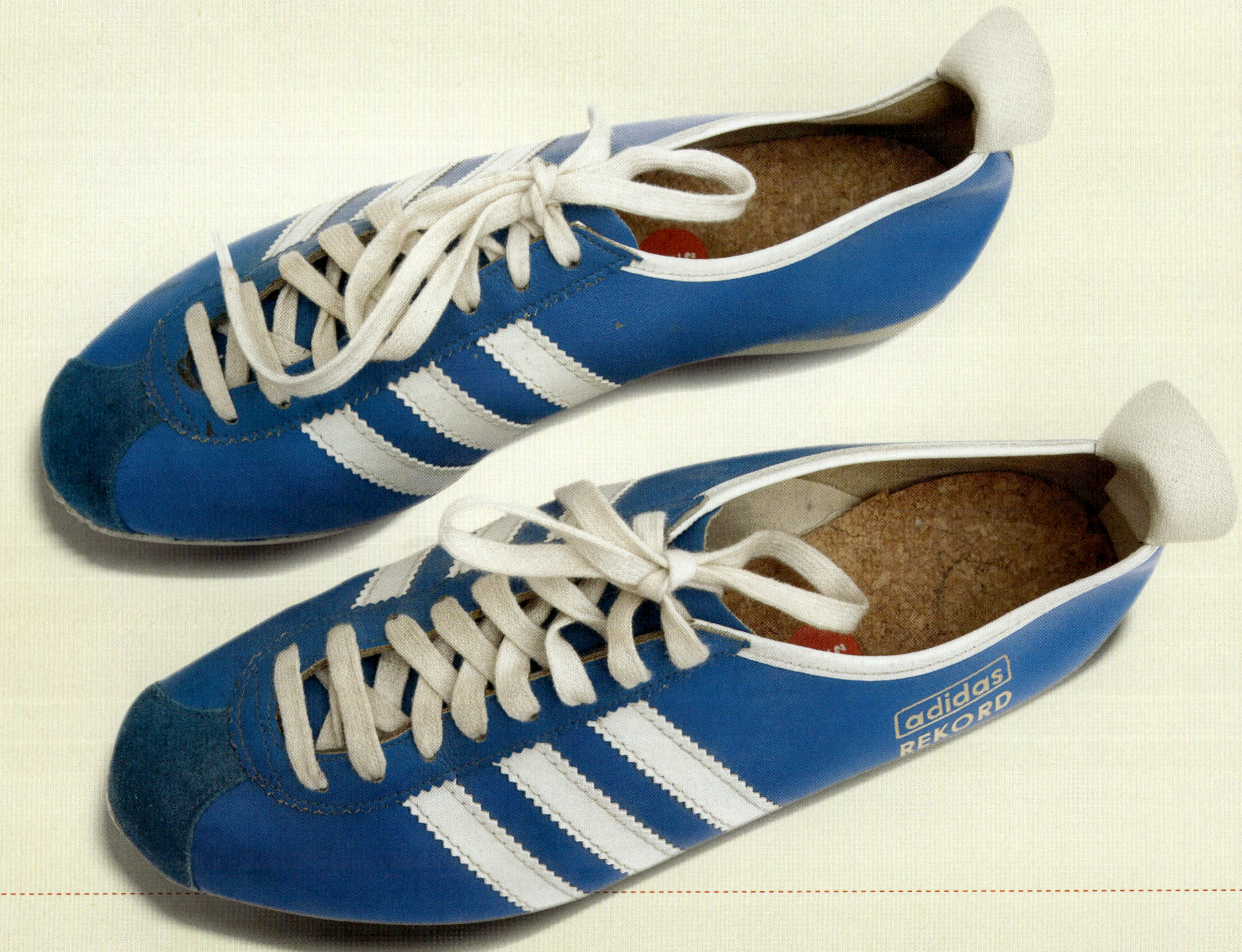

high-quality goods at a fraction of the price of their Western counterparts, which gave them a competitive edge in industries like electronics, automobiles, and textiles.

Before World War II, German companies like Leica, Zeiss, and Rolleiflex had long been known for their impeccable craftsmanship and optical excellence, producing high-end cameras that were used by professionals and serious amateurs alike. However, during the post-war period, Japanese camera makers began to challenge this dominance. Companies like Canon, Nikon, and later Minolta and Olympus began producing cameras that not only matched the quality of German models but also introduced new features and designs that made them more accessible to a broader audience. Japanese manufacturers focused on developing 35mm cameras that were more compact, easier to use, and, crucially, more affordable without sacrificing image quality. The global photography market began to shift as Japanese cameras offered more cutting-edge technology at competitive prices, while German cameras, though still superior in craftsmanship, were increasingly seen as expensive and less practical for everyday users. This reputation for quality at affordable prices also extended into sportswear with companies like Onitsuka Tiger (now ASICS).

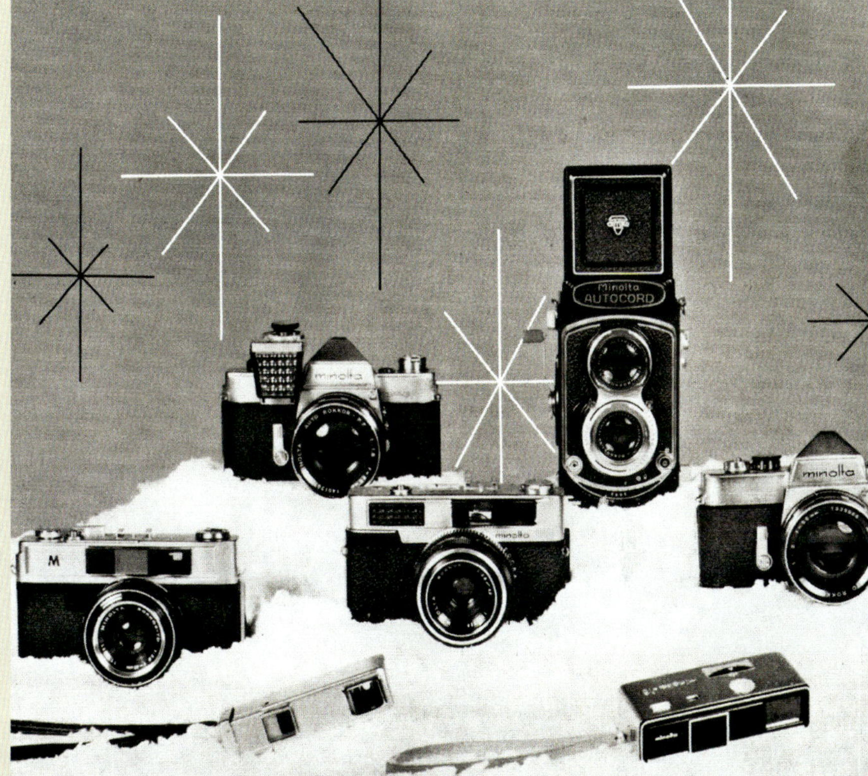

Phil's Stanford essay was the seed that laid down the foundations for one of the most iconic brands in sports history.

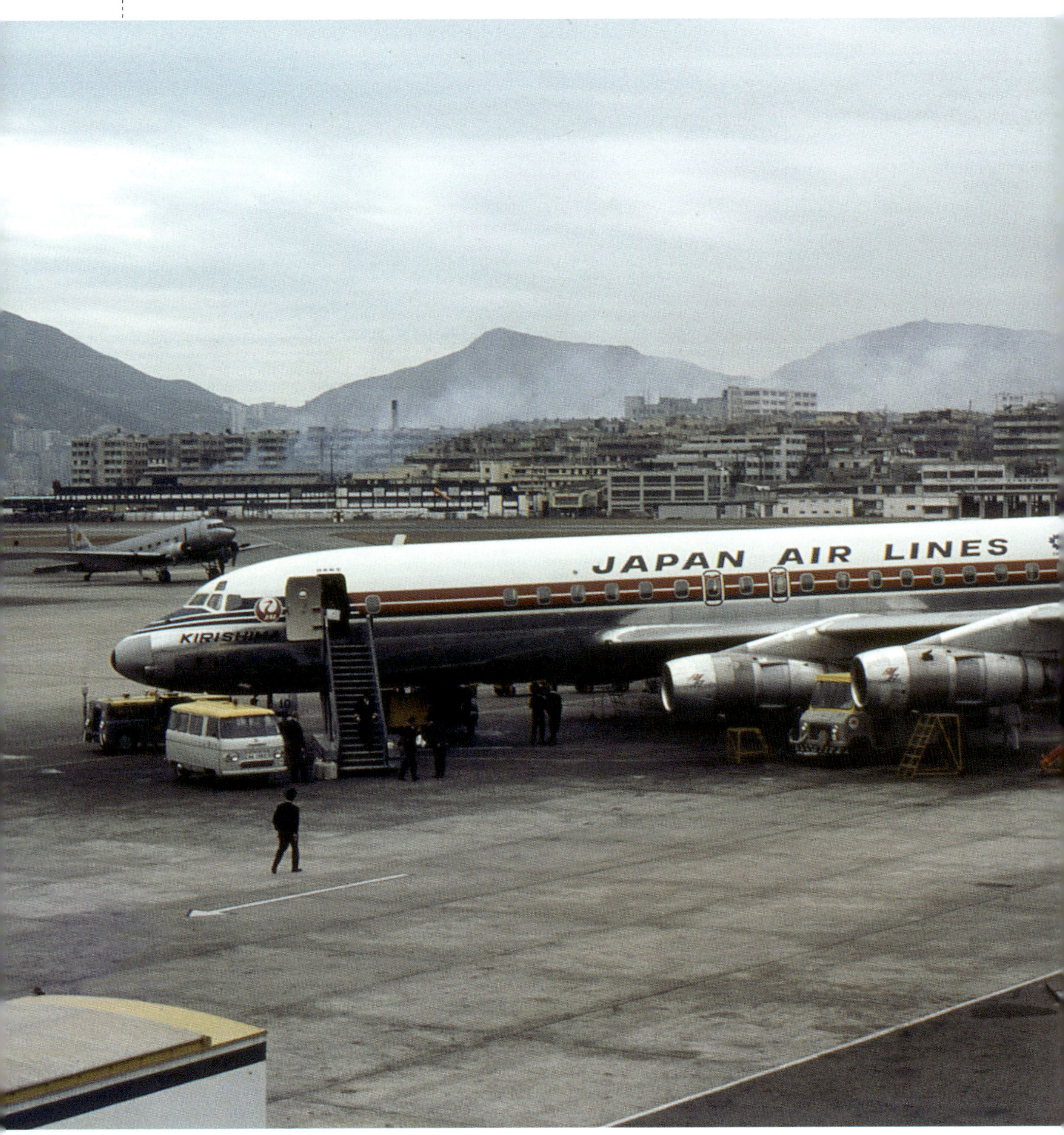

ABOVE: Phil Knight headed to Japan eager to make his mark

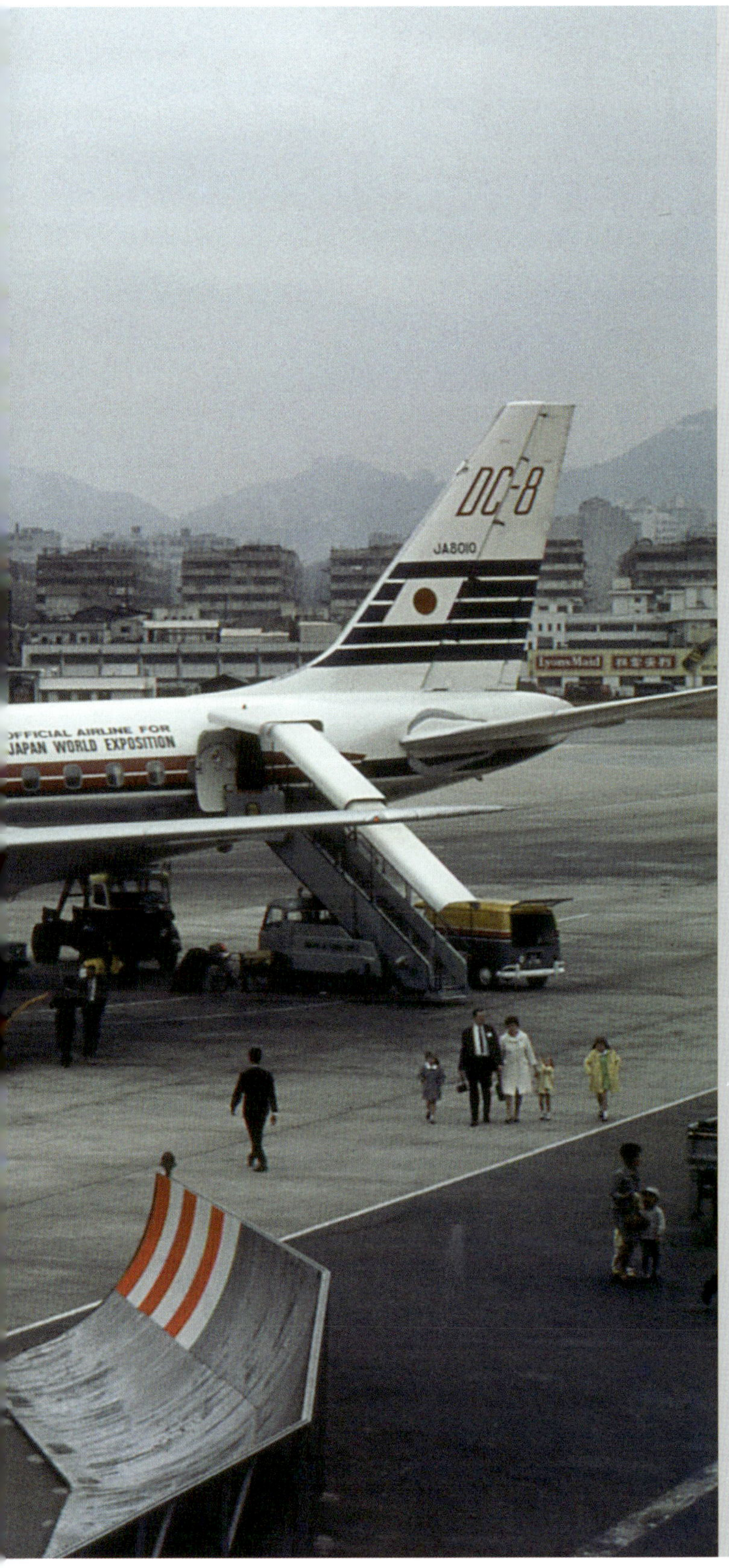

Unlike his peers, Knight didn't see this assignment as a simple academic exercise. As he became more and more enthralled in the research of his paper, Phil began to think that his idea might actually have some merit. "The idea interested me, then inspired me, then captured me" Phil later commented. "it seemed so obvious, so simple, so potentially huge". His professor must've also seen the potential for his business plan as he gave Phil an A for his essay. Still, it was just an idea.

Knight eventually got on with the rest of his course work and graduated from Stanford in the summer of 1962.

Phil was now a 24-year-old man, ready to get started with his new life as a young professional. The only problem was that he couldn't get his "crazy idea" out of his mind. "I wanted to leave my mark on the world", Knight later explained, "I hadn't smoked a cigarette, hadn't tried a drug. I hadn't broken a rule, let alone a law. The 1960's were just under way, the age of rebellion, and I was the only person in America who hadn't yet rebelled". So, one summer morning in 1962, on one of his daily runs, Phil decided to rebel and take a chance on himself. He was going to go to Japan, and he was going to meet with the head of Onitsuka Tiger (now ASICS), and he was going to put his theory into action.

A TRIP TO THE LAND OF THE RISING SUN

1962-1963

"The miracle isn't that I finished. The miracle is that I had the courage to start."

John Bingham

Phil decided that in order to leave his mark on the world, he would have to see it first. Before running a big race, you always want to walk the track, he reasoned. After weeks of reading, planning, and preparing, Knight set off on his Odyssey that would take him towards all corners of the world.

But first, he needed to make his way to Tokyo. So, on September 7th, 1962, Phil Knight boarded his first flight to Hawaii before eventually making his way to the land of the rising sun.

Once in Tokyo, Phil couldn't have felt more like a fish out of water. Everything around him was different: from the language to the food, to the smells. Luckily, his father had a few connections with some people at the United Press International and Phil figured that it couldn't hurt to get a few pointers on how best to conduct business with the Japanese. The overall consensus was that Japanese businessmen wouldn't respond well to the typical American "hard sell" way of doing business and that if Phil wanted any shot at going home with a deal, he needed to be less pushy and more sensitive.

After he had his fill of enough guidance, Phil had no choice but to take the train down to Kobe and meet the head of Onitsuka Co for real.

He was met in front of the Onitsuka factory by four executives including Ken Miyazaki. All five men proceeded to tour the factory before eventually settling down in a conference room and getting down to business.

After Knight presented his business proposition, quoting directly from his Stanford class assignment, Miyazaki took a moment to gather his thoughts. "What company are you with?", he asked. It was a simple question, but not a question Phil knew the answer to. In a moment of panic, he responded with "Blue Ribbon Sports".

OPP PAGE: Sunrise over Tokyo

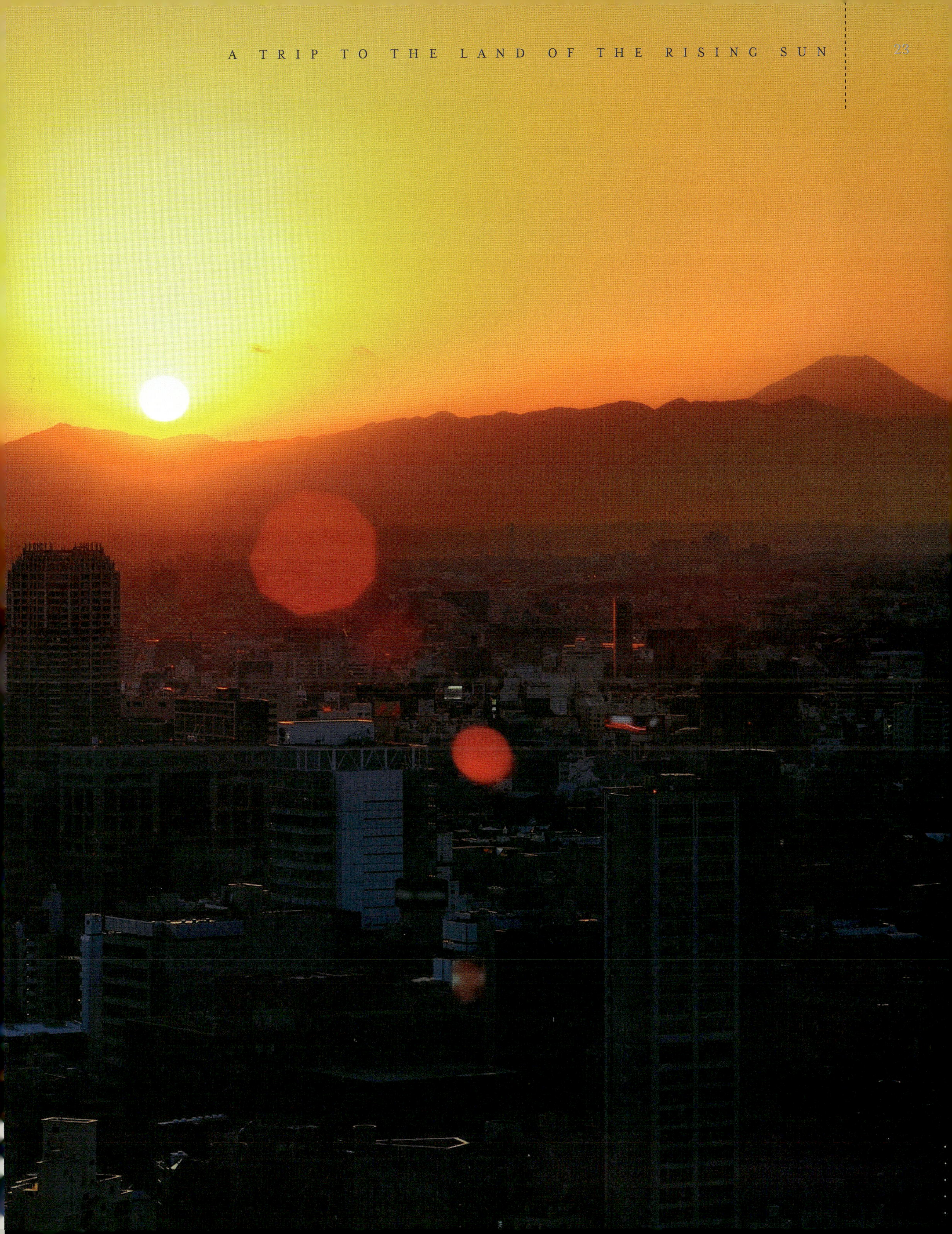

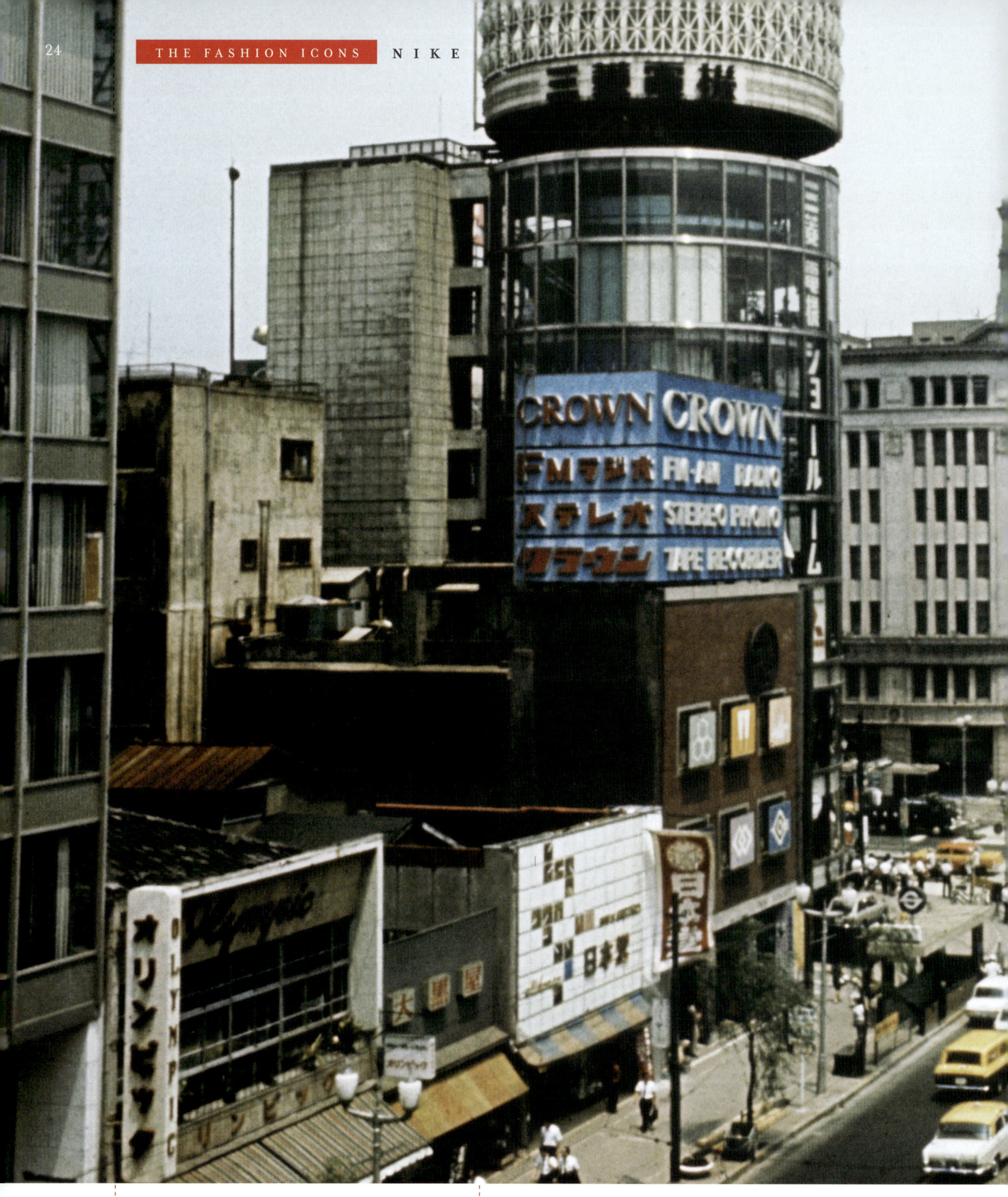

ABOVE: Ginza - The main business center of Tokyo

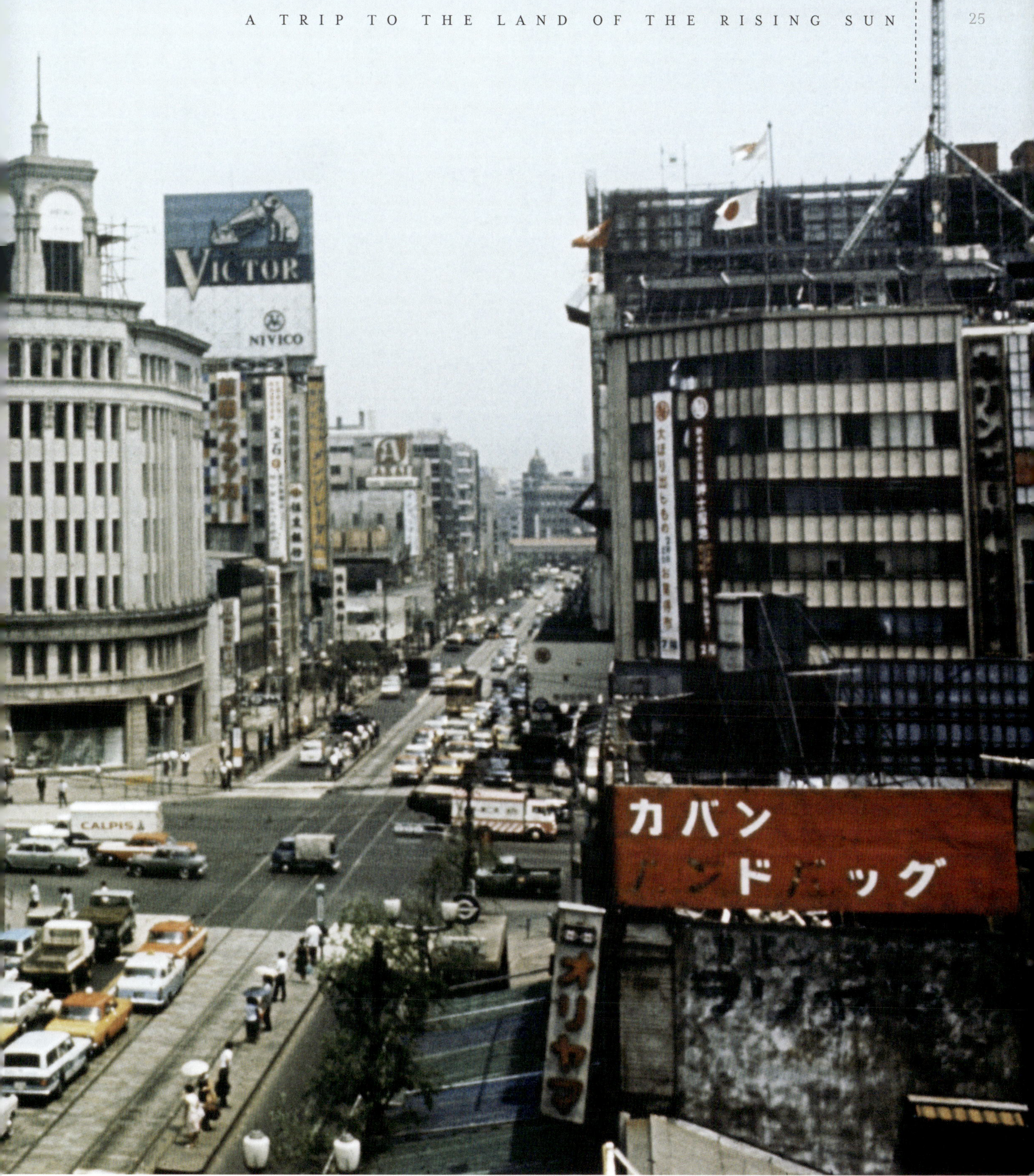
VICTOR
NIVICO
CALPIS
カバン
ハンドバッグ
オリヤマ

BLUE RIBBON SPORTS

Blue Ribbon Sports was the company founded by Phil Knight and Bill Bowerman in 1964 and would later come to be known under the name of Nike. Phil initially came up with the name Blue Ribbon Sports during his trip to Japan in 1962. He got the idea from the blue ribbons that adorned the walls of his childhood bedroom. The name was supposed to be a reflection of prestige and excellence, much like the blue ribbons awarded for first place in competitions. Initially, the company operated as a distributor for the Japanese shoe brand Onitsuka Tiger. It was a scrappy, grassroots operation in its early days, with a deep connection to the running community. This partnership set the stage for the future development of Nike as a leader in sports footwear innovation.

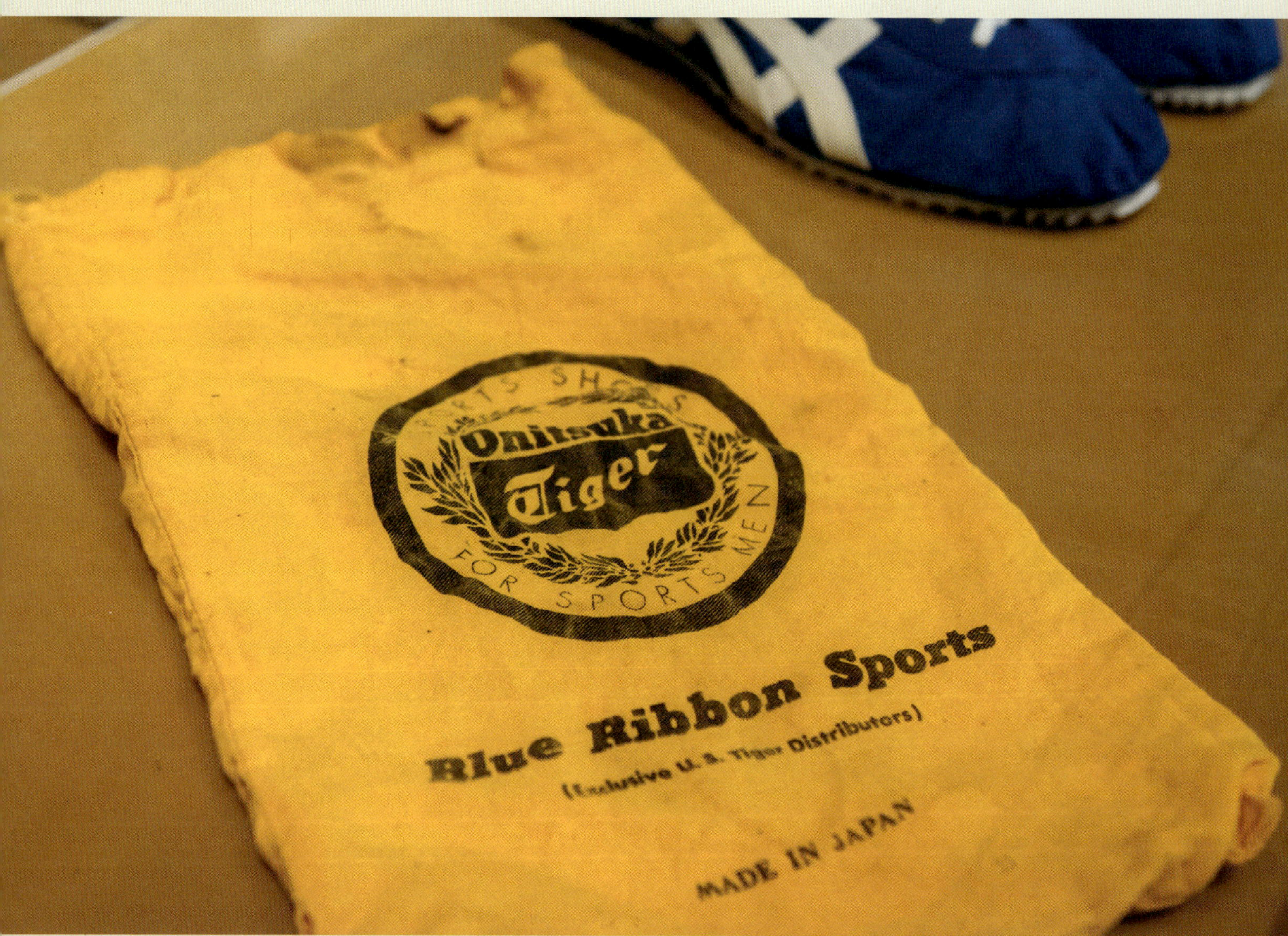

ABOVE: Branded shoe bag for Blue Ribbon Sport Exclusive U.S. Tiger Distributors
OPP PAGE: Panorama showing Alpenglow on the Himalayan Peaks

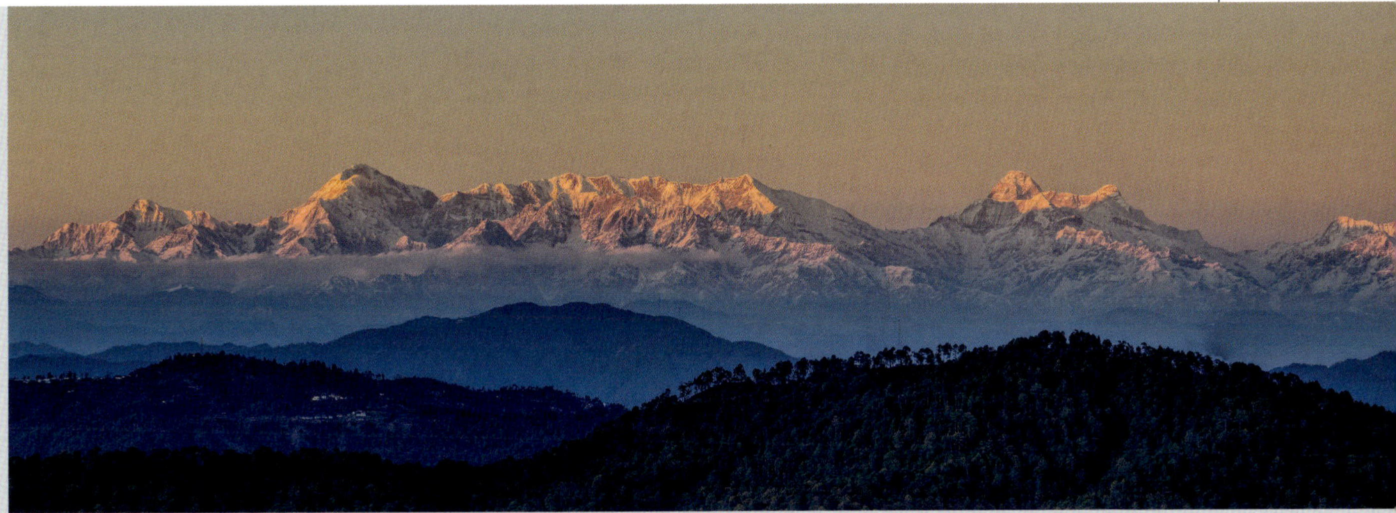

Phil left that meeting with a deal. Blue Ribbon Sports would be the first representative of Tiger shoes in the United States. His crazy idea didn't seem so crazy after all.

After his more than successful stay in Japan, Knight continued on his quest to see the world and went on to travel through China, The Philippines, Thailand, Vietnam, India, Nepal, Kenya, Egypt, Jerusalem, Turkey, Italy, France, Germany, Austria, England and Greece.

He hiked the Himalayas, ate blood rare buffalo meat with the Tibetans, took long rides into the African savannah, stood at the foot of the Sphinx, admired the Sistine Chapel and drank coffee in Hemingway's favourite Parisian café. He finished his 6-month trip in London before boarding his final flight back to Portland.

On February 24, 1963, his 25th birthday, Phil walked through the doors of the house he had been absent from for over half a year. His hair was now shoulder length, and his beard was unkempt, but the first thing he wanted, needed, to check was if his shoes from Japan had arrived.

It was almost a year later when Phil finally received his order from Onitsuka. On a whim he decided to send two pairs of the trainers to his old track and field coach, Bill Bowerman. After all, he was the man that made Phil first *really* think about what people put on their feet.

Bill Bowerman was instantly intrigued by these funny shoes, but he was even more intrigued by how inexpensive they were. He wrote back to Phil almost immediately, informing him that he would be in Portland the following week. On January 24, 1964, the pair met up for lunch at the Cosmopolitan Hotel. After a few minutes of polite conversation, Bill veered the conversation to what truly interested him: Blue Ribbons Sport. By the end of lunch, Bill Bowerman and Phil Knight had entered in a 50-50 partnership of the company.

PARTNERSHIPS AND RIVALRIES

1964

"The man who moves a mountain begins by carrying away small stones."

Confucius

Following the lunch that kicked off one of the most influential business partnerships to date, Phil decided he needed to get a job. Although the Tiger sneakers were selling fast and plentiful, the money he made from the sales was immediately reinvested into his company, leaving little to no profit for Phil to give himself an actual salary. Uncertain with what he wanted to do with his life and in desperate need for money, Knight decided to pursue a CPA (Certified Public Accountant). Phil took nine credit hours' worth of accounting classes at Portland State to qualify for his CPA exam and eventually secured himself a job as an accountant for the firm Lybrand, Ross Bros. & Montgomery.

Though his accounting job did teach him some valuable lessons in business, he didn't care much for the work. Going from being his own boss to having a boss wasn't an easy transition. Phil became increasingly frustrated by the fact he constantly had

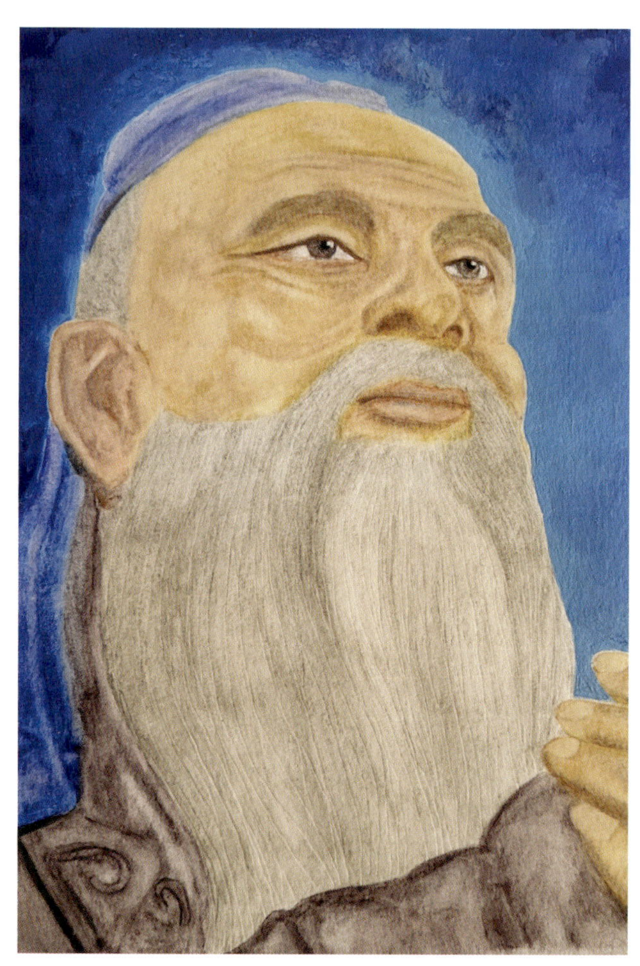

RIGHT: Confucius, the Chinese philosopher
OPP PAGE: Onitsuka Tiger signage

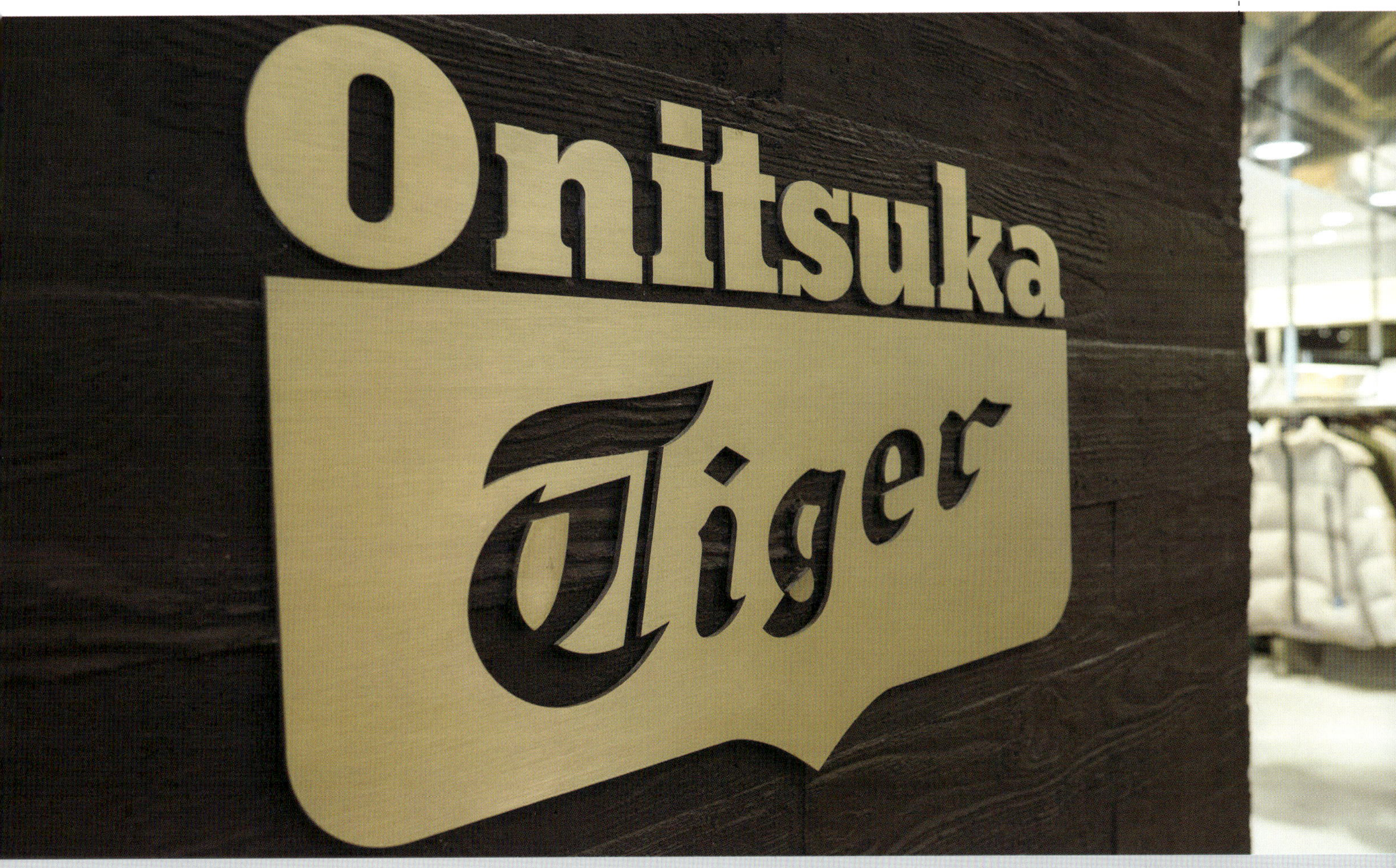

someone looking over his shoulder, but at least he had some decent money coming in.

A couple of weeks later, Knight and Bowerman met up with a lawyer to formalise their agreement and put it into writing. Following the advice of their lawyer, the partners decided to split the business 51% to 49%, so that Phil could retain full control of the company, while Bill would act primarily as a financial backer. With the paperwork all drawn up, the union was official. There was no going back now.

Phil decided it was high time to send a letter to Onitsuka and ask them to be the sole distributor of Tiger shoes on the West Coast of the US. While he was at it, he also made an order for $1,000 worth of Tiger shoes to be delivered as soon as possible.

In April, Knight received the shipment of shoes and got a letter from Miyazaki himself, confirming that Blue Ribbon Sports would be the only distributor of Onitsuka shoes in the Western United States. Overjoyed by this breakthrough, Phil quickly and rather eagerly quit his day job to fully dedicate himself to selling the sneakers.

GAME PLAN

Phil's initial strategy for promoting Blue Ribbon Sports and its shoes was rooted in direct, personal engagement with runners. In the early days, without a marketing budget or established distribution channels, Knight took on a grassroots approach. In order to move units, he would load up his recently acquired car with boxes of Onitsuka Tigers and drive to local track meets across Oregon and surrounding states, selling the shoes straight from his trunk. His goal was to sell the Tigers directly to the people who would benefit most from high-quality running shoes: the athletes, coaches, and spectators.

Phil's deep connection to the running world, through his own experience as a runner and his relationship with legendary University of Oregon track coach Bill Bowerman, gave him credibility. He knew that runners needed shoes that were light, comfortable, and durable and Tiger sneakers were the best. Rather than simply pitching the product, he often allowed runners to try the shoes out, emphasizing performance over salesmanship. After some time, Phil also started to receive letters and phone calls asking to purchase a pair of Tigers. On occasion, people even showed up at his parents' house.

Because business was going so well, Phil began to think about adding another salesman to his team. While selling shoes in California, he ran into Jeff Johnson, a fellow runner Knight had met at Stanford. Johnson was working as a social worker during the week but sold shoes for Adidas on the weekends. Phil offered Johnson a place in his new business venture but Jeff, who was about to get married at the time, thought it too risky. Although Johnson wouldn't be part of the Blue Ribbon Sports family right away, a few months later he would have a change of heart and become the first full-time employee of the company.

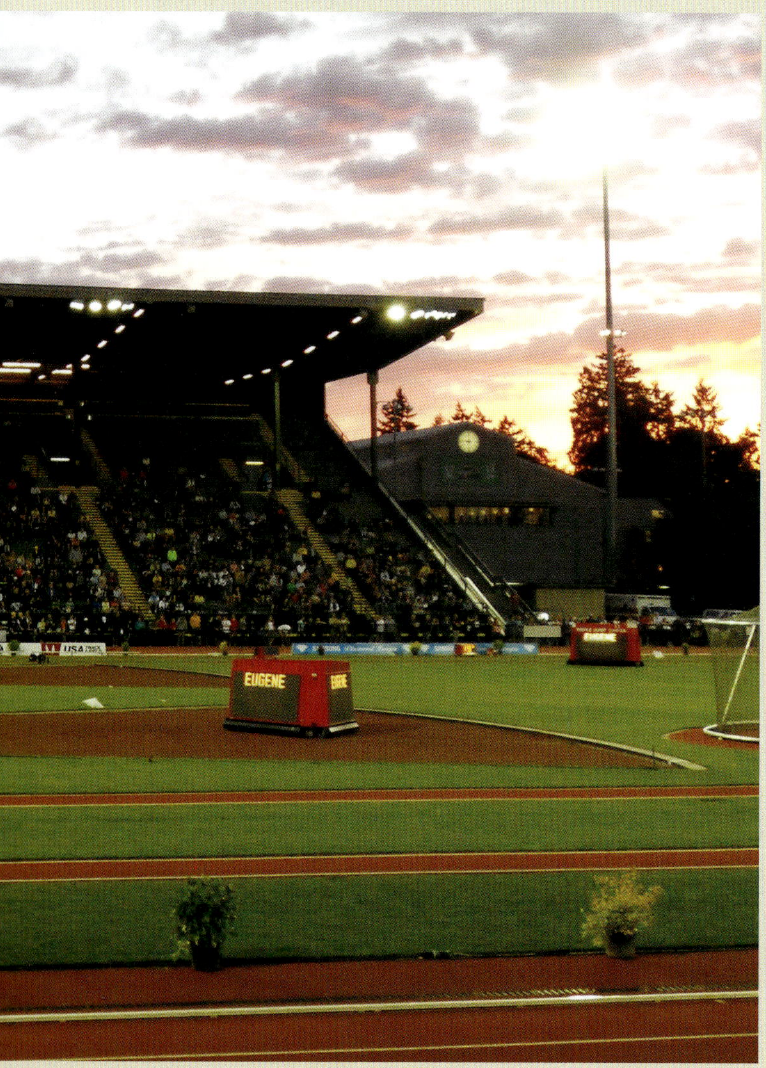

ABOVE: Hayward Field, where Phil and Bill's journey began
OPP PAGE: Tokyo hosted the Olympic Games in 1964, around the time Phil began traveling to Japan to pursue his own sporting dream

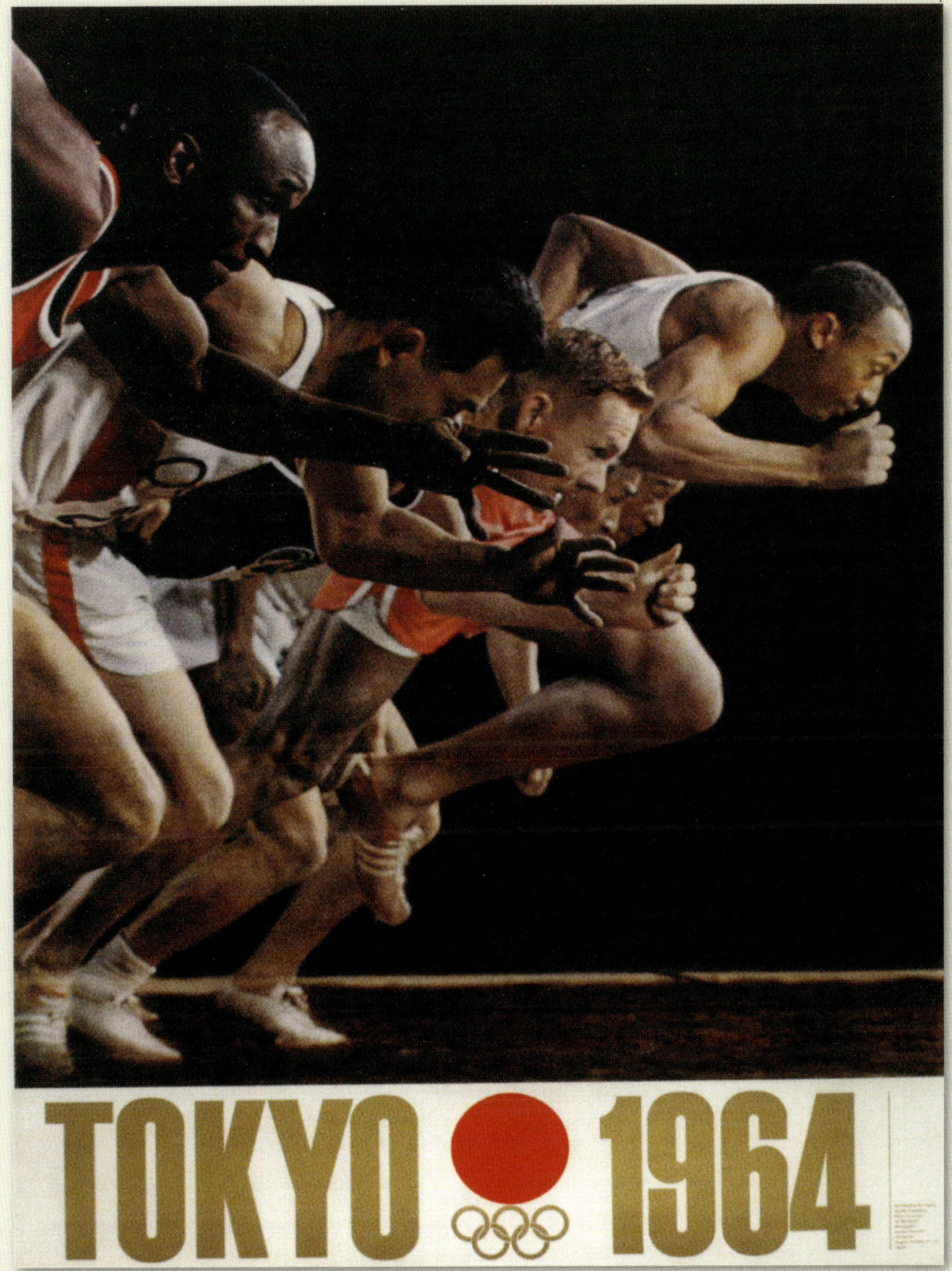
TOKYO 1964

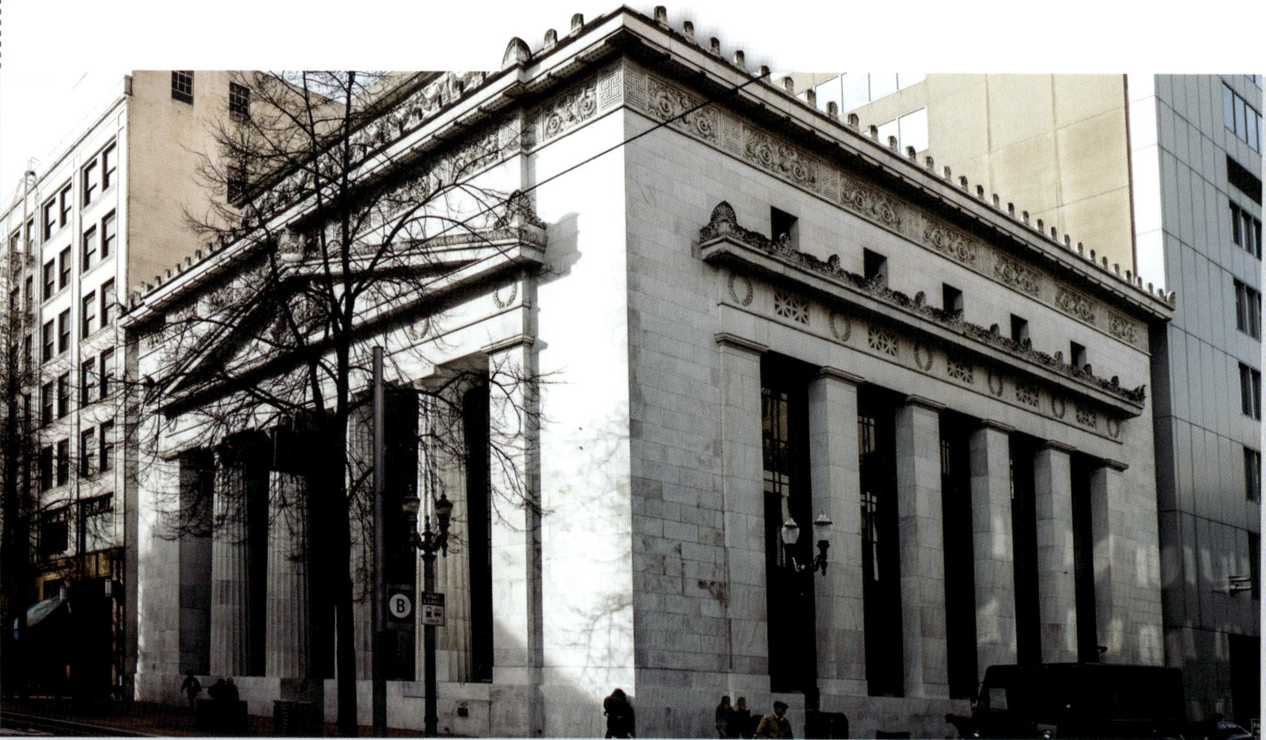

By July 4, 1964, Phil had sold out of his first shipment of shoes. He wrote back to Onitsuka, but this time he wanted a more significant shipment—$3,000 worth of goods to be exact. The only problem was that he couldn't afford the order, and his father had since refused to put any more of his money into his son's crazy idea. Phil had to do what anyone else looking for money did: he made his way to the First National Bank of Oregon in hopes of obtaining a loan. Thanks to Bill Knight's good name, he managed to leave the building with the necessary funds to make the order.

Unfortunately, this is where Knight's bad luck began to snowball. Shortly after his trip to California, he received a letter from a high school wrestling coach in Long Island claiming he was the exclusive distributor of Onitsuka Tigers in the USA. Understandably distressed by this information, Phil wasted no time to call his cousin, a lawyer, to get some advice. He also penned a panicked letter to Onitsuka in an attempt to figure out what on earth was going on. When he still didn't receive a reply by the end of summer, Phil decided that the only way to save his business was to fly to Japan and confront the Onitsuka executives directly.

Yet again, Phil found himself back on a plane to Tokyo.

Upon his arrival in Kobe, Phil was met by a man called Morimoto, Miyazaki's new replacement. The pair talked over a cup of tea at the hotel bar and by the next day, Phil had secured a meeting with Mr. Onitsuka himself. Thankfully, Mr. Onitsuka was impressed by the young man and by the end of their conversation, Phil was signing several contracts confirming that Blue Ribbon Sports indeed, had exclusive selling rights for the West of the United States. A huge sense of relief washed over Phil following that meeting. Crisis averted, he thought, at least for now.

ABOVE: First National Bank Building, Portland, Oregon
OPP PAGE: Onitsuka Tiger flagship store, Harajuku, Tokyo, Japan

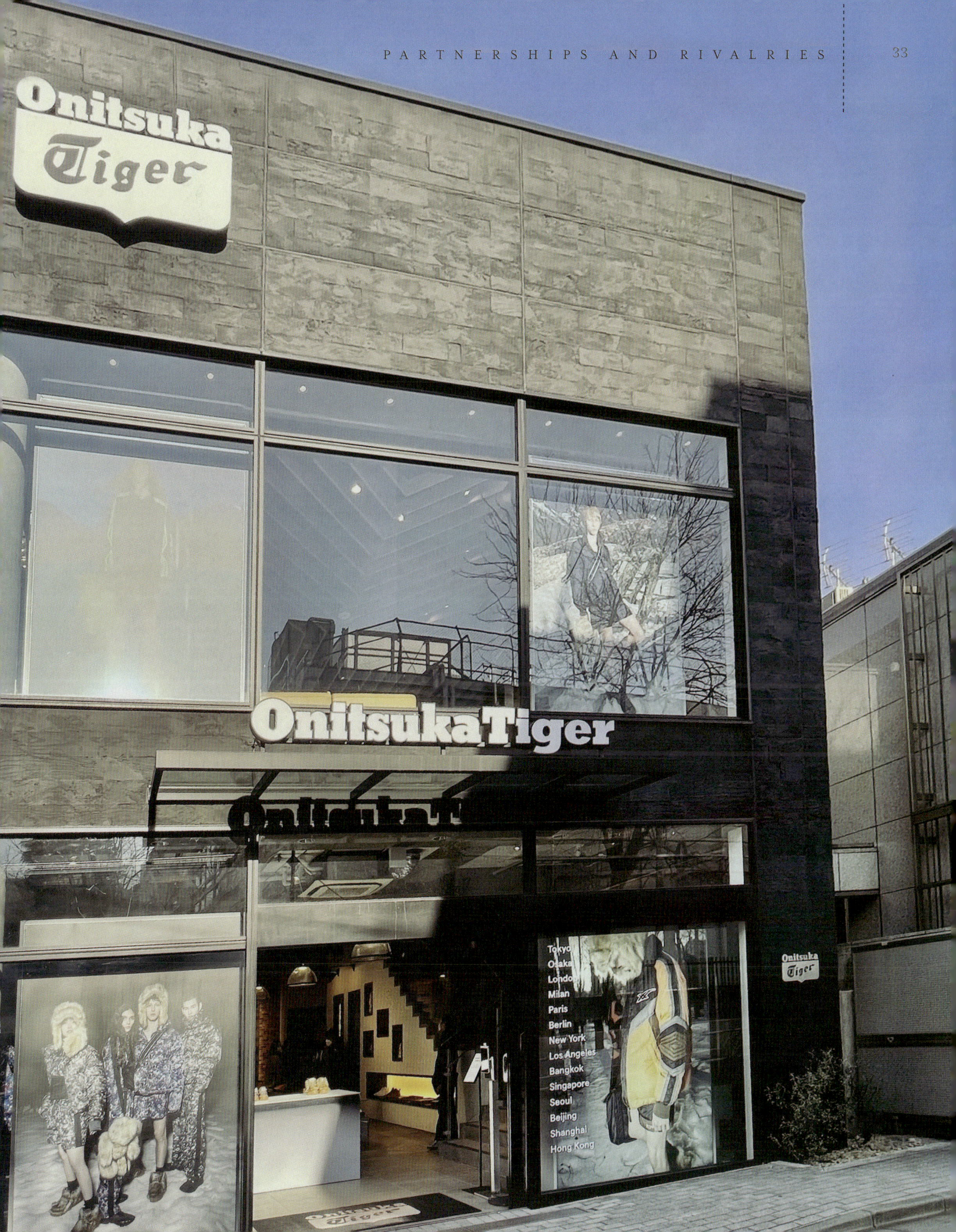
Onitsuka
Tiger
OnitsukaTiger
Onitsuka
Tokyo
Osaka
London
Milan
Paris
Berlin
New York
Los Angeles
Bangkok
Singapore
Seoul
Beijing
Shanghai
Hong Kong
Onitsuka
Tiger

EAST MEETS WEST

Following the formalisation of their business partnership, Bowerman decided it was time to forge his own relationship with the people at Onitsuka and more importantly, to share his ideas to help improve their shoes. The coach expressed his optimism in a letter to the Japanese factory in May 1964, saying *"I hope that your arrangements with Mr. Knight would be such that I would be free to turn over the ideas that I have worked out on track shoes"*.

By October, Bill Bowerman and his wife Barbara, found themselves standing amidst the bustling streets of Tokyo, where the city was alive with the energy of the 1964 Summer Olympics. Bowerman flew all the way to the land of the rising sun to support the members of the U.S. track-and-field team he'd coached. Two of his runners, Bill Dellinger and Harry Jerome would even go on to win Olympic medals that year.

However, Bill wasn't just there to witness the athletic feats on display but also to fulfil a mission that would soon prove crucial to the future of the company he had co-founded with Phil. After the Games, Bowerman switched hats and became an ambassador for Blue Ribbon Sports. He and his wife stayed an extra week in Japan so that Bowerman could meet Kihachiro Onitsuka, the visionary founder of Onitsuka Tiger, whose shoes Knight had been importing and selling in the U.S. for nearly two years. The meeting between Bowerman and Onitsuka was more than just a formality. It was an opportunity to solidify and strengthen the partnership that Phil had worked so hard to establish. Knight had already convinced Onitsuka to grant him the exclusive rights to distribute Tiger shoes in the U.S. market, but Bowerman's visit to Japan was an opportunity to take this relationship to the next level. Bowerman wanted to be involved not just in selling the shoes, but in helping to shape them. Bowerman, a no-nonsense man, appreciated Japan's efficiency and attention to detail. These qualities, he believed, were reflected in the shoes produced by Onitsuka Tiger.

When Bowerman finally met with Kihachiro Onitsuka, the two men hit it off almost immediately. Despite the language barrier and the cultural differences, they shared a common passion for innovation and improvement in athletic footwear. Onitsuka, like Bowerman, believed that shoes were a critical part of an athlete's success. During the factory visit, Mr. Onitsuka told Bowerman about how the inspiration for the unique soles on Tigers had come to him as he was eating sushi. While looking at the underside of the octopus's leg in front of him, he thought a similar suction cup might work on the sole of a runner's flat. Bowerman took note of this story and learned that inspiration could come from the most quotidian things, things you might even eat (more on that later).

As the 1964 Olympics came to a close, Bowerman left Japan inspired. The games had showcased not only athletic excellence but also the role of technology and innovation in achieving success. For Bowerman and Knight, the path forward was clear—Blue Ribbon Sports would continue selling Onitsuka Tiger shoes, but they would also start thinking about what came next. The trip to Japan had shown them that they could play a role in shaping the future of athletic footwear, and it wouldn't be long before that vision became a reality.

Bowerman continued corresponding with his new friend, Mr. Onitsuka, and suggesting modifications to their products to adapt them to the American market. "Though all people are the same under the skin, Bowerman had come to believe that all feet are not created equal. Americans have different bodies than Japanese do—longer, heavier—and Americans therefore need different shoes". However, Bill Bowerman soon discovered, same as Phil, that no matter how well you got along in person with the team at Onitsuka, things were different once you were back on your side of the Pacific. Most of Bowerman's letters went unanswered. When there was an answer, it was cryptic, or curtly dismissive.

Despite this slightly anticlimactic result, the seeds of Nike had definitely been planted in the heart of Tokyo, during that 1964 meeting between Bowerman and Onitsuka, though it would take a couple of years to really blossom.

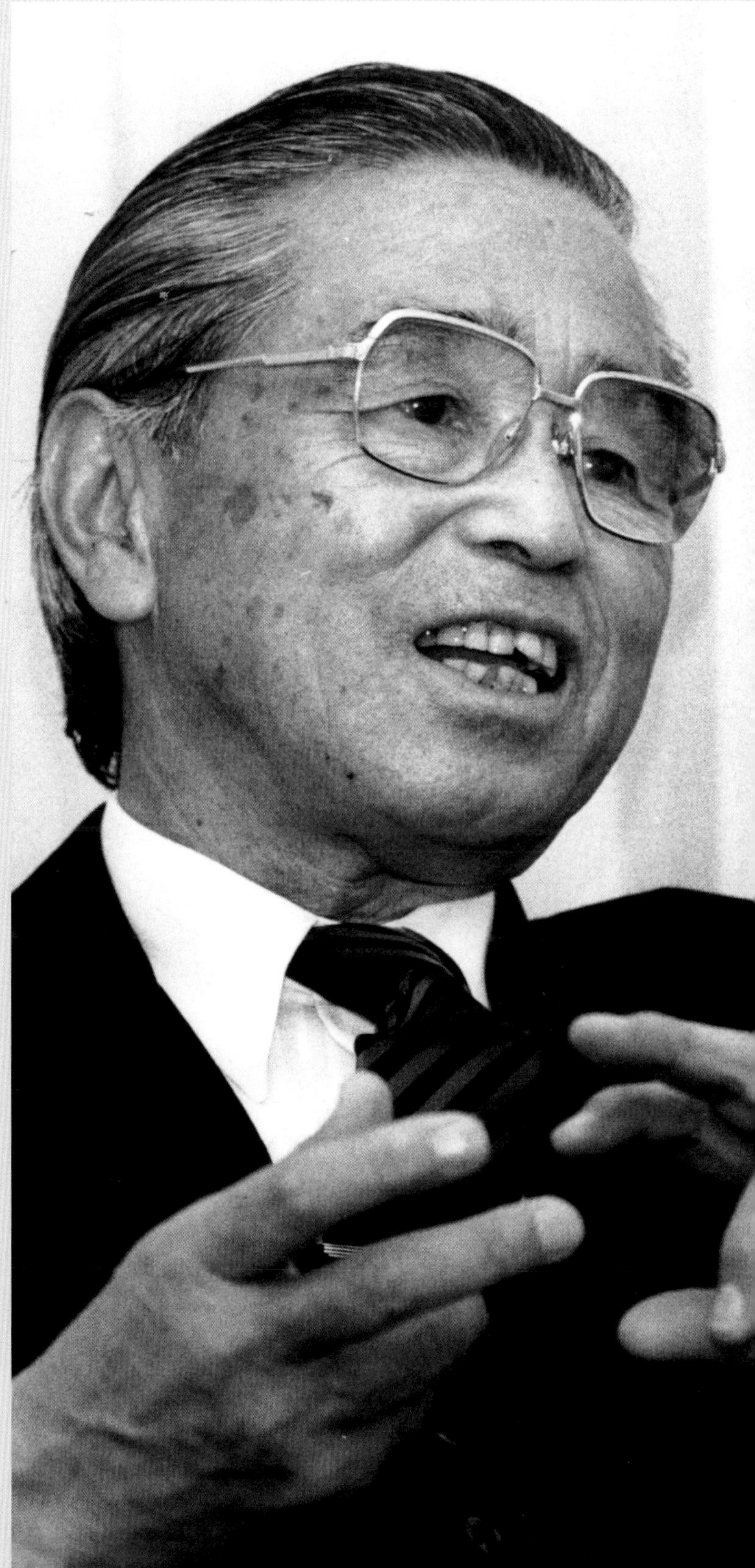

BLOOD, SWEAT, & SNEAKERS

1965-1967

"Life is growth. You grow or you die."

Phil Knight

At the beginning of 1965, Phil received a letter from his former running buddy from Grad School, Jeff Johnson. Following their chance meeting at a track and field event in California, Phil sent the fellow Stanford alumnus a pair of Tiger shoes to try out. Jeff instantly fell in love with sneakers and even got some of his own running mates hooked on them as well. At that point, Knight was slowly but surely putting together a crew of part time sales representatives and offered Johnson a post as a "commissioned salesman" at Blue Ribbon Sports, which he immediately accepted. Jeff spent his weekends selling the batch of Tiger sneakers with the kind of enthusiasm usually reserved for children opening presents on Christmas day. Phil later recalled that Johnson's relationship to running was unlike anything he'd ever seen before… "In his heart of hearts Johnson believed that runners were God's chosen, that running done right, in the correct spirit and with proper form, is a mystical exercise, no less

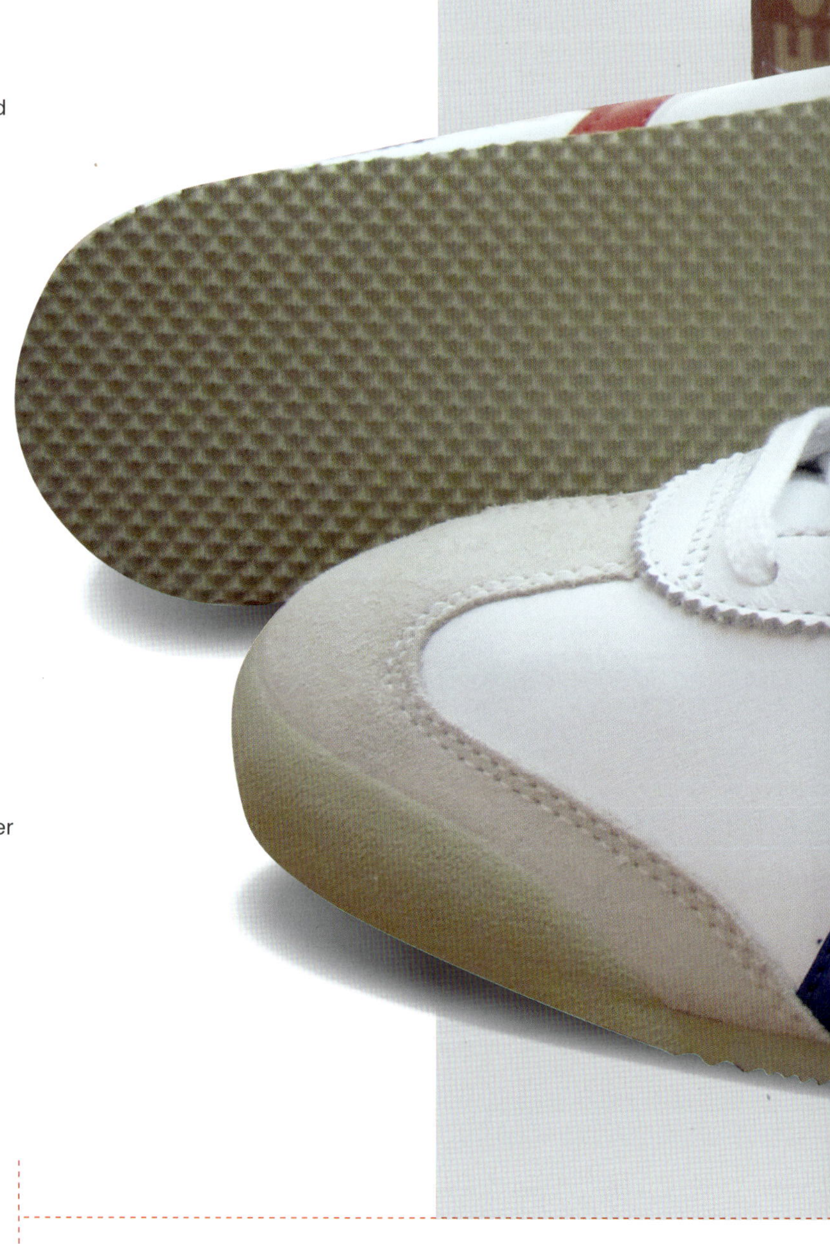

RIGHT: Onitsuka Tiger Mexico 66 in white, blue and red

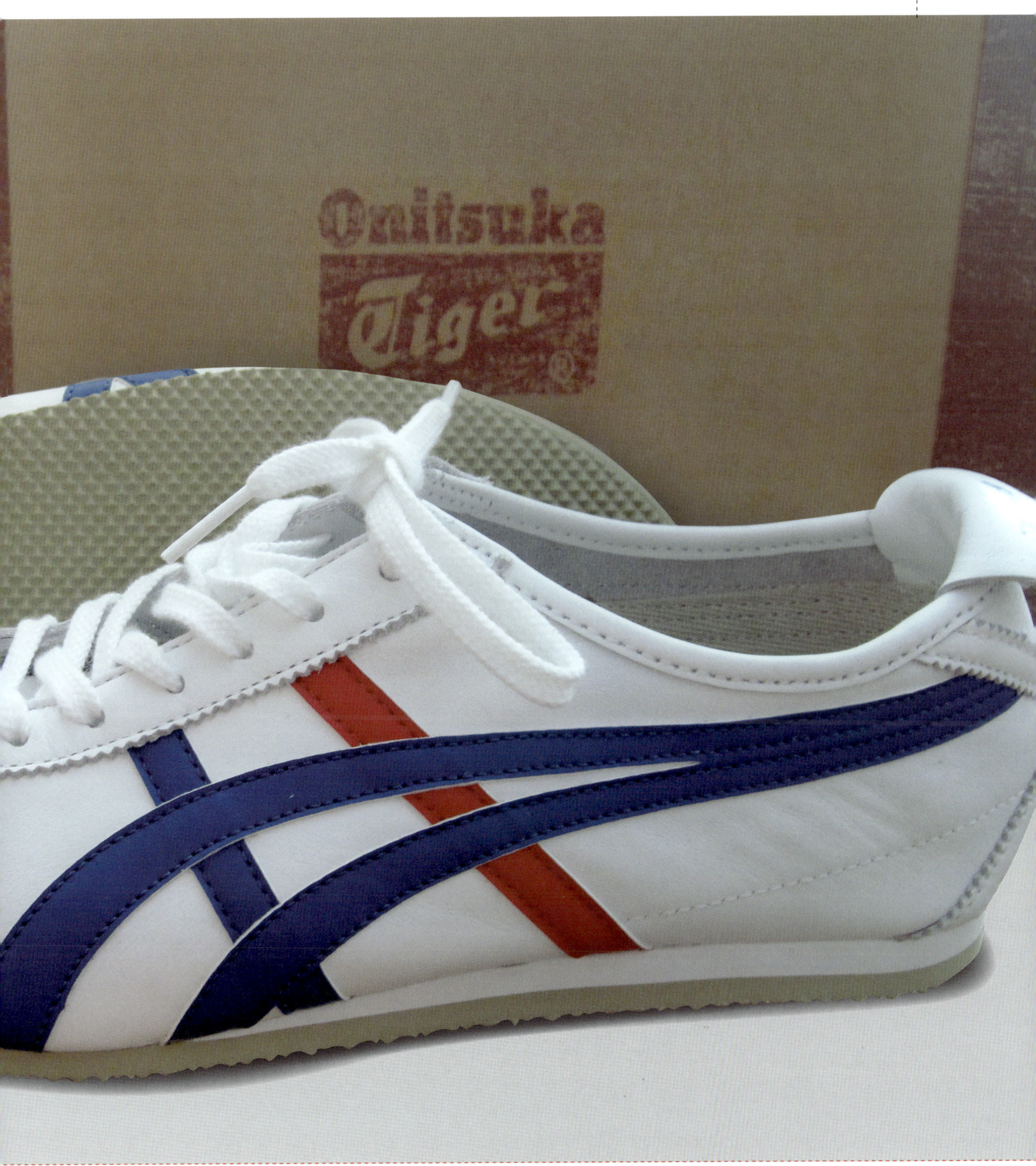
Onitsuka
Tiger

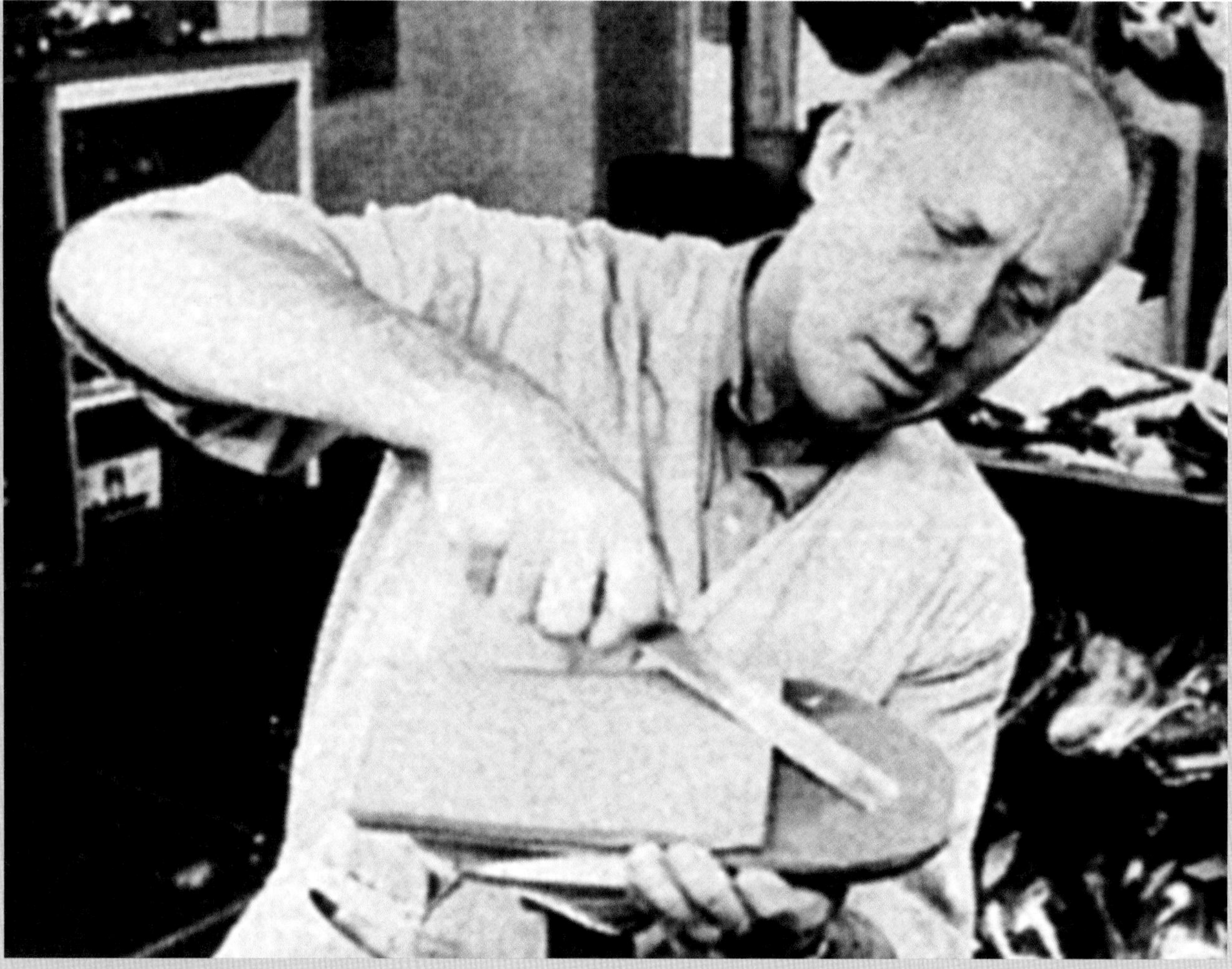

than meditation and prayer, and thus he felt called to help runners reach their Nirvana". Despite Phil's connection to the running world, he had never heard of such a romanticised way of looking at the sport. In 1965, running wasn't a popular sport, but running for pleasure was simply unheard of or at the very least, ridiculed. Though Jeff had somewhat of an eccentric personality, Knight admired his colleague's passion for the business. By the summer, Jeff Johnson was the first full-time Blue Ribbon Sports employee.

Though the company had experienced considerable growth over the past year, Blue Ribbon Sports was struggling financially. His banker at the time would often warn Phil against the dangers of growing off a balance sheet, and how growth without enough equity could have catastrophic consequences for the business. Despite his impressive background as a businessman, Knight couldn't understand how growth could be bad... He needed to grow to retain his role as sole distributor of Onitsuka shoes in Western United States, he couldn't afford to stop. On top of his financial woes, the Tiger shipments were taking longer and longer to reach him, which in turn gave

ABOVE: Bill Bowerman hard at work perfecting a shoe design

OPP PAGE: 1966 Oregon Ducks and Oregon State Beavers track and field dual meet at Hayward Field

Blue Ribbon Sports less and less time to sell them. The future of the company was starting to look bleaker. The only thing to do was to get a job... again. A couple of weeks later, Phil was hired as an accountant for the firm Price Waterhouse. With his new job, he could reinvest a healthy portion of his salary into Blue Ribbon Sports and sort out his company's cash balance problem. All in all, things were looking up.

Bill Bowerman, on the other hand, didn't let his unanswered letters to Onitsuka dim his spirits or more importantly, his experiments. He continued to tear apart Tigers and use the young men on his track teams as lab mice. During the autumn track season of 1965, every race had two results for Bowerman. There was the performance of his runners, and there was the performance of their shoes. Bowerman would note how the arches held up, how the soles gripped the cinders, how the toes pinched, and the instep flexed and send his observations to Japan. Eventually he broke through. Onitsuka made prototypes that conformed to the coach's vision of a more American shoe, including a soft inner sole, more arch support, heel wedge to reduce stress on the Achilles tendon. He then handed these experimental shoes out to all his runners, who used them to crush the competition.

In 1966, two years after the creation of Blue Ribbon Sports, Phil decided that his parents' basement was no longer a big enough space from which to launch his operations. He needed to find a more appropriate headquarter for his business. Phil rented

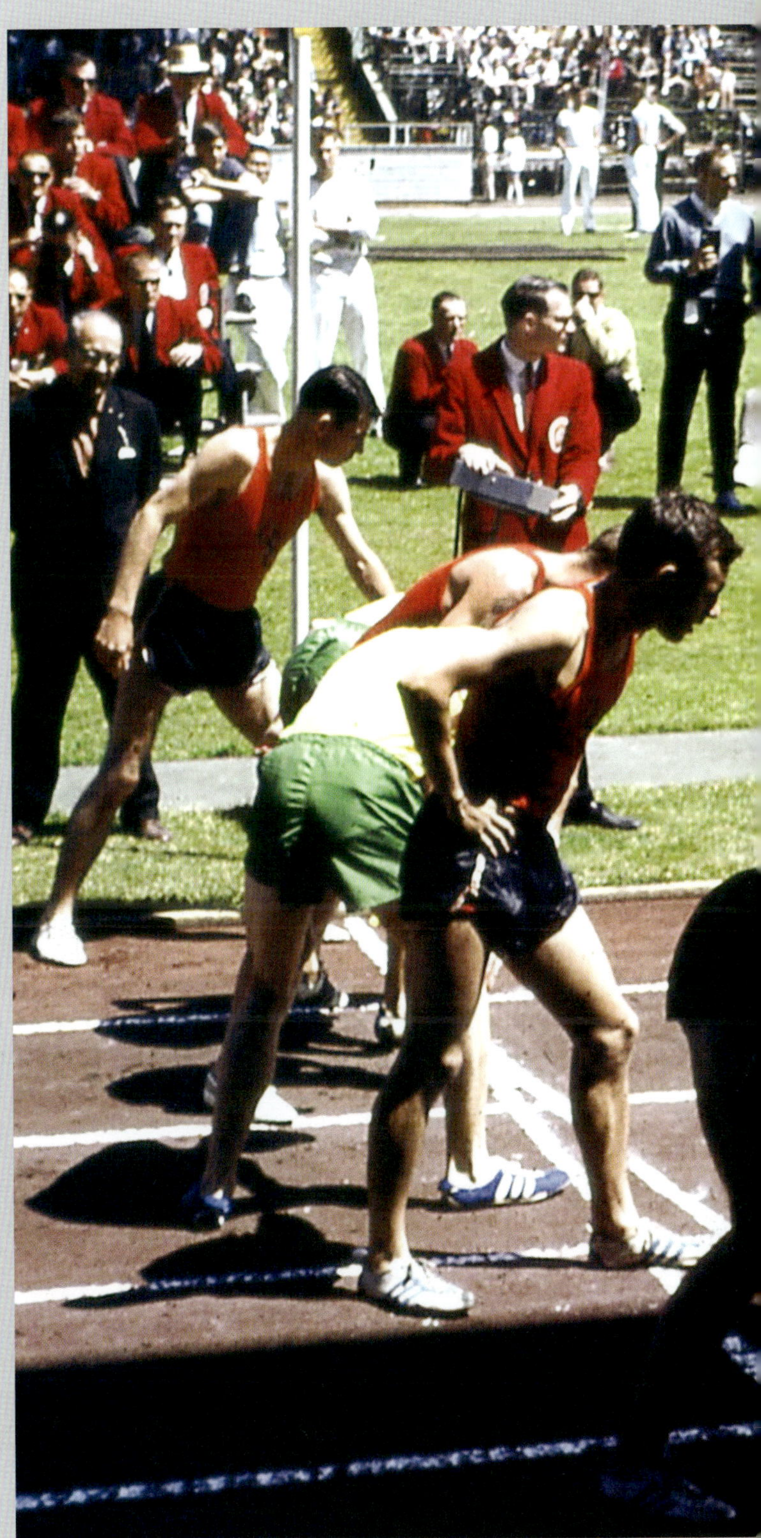

a one- bedroom apartment in a new high rise in down town Portland, and even rented some essential furniture such as a desk and chairs to furnish his new home and office. A few months later, Phil decided he needed to expand further and leased a small retail space in Santa Monica and opened his first ever retail store. The store was designed and decorated to be a mecca for runners, a space for them to meet up and enthuse about the joys of the sport. The shop's walls were lined with books all runners should read, straight form Phil's own personal library. He even distributed some "Tiger" merch to some of his best customers.

Despite this much awaited progress, there's only so high one can fly before eventually getting burned by the sun. Phil received a troubling letter from Jeff Johnson, saying that

one of his pen pals, a kid from Long Island, had revealed that his track coach was thinking of acquiring Tigers from a new source. The man that had plagued Phil's life only a few short months ago was back, and now he was poaching the clients he and Jeff had spent a long time acquiring.

Knight had no choice but to go back to Japan and demand his rights. He paid for the airfare with his credit card, 12 months to reimburse the ticket felt reasonable, and hopped on a plane to Tokyo. Upon landing, Phil met up with Onitsuka's export manager and told him, along with other executives, that Blue Ribbon had done a remarkable job so far, that they had sold out every order while developing a robust customer base, and expected this solid growth to continue. Blue Ribbon Sports had forty-four thousand dollars in sales for 1966, and was projected to have eighty-four thousand dollars in 1967. Phil plead his case and asked for exclusive distributor rights for the US and got it for a three-year contract. The only problem was that to get the exclusive rights, he told the people at Onitsuka that his company had offices on the East coast. That wasn't true, but Knight hadn't gotten this far by telling the complete truth and he wasn't going to change now.

When he got back to Oregon, Phil was tasked with the duty to inform Johnson that he would be moving across the country to open Blue Ribbon Sports' first office on the East coast of the United States. As a Californian native, Jeff didn't take the news quite as good humouredly as he was usually accustomed to. But off he went to start a new chapter of life for the company in Boston.

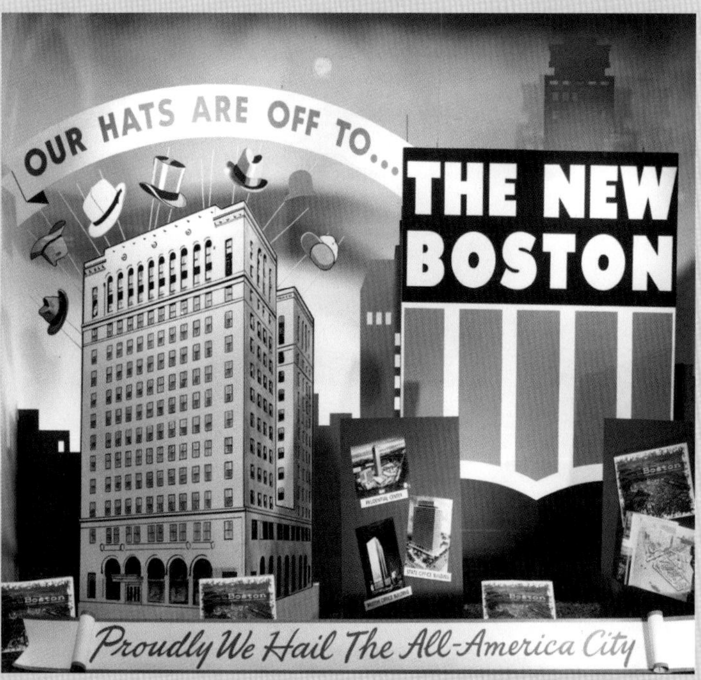

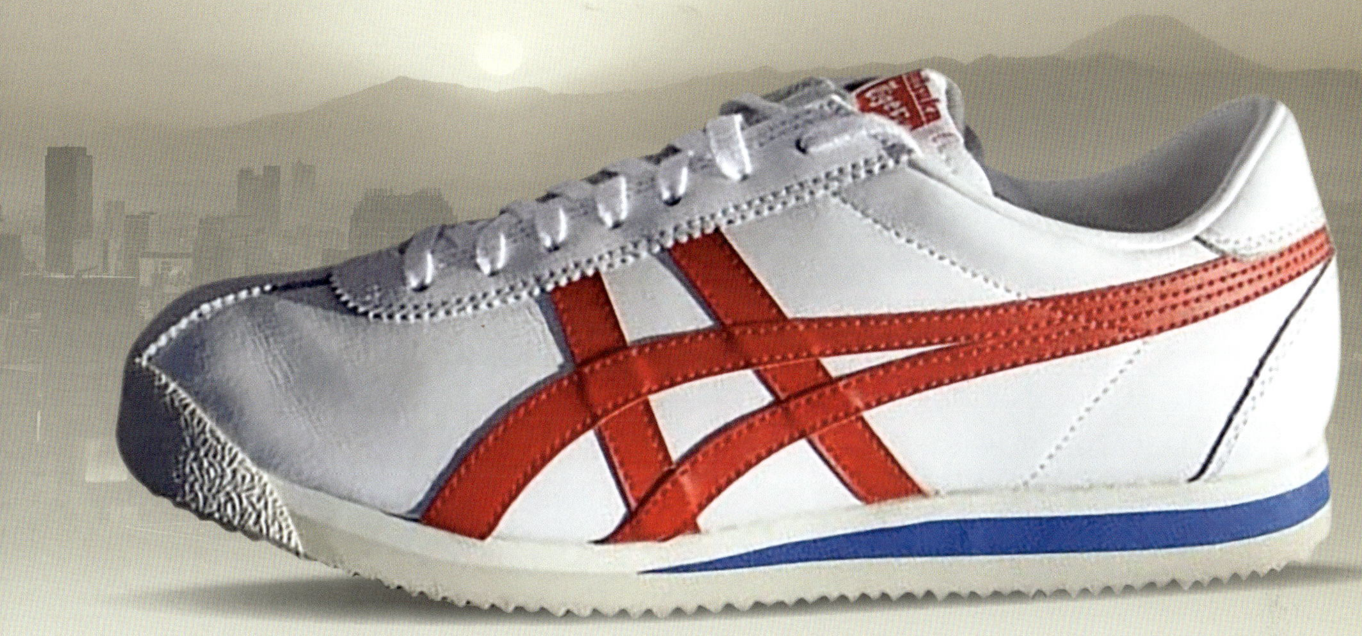

THE BIRTH OF THE TIGER CORTEZ

In 1967, Blue Ribbon Sports was still operating on the slimmest of margins, with Phil Knight and Bill Bowerman tirelessly working to introduce the American market to high-performance running shoes. Yet, in a modest Oregon workshop, Bill Bowerman was busy experimenting with a shoe that would become one of the most iconic models in sneaker history: the Tiger Cortez.

Bowerman, driven by a relentless passion for improving athlete performance, was constantly looking for ways to make shoes lighter, more durable, and better suited for long-distance running.

In his experiments, Bowerman had focused on adding more cushioning to the midsole without compromising the shoe's stability and weight. He recognized that runners needed a shoe that could absorb impact, reduce strain on the legs, and still provide enough support for high-performance running. This idea became the foundation for what would eventually be called the Tiger Cortez.

Using his own handmade prototypes, Bowerman tested various materials and designs, adding layers of rubber and foam to create a midsole that offered both support and shock absorption. His idea was straightforward but revolutionary: a shoe that could deliver comfort for marathon distances, whether on a track or the open road. His design had a thicker heel to reduce impact with each stride and a well-cushioned arch to support runners' foot shapes. This attention to detail marked the Tiger Cortez as one of the first truly ergonomic running shoes, tuned specifically to the needs of athletes.

Once Bowerman had refined his prototype, he presented it to Kihachiro Onitsuka of Onitsuka Tiger, hoping the company would produce the model. At this point, Blue Ribbon Sports was still distributing Onitsuka Tiger shoes in the United States, and Onitsuka had developed a respect for Bowerman's expertise and track record. Bowerman's passion for performance innovation caught Onitsuka's attention, and he agreed to work with him on the design, recognizing the potential appeal of the shoe for American athletes.

In 1968, the Tiger Cortez was officially launched. Originally, Phil and Bowerman had considered naming the shoe "Aztec," referencing the powerful ancient civilization of the Americas to emphasize strength, endurance, and conquest. It was also a nod to the 1968 Olympics that were going to be held in Mexico. However, Adidas were already preparing to release a shoe called the "Azteca Gold," and trademark issues were likely. In a clever twist, the dynamic duo instead opted for "Cortez," named after the Spanish conquistador Hernán Cortés, who famously defeated the Aztec Empire. The name was a playful dig, suggesting that their new shoe would "conquer" the market, competing directly with Adidas and other brands.

The choice of name signalled a bold, conquest-like ambition for Blue Ribbon Sports, representing Bowerman's and Phil's shared dream of making a mark on the running world. The Cortez rapidly became popular, thanks to its comfort, durability, and striking design. Runners, both casual and professional, found that the Cortez not only improved their performance but also brought a new level of comfort, allowing them to go farther with less strain on their bodies.

The release of the Tiger Cortez marked a major turning point for Blue Ribbon Sports. The shoe's success fuelled demand, allowing the company to grow beyond Knight's garage and develop a reputation in the running community. It was a monumental moment that showed Bowerman and Knight the power of design and innovation to disrupt an entire market.

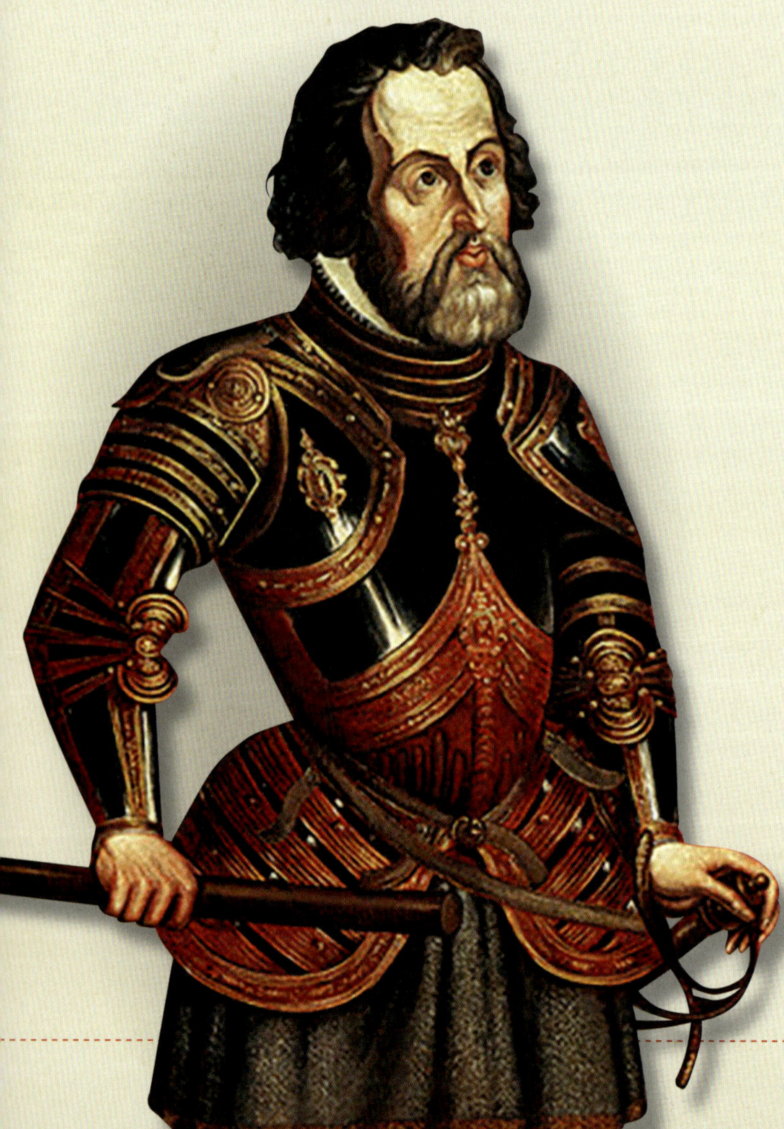

However, the story of the Cortez didn't end there. As Blue Ribbon Sports expanded, tensions grew with Onitsuka, leading to legal disputes over control of the design. The Cortez, which had originally launched as a Tiger model, would become one of Nike's first independent designs and a lasting symbol of the brand's commitment to performance and innovation.

Bowerman's creation of the Tiger Cortez wasn't just the story of a shoe; it was the beginning of a philosophy that would drive Nike's future. His hands-on approach to innovation and dedication to athletes would define Nike's ethos, leading to decades of technological advancements and some of the world's most iconic footwear.

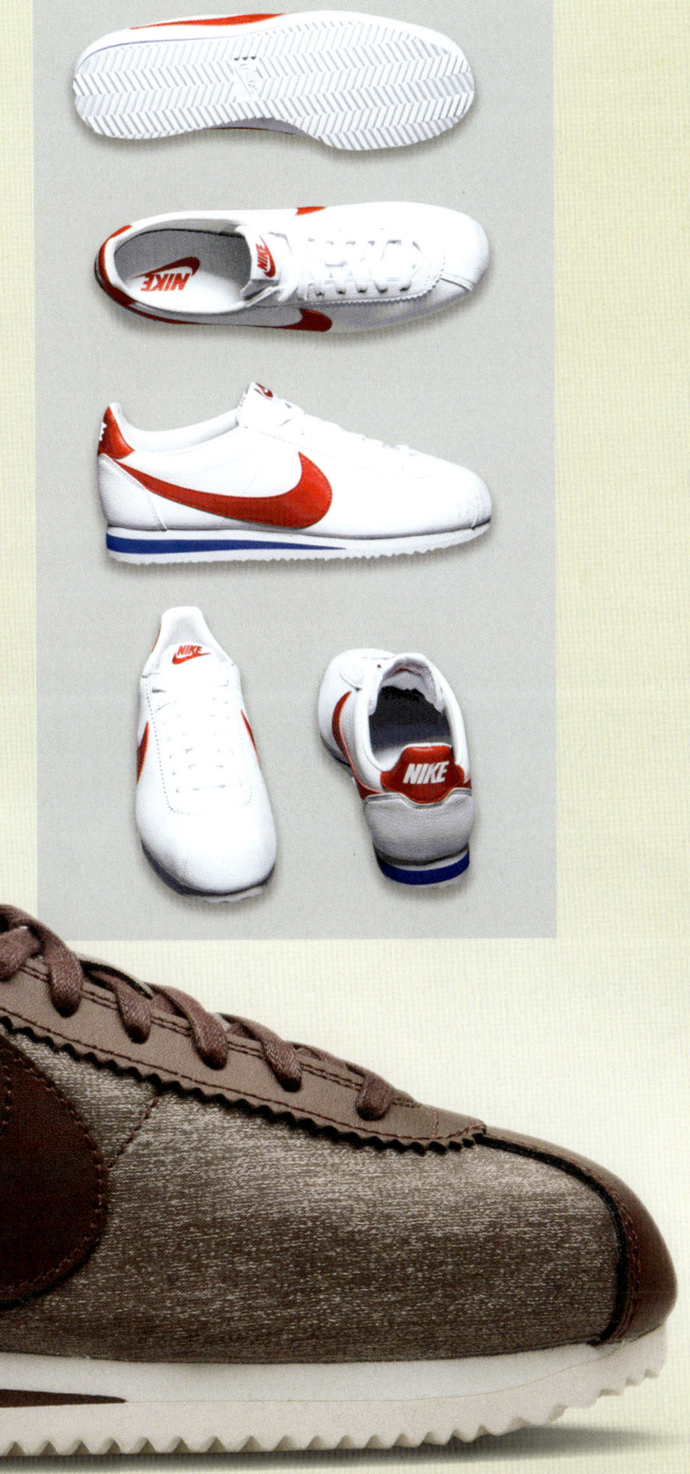

OPP PAGE: Hernán Cortés
ABOVE: (TOP) Profiles of the original Nike Cortez design and (BOTTOM) A modern Nike Classic Cortez Premium Metallic Mahogany

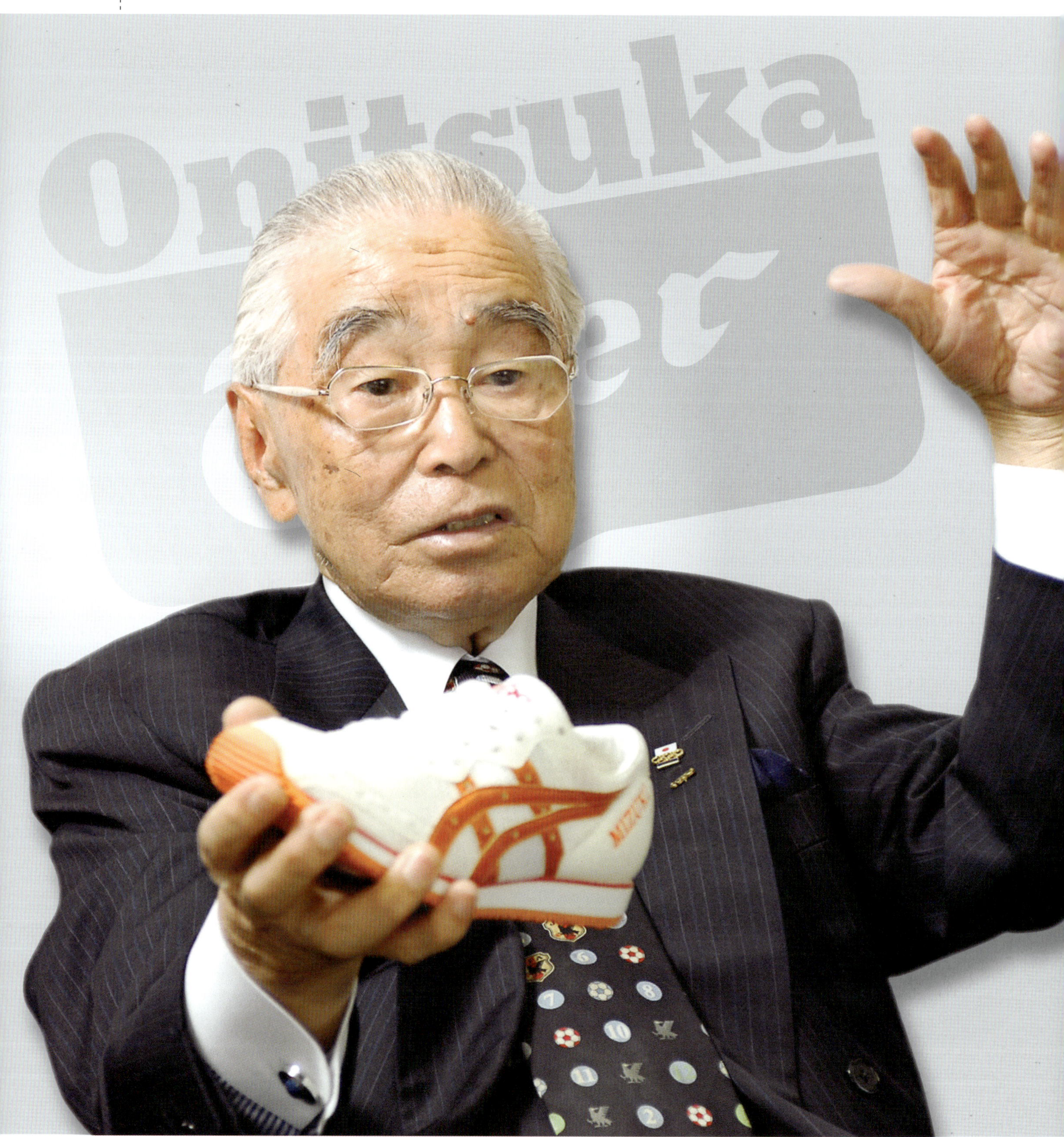

ABOVE: Onitsuka Tiger founder Kihachiro Onitsuka speaking in 2006

OPP PAGE: A comparison of the Onitsuka Tiger Cortez (renamed Corsair) and the Nike Cortez

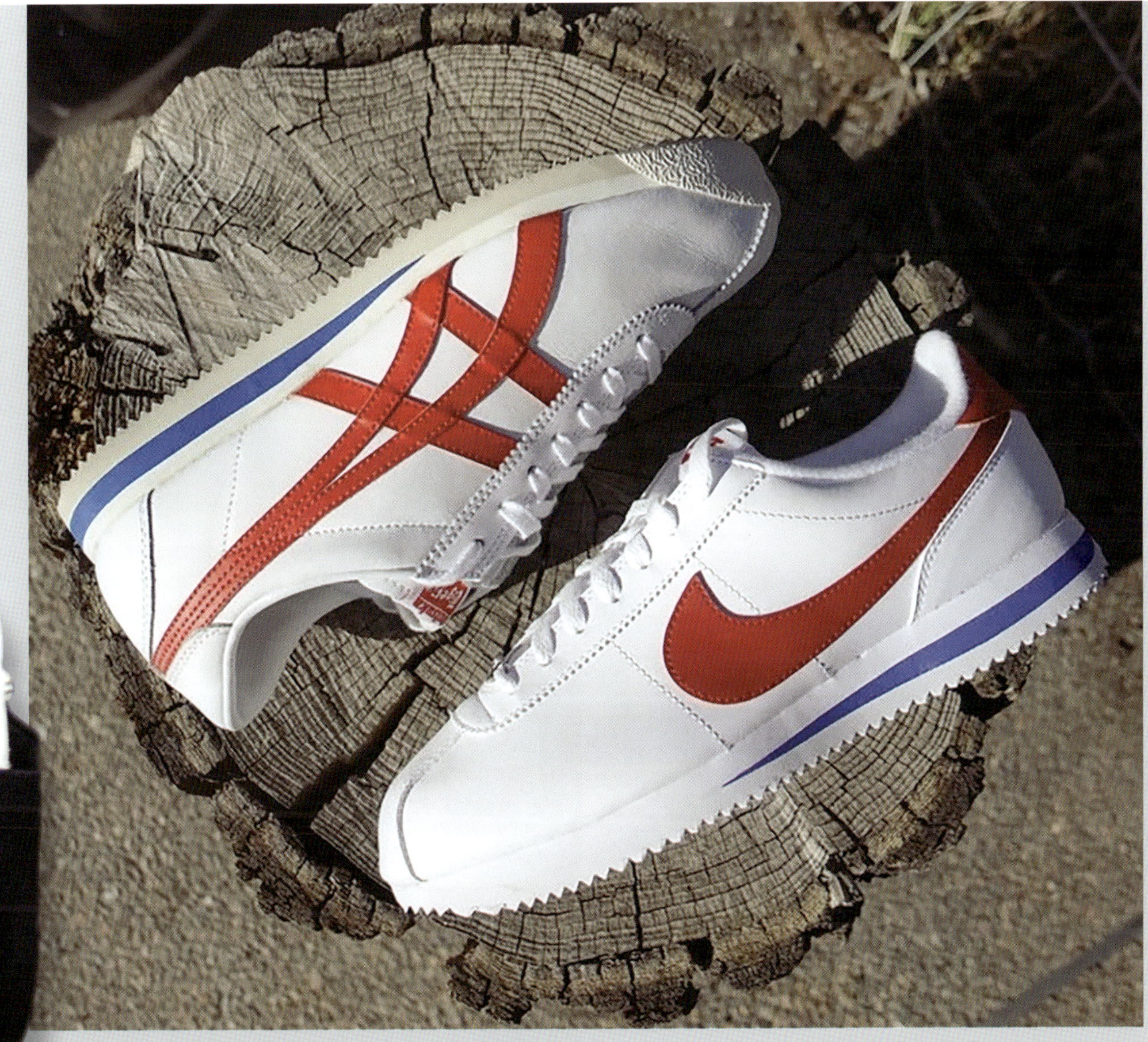

Largely in thanks to Bowerman's Cortez, Blue Ribbon Sports closed the year of 1968 in a blaze, meeting the eighty-four thousand dollars expectation of revenue. It was safe to say that Phil no longer dreaded his meeting with his banker as much as he used to.

Also, by the end of the year, Knight decided that he no longer wanted to work for Price Waterhouse. He didn't dislike the work necessarily but the hours were long and he couldn't give enough of his time to his budding business. He got a job teaching accounting at Portland State University, much to his father's dismay. Though his classroom was a far cry from the life he had initially conceived from himself, it was within those four, rather sad looking walls, where he would meet a young woman with the name of Penelope Parks.

THE TIGER'S BITE
1968-1970

*"Hard work is critical, a good team is essential,
brains and determination are invaluable,
but luck may decide the outcome."*
Phil Knight

Penelope "Penny" Parks was an accounting student at Portland State University where, rather serendipitously, Phil was also teaching. Knight later recalled his first meeting with his soon to be wife and how he was instantly enamoured by her beauty, saying, "she had long golden hair that brushed her shoulders, and matching golden hoop earrings that also brushed her shoulders. I looked at her, and she looked at me [...] She gave a half smile [...] Penelope, like the faithful wife of world-traveling Odysseus". The pair immediately struck up a friendly relationship, with Penny being drawn to Phil's dry humour and intense, slightly enigmatic personality, while Phil was completely captivated by Penny's warmth, intelligence, and quiet confidence. A couple of weeks after the start of the Fall semester, Phil offered her a job as a bookkeeper at Blue Ribbon Sports.

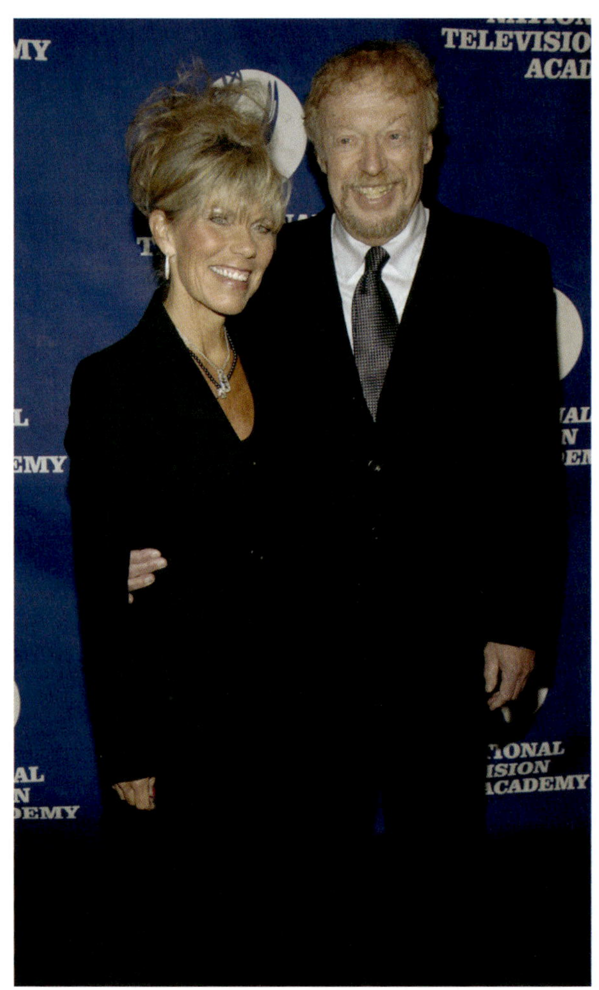

RIGHT: Penny Knight and Phil Knight pictured during the 26th Annual Sports Emmy Awards in 2005
OPP PAGE: Onitsuka Tiger store front

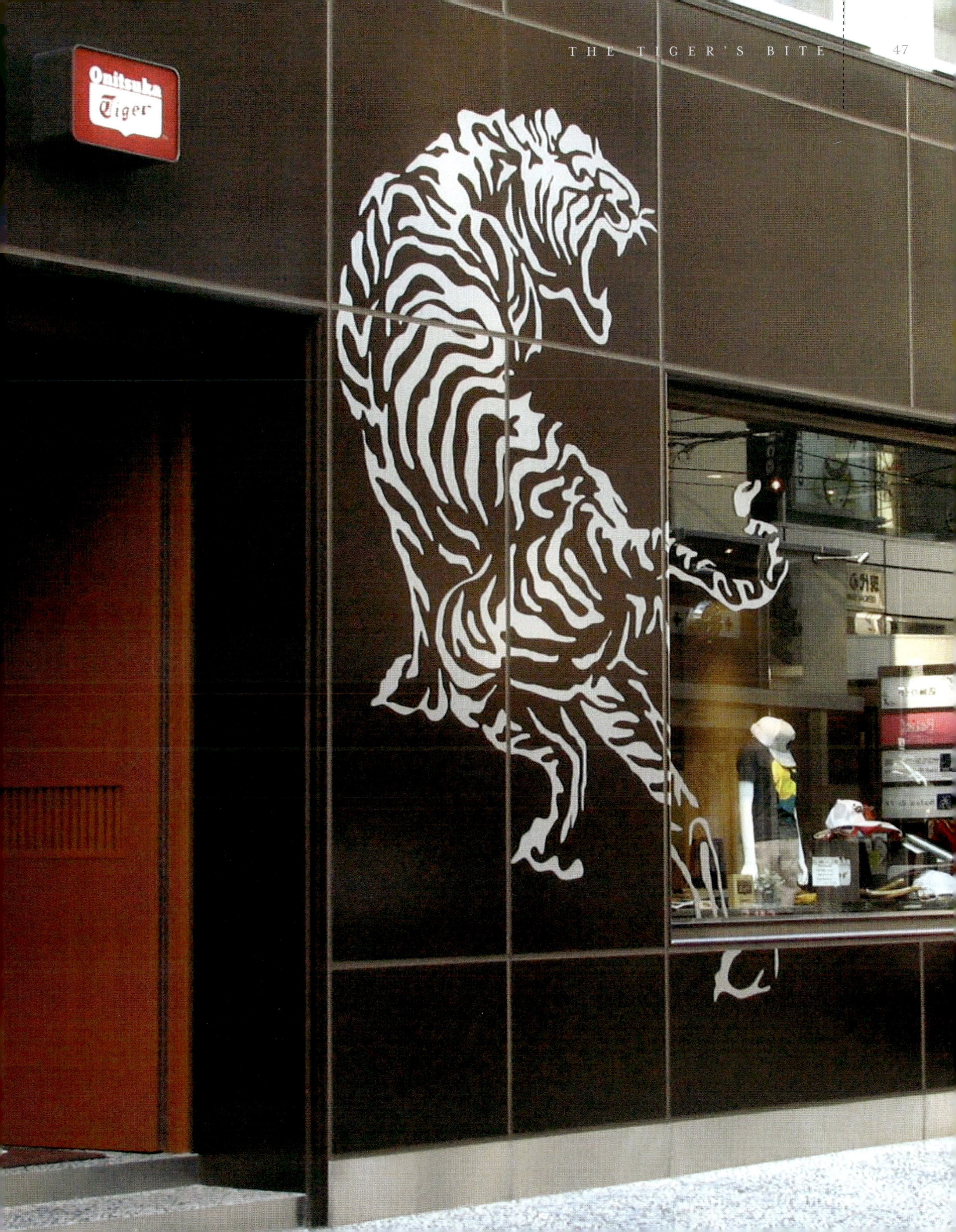

Onitsuka
Tiger

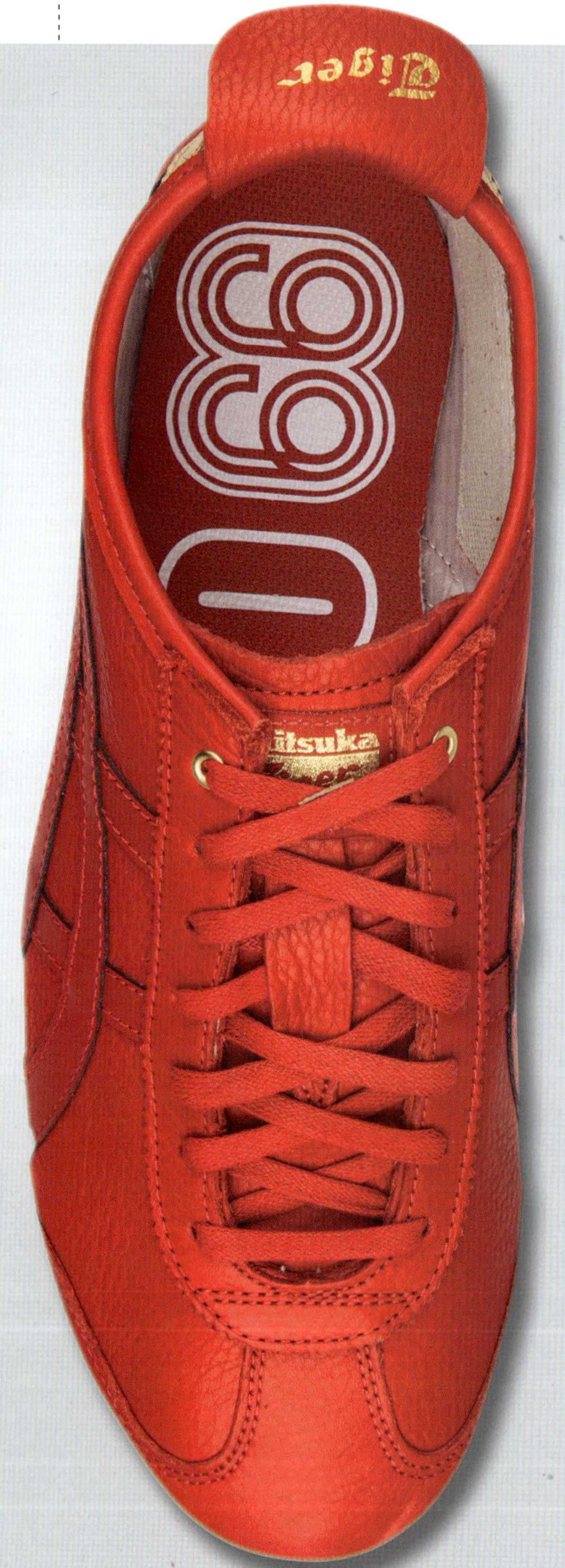

From there, their friendship grew into a steady relationship, a refreshing counterpoint to the pressures Knight faced in building his young company. Despite the demands of Phil's entrepreneurial life, Penny remained supportive and grounded, valuing his dreams and understanding the drive that fuelled him. In her, Phil found a partner who could stand by him through the highs and lows of his business journey. The two were married in a small, intimate ceremony in September of 1968, marking the beginning of a lifelong partnership that would prove essential in both Phil's personal life and his journey to build Nike.

Phil never considered himself an overly optimistic person, nor a particularly pessimistic person for that matter, he just tried to stay somewhere between the two. But over the last two years, his company was by all metrics flourishing. In 1968 the company posted $150,000 in sales and in 1969 Blue Ribbon Sports was on its way to making just under $300,000. Rising sales enabled Phil to hire more employees, meaning a whole new cast of characters were now wandering in and out of the office, including Carolyn Davidson, a young art student from his university. She was tasked with the job of advertising Blue Ribbon Sports and its products. The increase in profits also allowed Knight to finally give himself a salary and eventually leave his teaching position at Portland State University.

ABOVE: Onitsuka Tiger Mexico 66 Red, released 2 years before the Mexico Olympics in 1966
OPP PAGE: Poster from the Mexico Olympics 1968

MEXICO CITY '68 – THE GAMES THAT SHOOK THE WORLD

As the 1968 Olympics unfolded in Mexico City, Bill Bowerman arrived not as a spectator but as an assistant coach for the U.S. track and field team. Bowerman witnessed firsthand the remarkable athletic achievements that arose from these challenging conditions. He marvelled at Bob Beamon's world-record long jump, a breathtaking leap that defied convention and seemed to hover beyond belief. He also played a pivotal role in the U.S. winning more gold medals than any team, from any nation, ever. Phil Knight's partner was more than famous; he was now legendary. But more importantly, Bowerman was there to experience one of the most politically charged cultural moments in sports history. On the 16th of October 1968, African American sprinters Tommie Smith and John Carlos, the gold and bronze medallists in the men's 200-meter race, took their places on the podium for the medal ceremony wearing human rights badges and black socks without shoes, lowered their heads and each raised a black-gloved fist as "The Star Spangled Banner" was played, in solidarity with the Black Freedom Movement in the United States. Both were members of the Olympic Project for Human Rights. The International Olympic Committee (IOC) president Avery Brundage, deemed the act to be a domestic political statement unfit for the apolitical, international forum the Olympic Games were intended to be. In response to their actions, he ordered Smith and Carlos to be suspended from the US team and

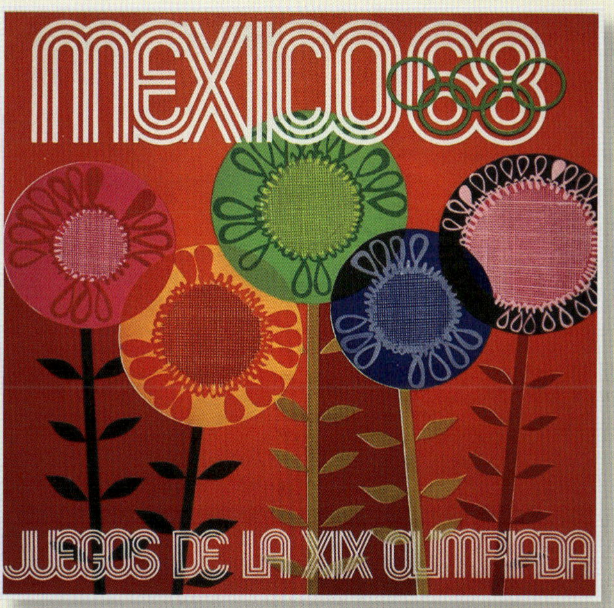

banned from the Olympic Village. When the US Olympic Committee refused, Brundage threatened to ban the entire US track team. This threat led to the expulsion of the two athletes from the Games. Although he was a patriot, Bowerman respected the power of their protest, seeing it as a courageous stand that went beyond sport.

Returning from Mexico City, Bowerman was more committed than ever to creating innovative tools and training methods for athletes. He had witnessed history in Mexico, not only in athletic achievement but in a broadening sense of purpose for sports as a platform for change. For Bowerman, Mexico City '68 was a powerful reminder that sports could inspire, unite, and even disrupt, and he carried these lessons into every shoe he crafted, every athlete he coached and decision he would take to shape Nike into a brand not only of performance but of identity and expression.

Almost a year after Phil and Penny's wedding, the couple welcomed their first child, a boy named Matthew Knight on the 11th of September 1969. The new family of three moved into a quaint but beautiful home in the neighbouring town of Beavertown, Oregon. At the same time that Phil and his family outgrew their apartment in downtown Portland, so did his business. Knight obviously couldn't afford to lease a whole office building yet, but he did manage to rent out a corner of a floor in a building occupied by an insurance company. The change of address was a clear signifier that Blue Ribbon Sports was slowly but surely establishing itself as one of the most promising and exciting small companies around.

Although business was continuing to boom, by the end of 1969, Phil's relationship with Onitsuka Tiger began to unravel, bringing Blue Ribbon Sports to a defining crossroads. For nearly five years, Knight and his small team had poured their blood, sweat and tears into building a market for Onitsuka Tiger shoes in the United States, introducing American runners to affordable, high-quality footwear and watching their company grow beyond anyone's wildest dreams. But with the company's success came growing tensions. The people at Onitsuka were constantly late sending over shipments and when they did eventually arrive, very often the shoes wouldn't be in the right sizes. This created financial strain for Blue Ribbon Sports as they were unable to sell as much product as they needed to meet their sales objectives for the year. Additionally, contact between the two companies was becoming more and more scarce, with Phil going weeks even months with his letters left unanswered. By the end of the decade, Phil sensed that the partnership with Onitsuka, once strong and full of promise, was headed toward a rocky end that would change everything.

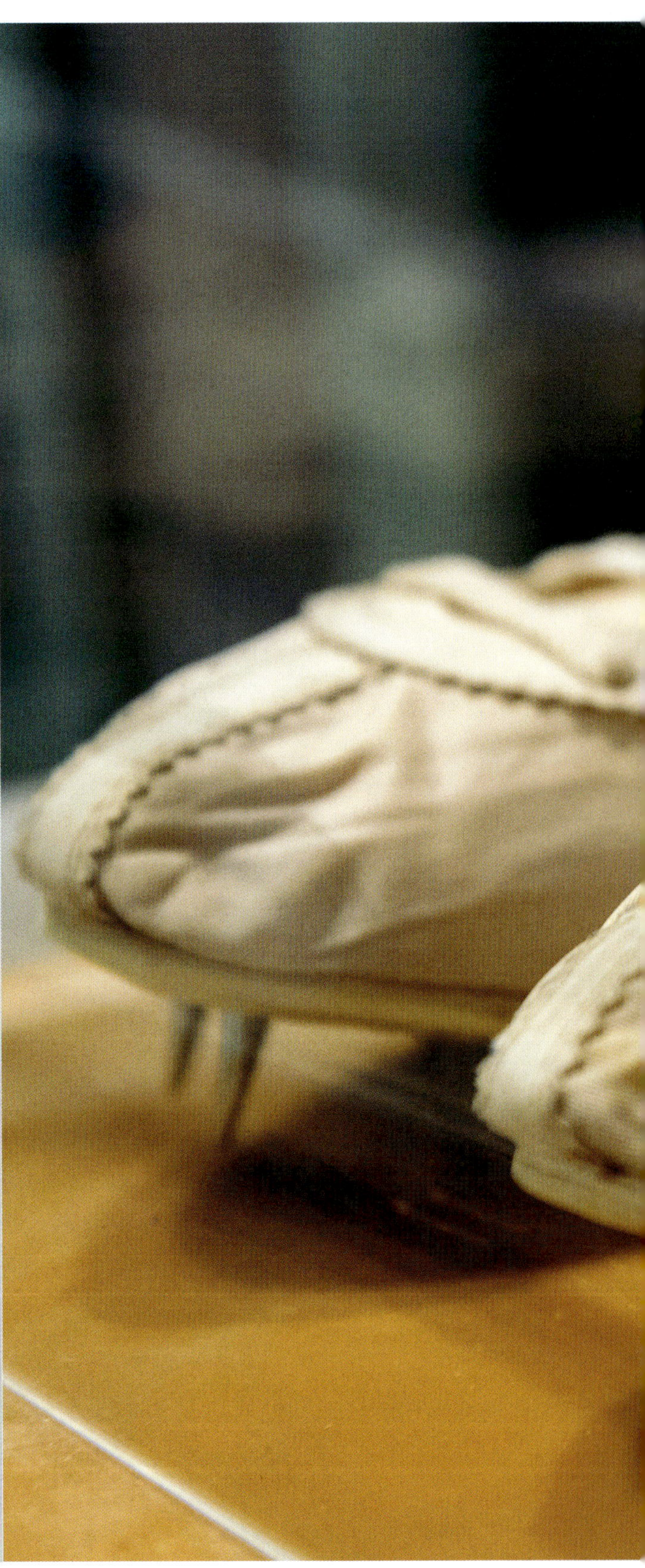

RIGHT: Onitsuka Tiger TG-4 Marathon and Nylon spikes, 1968-72

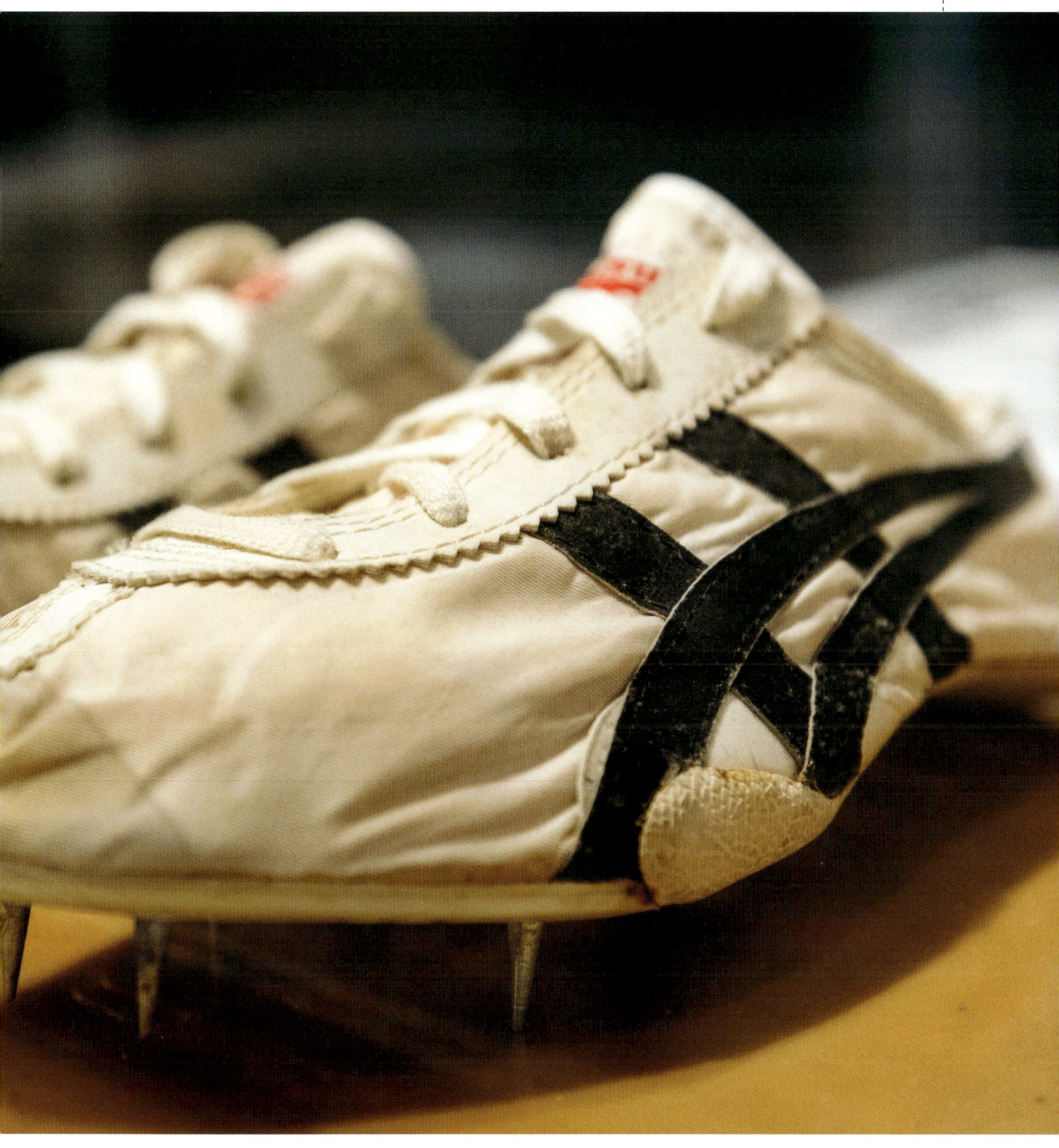

THE GODDESS OF VICTORY

1971 PART 1

"The single easiest way to find out how you feel about someone. Say goodbye"

Phil Knight

In 1971, Knight was still hopeful he could salvage his relationship with Onitsuka. He reasoned with himself that better the devil you know than the devil you don't. Besides, they had seven years of history and that alone was worth fighting for. Phil decided that in order to restore Onitsuka's faith in him, he would just need to remind them of what Blue Ribbon Sports was all about, which meant inviting Kitami to the United States for a friendly visit. Kitami accepted the invitation and in March of that year, Phil was face to face with his former friend. Little did he know that this meeting would mark a turning point in both his business and his life.

During their chat, Kitami got up to go to the bathroom, leaving his briefcase wide open on Phil's desk. Unable to contain his curiosity, Knight immediately jumped up from his seat to riffle through the contents of the folder. As he quickly scanned the documents, Phil's greatest fears were realised when he stumbled upon a list of

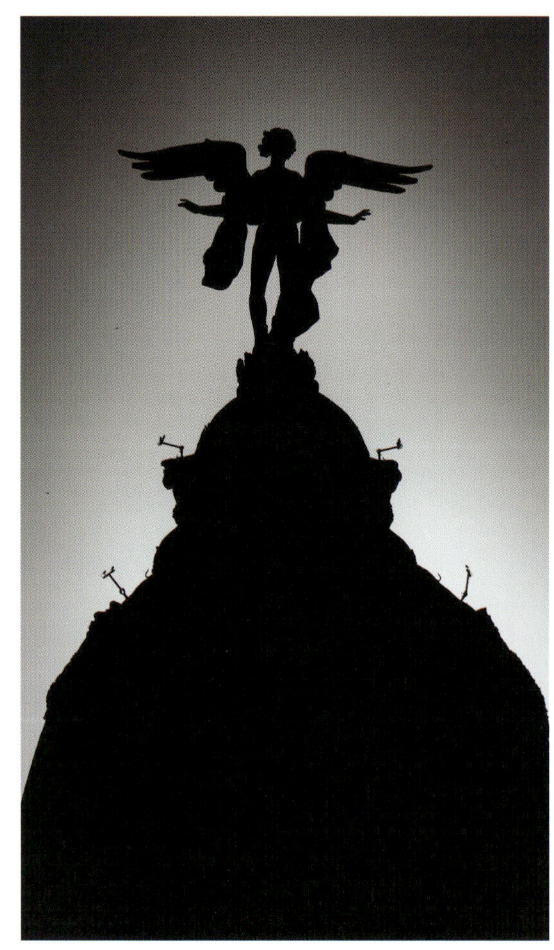

RIGHT: Nike was the Greek goddess of victory to whom Olympic athletes made offerings and prayers at the Temple of Zeus

OPP PAGE: Nike goddess mural on a partially-demolished building

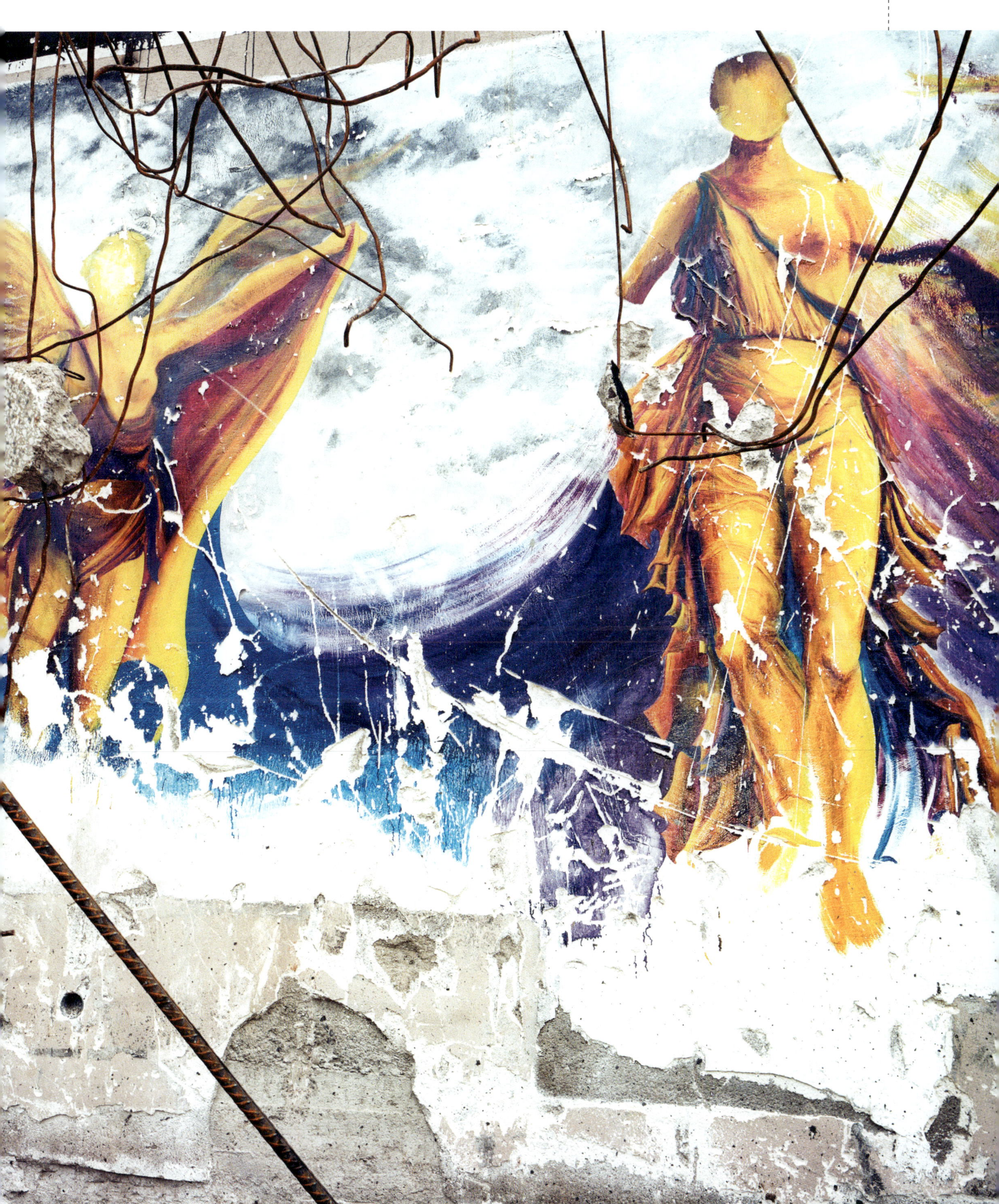

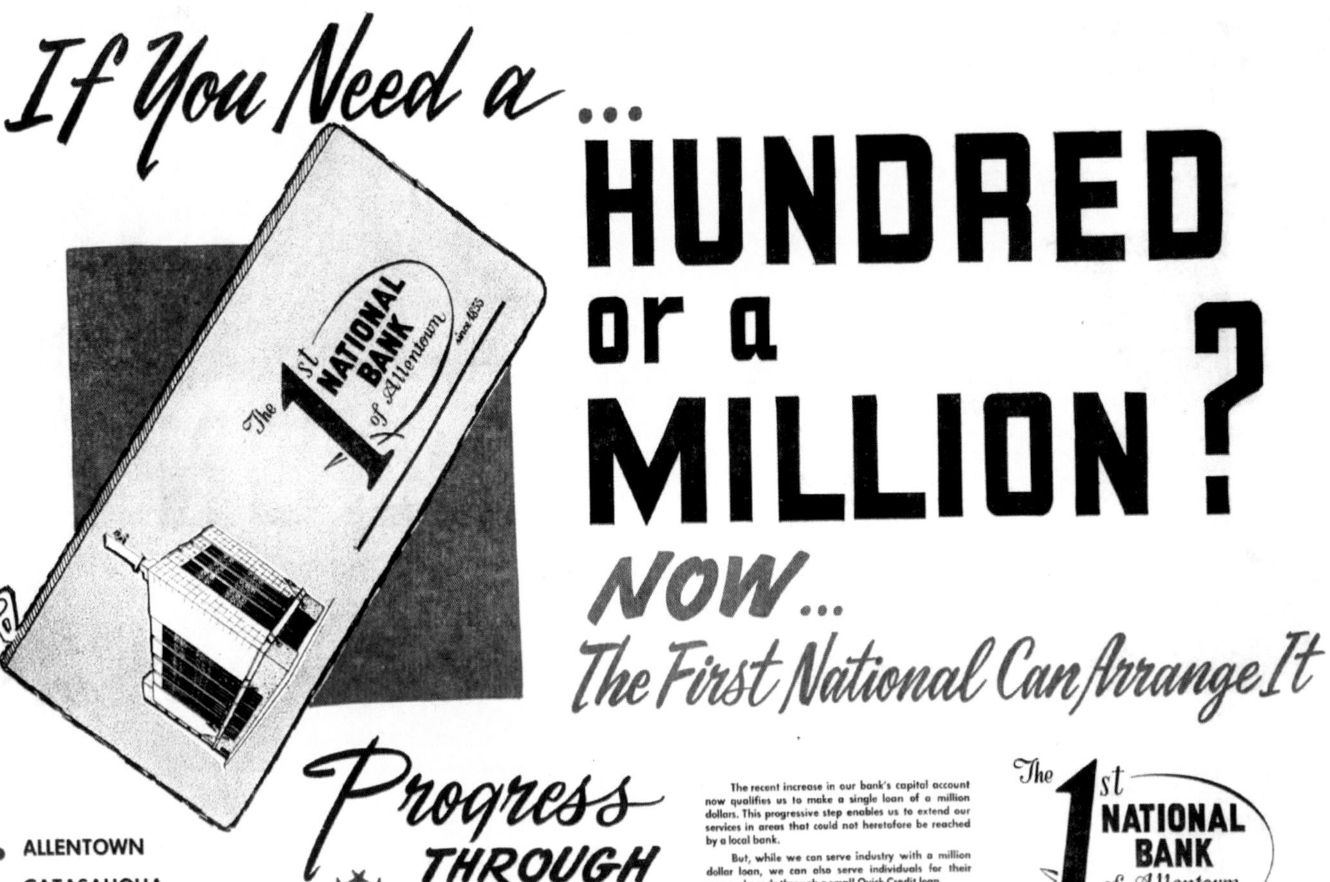

eighteen athletic shoe distributors across the United States as well as a schedule of appointments with over half of them. Knight had always seen himself as more than a distributor for Onitsuka. Since the day he'd pitched his "crazy idea" to the Japanese executives, he'd nurtured a vision of building a brand that would elevate athletic performance and the art of running itself. But now, him and his efforts were being undermined.

Phil later commented on this watershed moment by saying, "I was outraged, of course. But mostly hurt. For seven years we'd devoted ourselves to Tiger shoes. We'd introduced them to America; we'd reinvented the line. Bowerman and Johnson had shown Onitsuka how to make a better shoe, and their designs were now foundational, setting sales records, changing the face of the industry—and this was how we were repaid?".

ABOVE: First National Bank advertisment, 1963
OPP PAGE: A buyer for Nissho-Iwai at the Sydney Wool Sales, 2 September, 1971

This move felt like a betrayal. To Phil, it was clear that Onitsuka had come to view Blue Ribbon as expendable. Feeling sidelined, he realized that Onitsuka was no longer a company he could trust—or rely on for his business's future. It was time for them to go their own way.

To compound problems, Blue Ribbon Sports' relationship to First National Bank had reached the end of the line. The bank said they would no longer issue any more letters of credit to Phil or his business which meant that when they had paid off the remaining bills, the Blue Ribbon account would be terminated. Phil's company, born from nothing, and now finishing 1971 with sales of $1.3 million, was on life support. Knight did manage to get a small loan from a Californian bank, but it was still a short-term solution to a growing problem. What he really needed was money from a partner that understood the importance of growth.

A couple of weeks later, in the most miraculous of timings, Tom Sumeragi, a representative of the Japanese company Nissho Iwai, stepped in as Blue-Ribbon Sports' financial lifeline. This serendipitous backing allowed Phil to continue operations, import shoes, and even expand at a time when traditional financing was difficult to secure.

This new relationship was an opportunity for Phil to create something uniquely his own, a company that embodied his vision and could serve athletes without

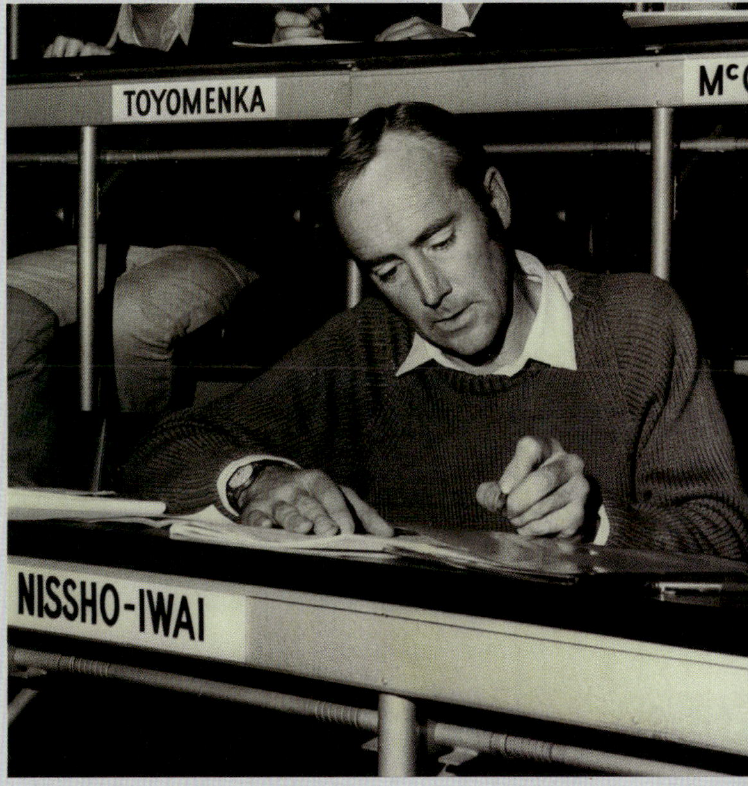

restriction. While he was still technically under contract with Onitsuka, Phil began quietly preparing to sever ties for good, laying the groundwork for a future without the Japanese brand. He signed a contract with a factory in central Mexico and placed an order for three thousand leather shoes he planned to sell as football boots.

Amid all this change, Phil saw it as the perfect time to redefine his company. He set out to create a fresh identity, crafting a new logo, name, and product line that aligned with his vision for the future. In fact, it is under this reinvention that Phil Knight and formerly Blue Ribbon Sports, will come to be known throughout the world and for many generations to come.

A SWOOSH TOWARDS VICTORY

In 1971, as Phil Knight and his team at Blue Ribbon Sports prepared to launch their first independent line of shoes, they faced a new and crucial challenge: creating a brand identity that would capture their vision and stand out against industry giants like Adidas and Onitsuka Tiger. Knight knew the brand needed more than just a good product. It needed a name that conveyed power and uniqueness—and a logo that could leave a lasting mark on athletes and consumers alike.

As he brainstormed ideas, he remembered a talented young artist he'd met at Portland State University, Carolyn Davidson, who had done graphic work for Blue Ribbon before. He invited her to the office, explained his vague concept, and asked her to create a logo that would evoke movement. "Something that says speed," he told her, though he admitted he wasn't sure exactly what he wanted. Davidson, after a couple of weeks, returned with her first sketches, though none quite hit the mark. Phil and his team debated various options and ultimately selected a simple design—a swoosh that looked like a wing in motion. Davidson's sketch wasn't what Knight initially had in mind, but it conveyed a sense of energy and movement that felt promising. "It looks like something a runner might leave in his wake", someone remarked. The swoosh symbolized speed, the swiftness of athletes, and the spirit of motion that Blue Ribbon Sports wanted to champion. For her work, Davidson was paid $35—a modest sum for what would become one of the world's most recognizable logos.

With a logo in hand, Knight and his team turned to the equally daunting task of selecting a brand name. After hours of brainstorming, they had only a shortlist of ideas. Knight's suggestion, "Dimension Six," was his favourite, but the team found it uninspired. Another suggestion, "Falcon," had potential, but it still didn't quite feel right. As the production deadlines loomed, the team grew frustrated, churning through suggestions from every employee and seemingly every animal name in the dictionary. Finally, in a last-minute burst of inspiration, Blue Ribbon's first employee, Jeff Johnson, called in with a name that had come to him in a dream: "Nike," after the Greek goddess of victory.

At first, Knight was hesitant. He didn't love the sound of it, but with production schedules and marketing plans on the line, he had little choice but to decide quickly. Knight reflected briefly on the goddess Nike, the symbol of victory, and realized the significance. Victory was at the heart of his own journey with Blue Ribbon Sports—a small company, up against giants, competing against the odds. "Nike" represented triumph, a fitting identity for the brand Phil wanted to build. He decided, reluctantly, to approve it.

Thus, Nike was born. It was a name that, Knight hoped, might grow on him over time. With the Swoosh logo and the goddess-inspired name, Phil felt both liberated and anxious. They had the building blocks of a new brand, one that was uniquely theirs, and a future that was now completely in their hands.

OPP PAGE TOP: The evolution of the Nike swoosh, 1971-1996
OPP PAGE BOTTOM: A large Nike swoosh on the outside of the Nike Store, Deer Park, New York

LOGO EVOLUTION

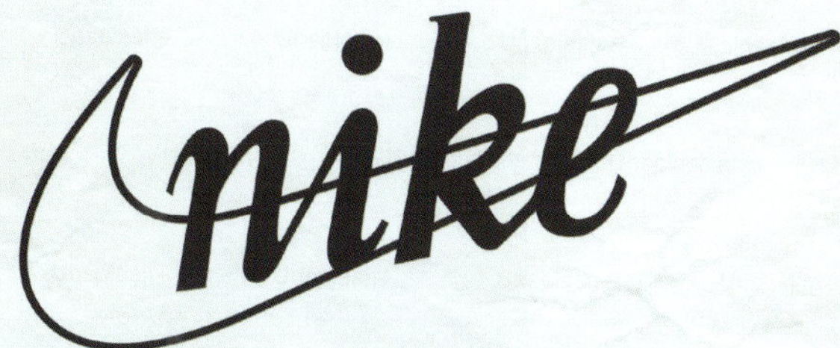

1971

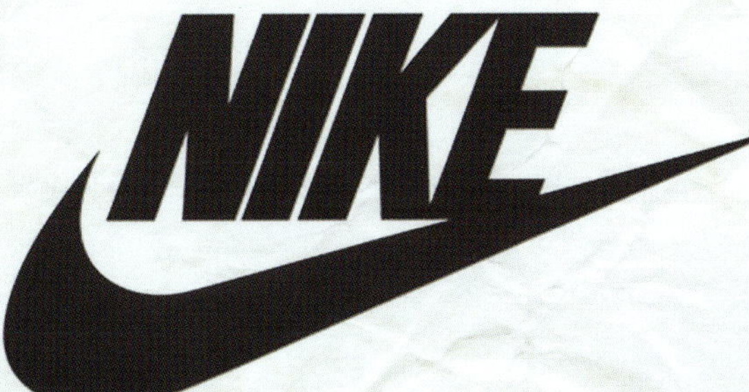

1978

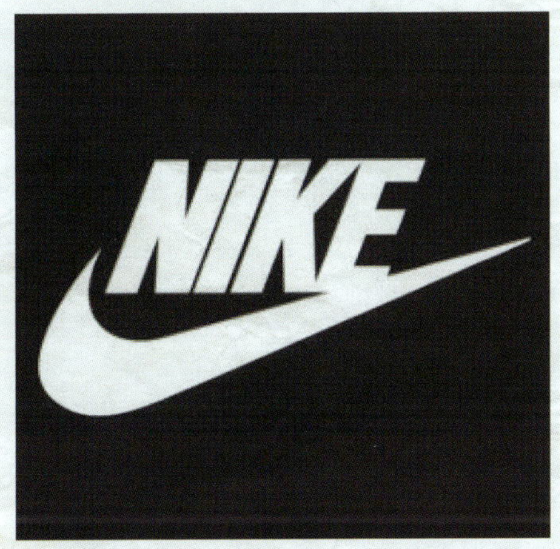

1985

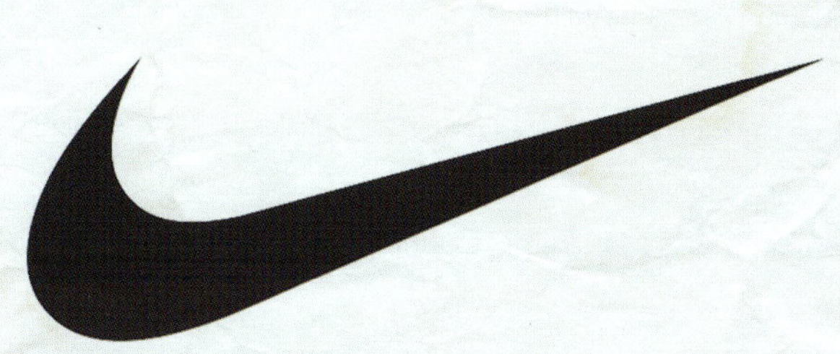

1995

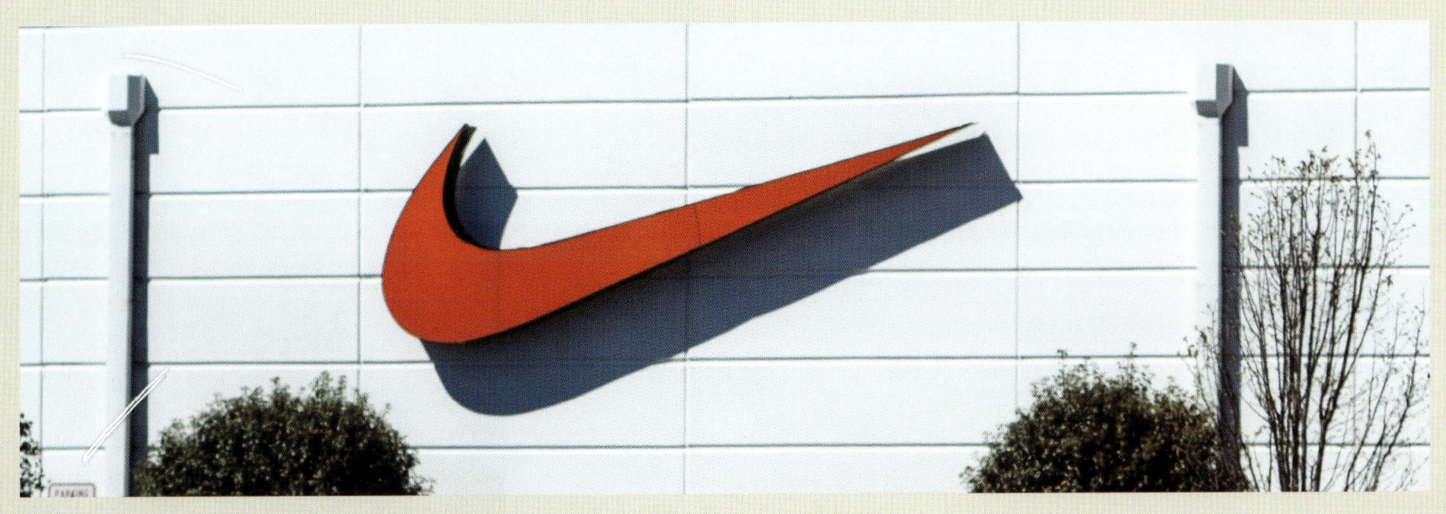

THE WAFFLE IRON REVOLUTION
1971 PART 2

"If we're going to succeed, or fail, we should do so on our own terms, with our own ideas—our own brand... Let's look at this as our liberation. Our Independence Day."

Phil Knight

In the early days of the relationship with Nissho, the promise of cash injections was undeniably exciting, but Phil remained cautious, mindful of how his partnership with Onitsuka had ultimately soured. To safeguard Blue Ribbon Sports, now Nike, future, he prioritized diversifying cash sources, which led him to the prospect of a public offering. Learning from his first attempt, Phil decided to promote the company more assertively, opting for convertible debentures instead of traditional stock options. Put simply, the public loans money to a company in exchange for quasi

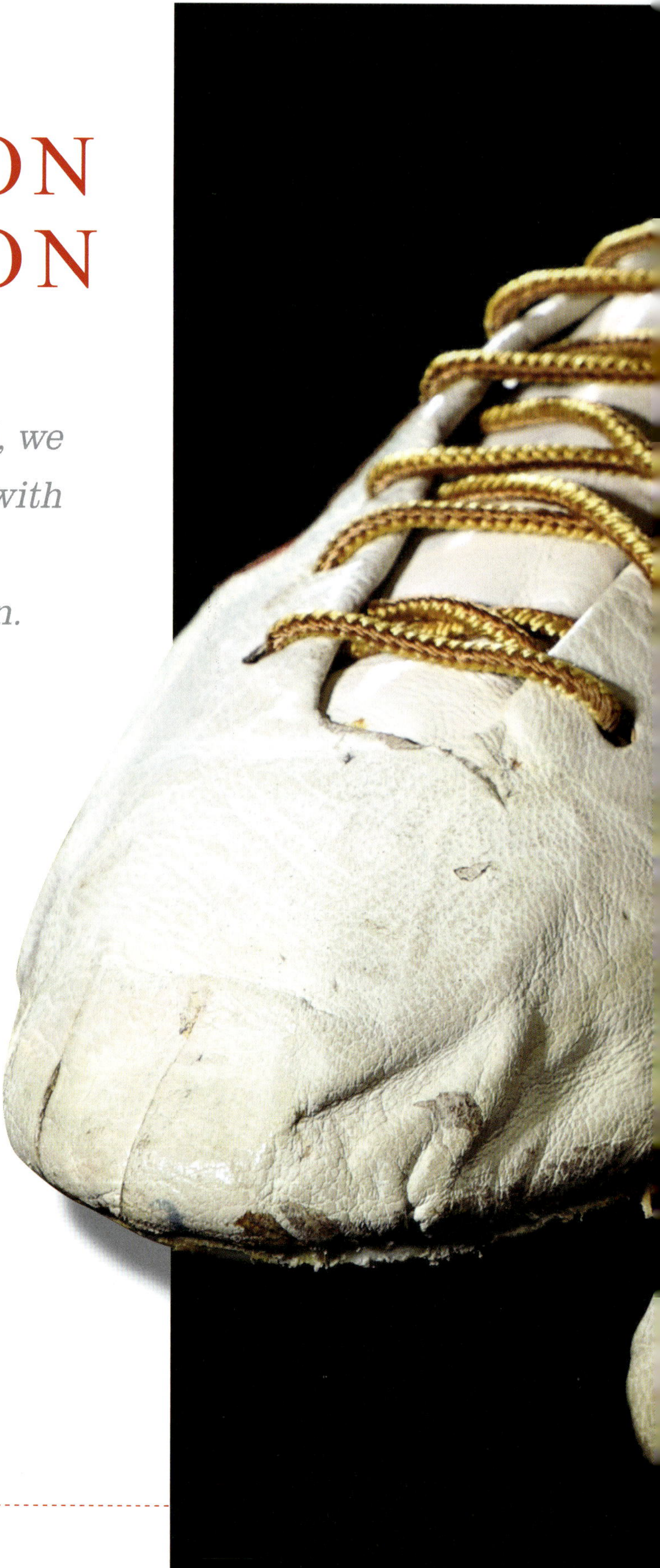

RIGHT: Bill Bowerman's handmade prototype track spikes with the waffle sole on display at *The Olympic Collection* at Sotheby's

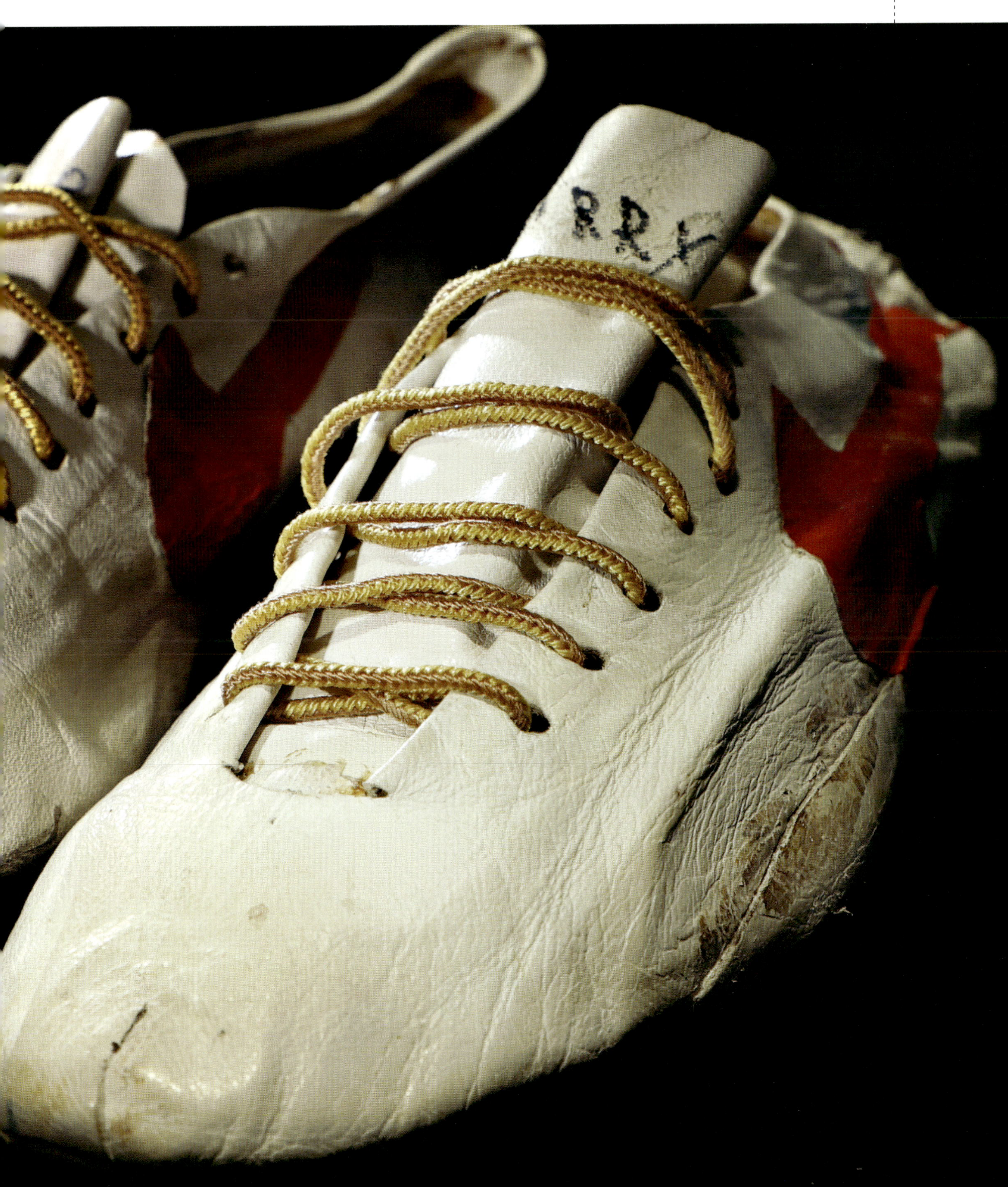

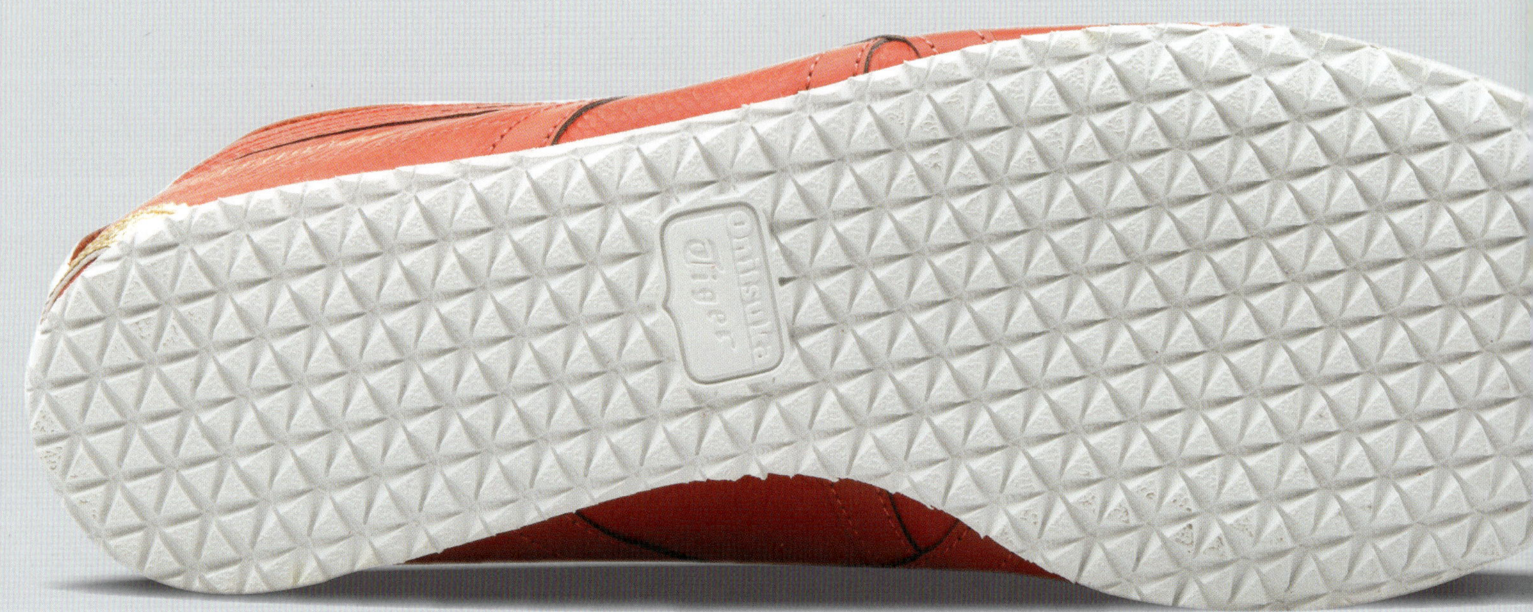

stock in that business. Its quasi because debenture holders are incentivised to hold their shares for five years and after that they can trade them in for actual stock or get their money back with interest. Because of its risk adverse properties and with the help of a hard driving salesmen, the launch of these convertible debentures was a total success.

Following this victory, almost like clockwork, things started to go awry in Mexico. The new leather football shoe that Phil commissioned from the factory in Guadalajara, though aesthetically appealing, turned out to be fragile in colder weather. The soles of the shoes would just split and crack, a misstep that prompted a change in manufacturer. Nissho were more than happy to provide Phil with access to various factories and connect him with an experienced shoe expert, a man called Sole. Though Knight was very grateful for all the help, the partnership with Nissho

came with inherent risks, as working exclusively with them could lead to dependency.

Phil decided to seek some advice and reassurance from industry veterans on how best to handle the situation. He reached out to Chuck Robinson, the CEO of Marcona Mining. In their conversation, Chuck advised Phil to set firm boundaries with the Japanese company to avoid a redo of the Onitsuka debacle. And that's exactly what he did. He notably communicated to Nissho that under no circumstances were they to take any equity stakes in Nike. With all that cleared up, Phil was free to go to Japan and meet with the shoe expert.

Once he got to Japan, Sole's son brought Knight up and down the country to tour various promising factories. They ended up in Kurume, a city on the island of Kyushu to visit Nippon Rubber, a Japanese

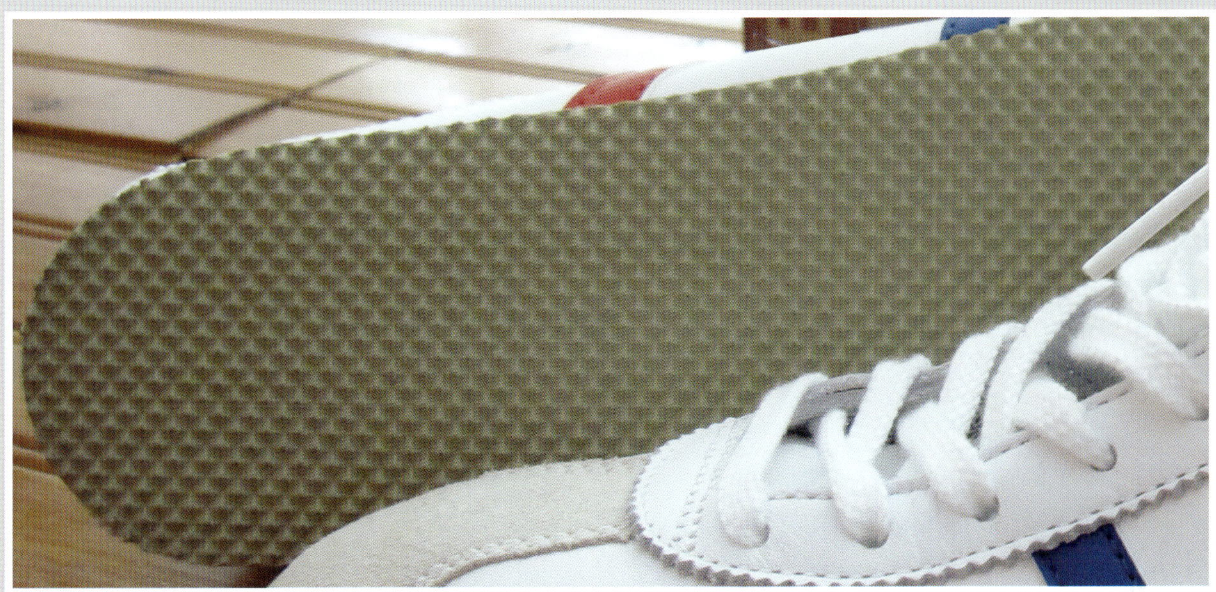

factory. Phil explained to the factory officials exactly the type of shoe he wanted, showing them the model. The officials nodded gravely, though Knight wasn't sure they fully understood. After lunch, they returned to the conference room, where he found a brand-new Cortez on the table, complete with the Nike side stripe, fresh from the factory floor. It felt like magic.

Phil spent the rest of the afternoon describing additional models he envisioned: tennis shoes, basketball shoes, high-tops, low-tops, and several more types of running shoes. The officials insisted that producing any of these designs would be no problem.

The only thing to do was to wait for the samples to be delivered to Nissho's offices in Tokyo. A couple of days passed before a box of all the shoes he had commissioned came into his possession. The shoes weren't perfect—one logo wasn't quite straight, another midsole was too thin, and a different pair needed more lift. Knight made detailed notes for the factory officials. Despite these minor flaws, the samples were impressive. After a three-week stay in Japan, Phil made his way back home to Oregon with a renewed sense of optimism.

A couple of weeks later, Phil found himself sitting in Bowerman's office one rainy afternoon, discussing the future of the company and their frustrations with the running shoes they had on hand. Nothing new there. Knight spoke about durability and performance, remarking that the soles of shoes hadn't changed in over fifty years and the necessity for change. This conversation triggered something in Bowerman that would soon change the running world forever, but at first, the spark remained just that: a faint idea. Bowerman knew he wanted to improve traction, but he wasn't sure how.

HOT OFF THE IRON

The big breakthrough came from the Bowerman family breakfast table. Then, on an otherwise ordinary Sunday morning, as his wife Barbara was preparing breakfast, Bowerman's eyes caught sight of an old appliance on the kitchen counter: their family's waffle iron. The small, square ridges and grooves of the iron's surface held his attention. The texture reminded him of something that could be both pliable and supportive, just what a runner needed in a shoe sole. He realized that the waffle's unique grid might offer a new type of traction—a sole with built-in grip and resilience without the traditional heavy, flat materials most shoe companies used.

Without hesitation, Bowerman sprang into action. He rushed to his workshop, the old waffle iron in hand, grabbing a tube of urethane—a substance he'd been experimenting with in his quest to find lighter materials for shoes. If he could shape the urethane into a sole that mimicked the waffle iron's grid, it could provide grip, cushioning, and flexibility, all while cutting down on the shoe's weight.

The first experiment didn't go smoothly. Bowerman poured urethane onto the waffle iron, hoping to create a single, moulded sole. But as the urethane heated, the mixture overflowed, seeping down the sides and hardening onto the iron itself. Smoke filled the kitchen, the smell of burning plastic mingling with the aroma of breakfast. Barbara was unimpressed, and the waffle iron was, for all intents and purposes, ruined. But Bowerman was undeterred—he knew he was onto something.

After several attempts, Bowerman finally had a prototype that he could test.

He shared his prototype with Knight, who was immediately captivated by its potential. Unlike the bulky soles of most running shoes on the market, this one was remarkably lightweight, but the real marvel was its texture. The waffle pattern felt innovative— engineered not just to support a runner's foot but to

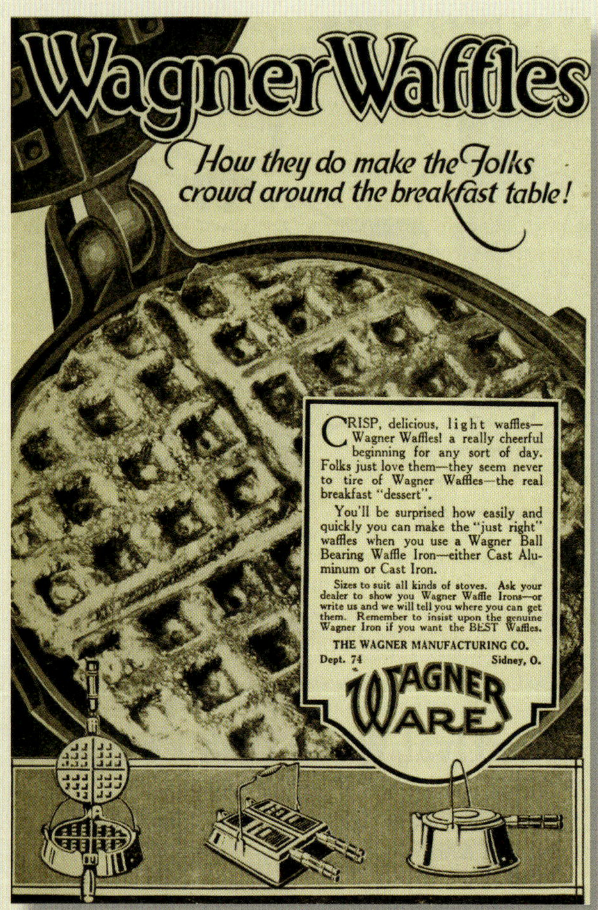

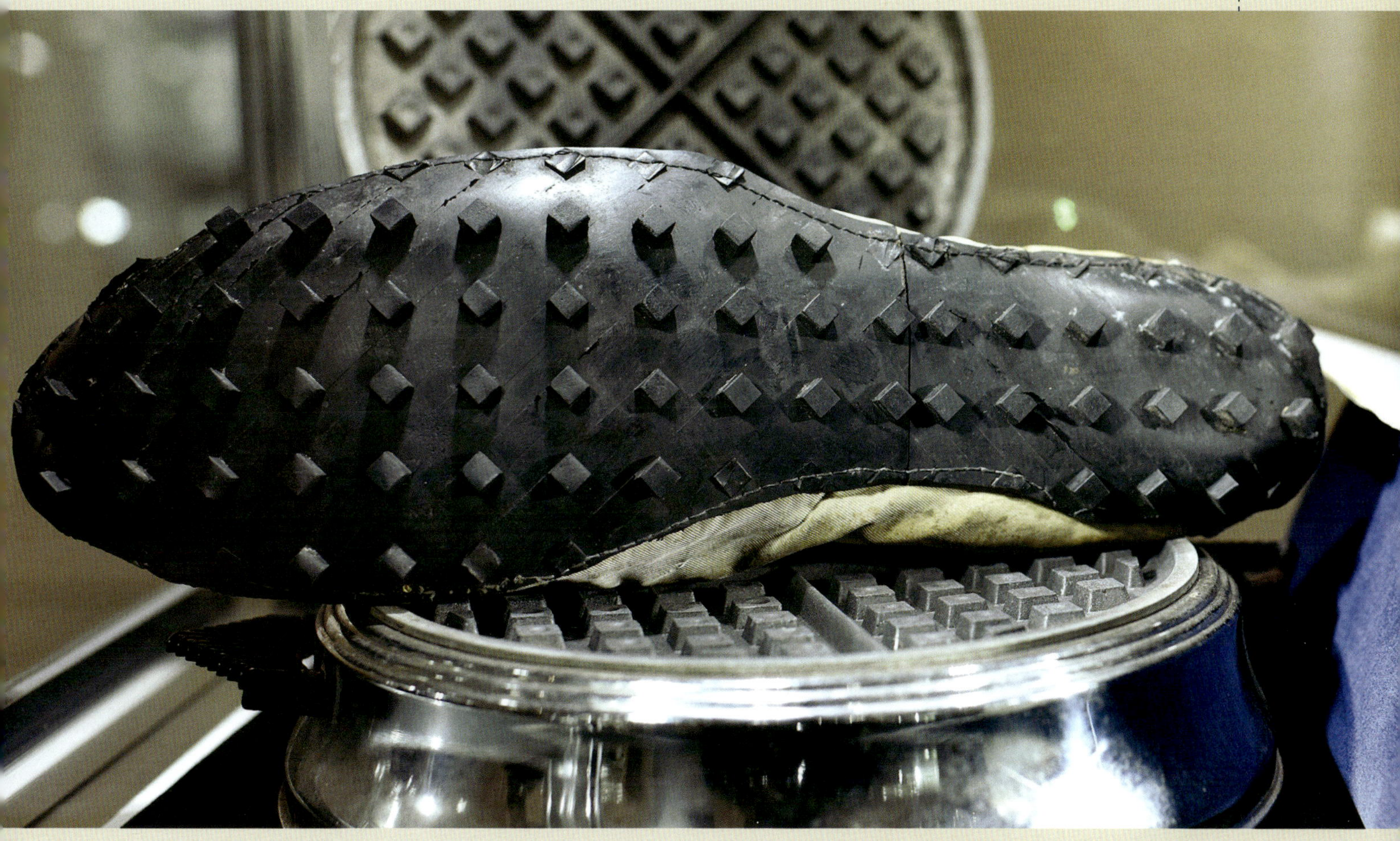

work with it. They quickly filed for the patent for their invention, the aptly named *Nike Waffle Trainer*. It would take another year or two for the *Waffle Trainer* to hit the shelves, but when it did, it quickly captured the attention of the running community.

Runners across the country and around the world recognized the innovation as more than a novelty—it was a genuine leap forward in footwear technology. The waffle sole wasn't just about function; it was about an aesthetic that said, "This is different. This is progress." For Bowerman and Knight, it was proof that thinking outside the box—or inside the waffle iron—

could produce something revolutionary.

The "Waffle Revolution" had begun, and it wouldn't stop there. Bowerman's discovery transformed Nike's approach to design, pushing them to constantly question the status quo, to seek new solutions in unconventional places, and to listen to the needs of athletes. The Waffle Trainer's sole became iconic, an emblem of both Bowerman's relentless creativity and Knight's determination to bring innovation to the masses. Together, they'd created something extraordinary—a shoe that, as it turned out, was only the beginning.

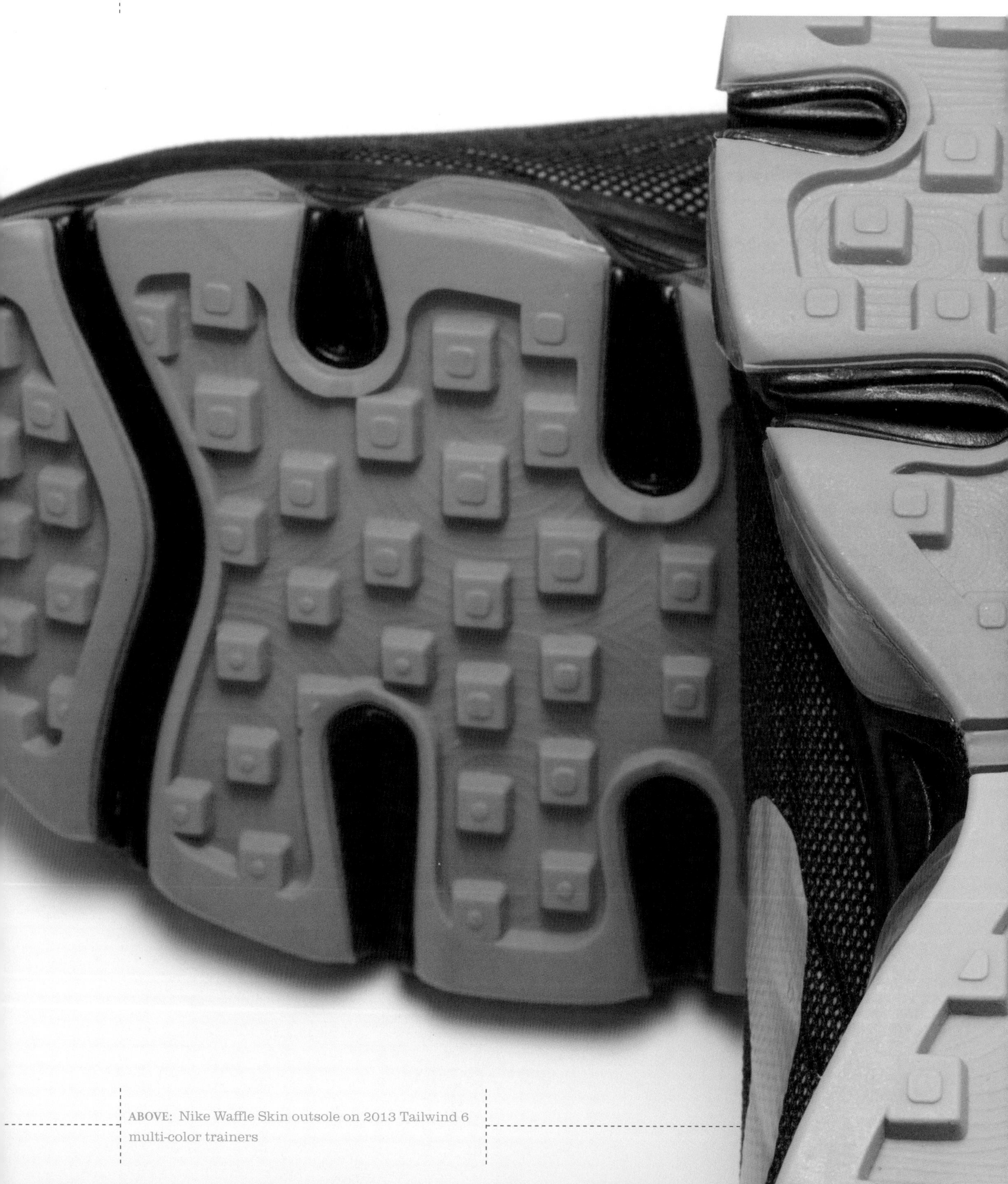

ABOVE: Nike Waffle Skin outsole on 2013 Tailwind 6
multi-color trainers

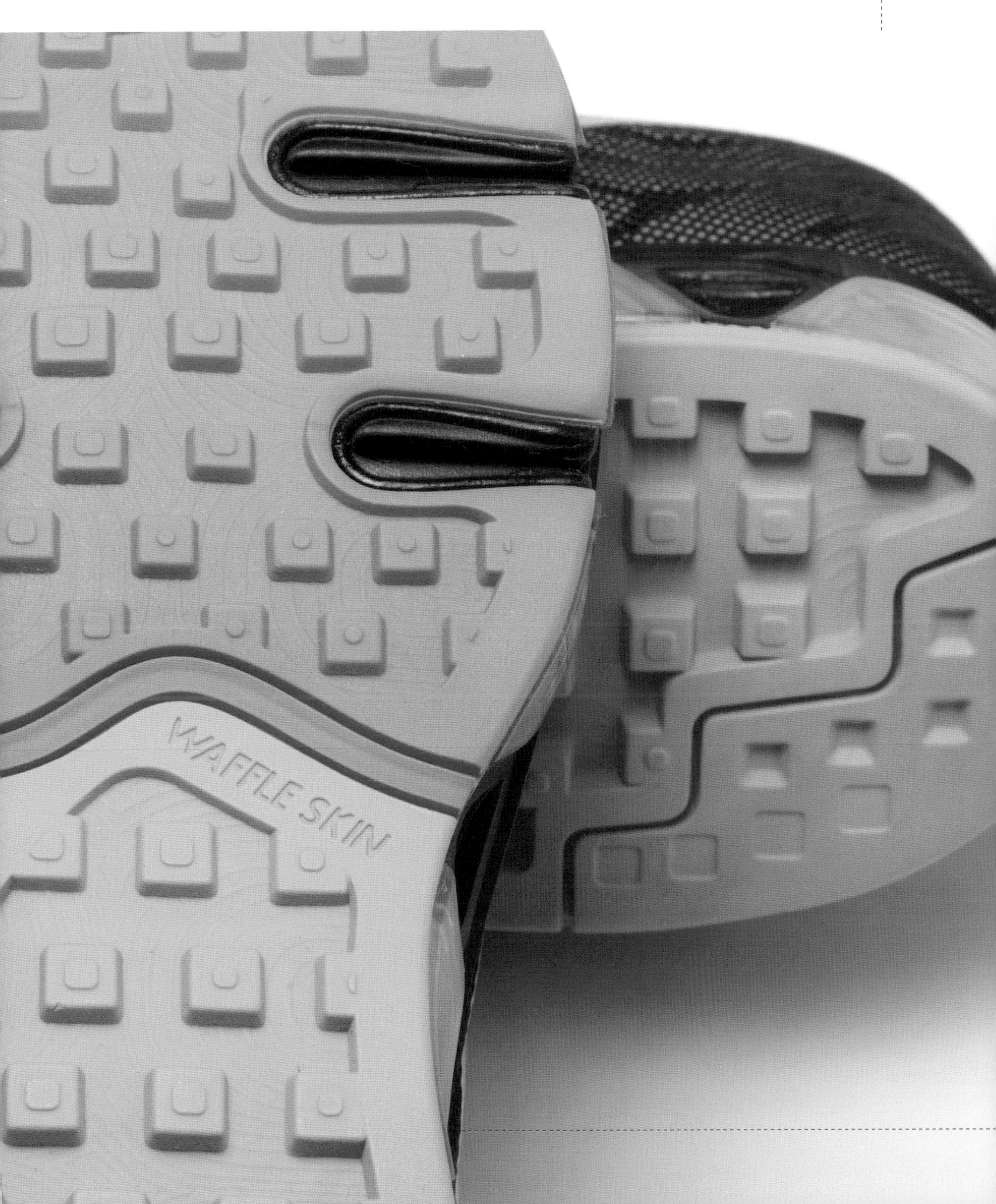
WAFFLE SKIN

ATHLETES AND ADVERSITY

1972- 1973

"To give anything less than your best, is to sacrifice the gift"
Steve Prefontaine

In 1972, Phil was deeply embroiled in an acrimonious legal battle against his former partner, Onitsuka. Upon learning of the Nike project, the Japanese manufacturer challenged Blue Ribbon Sports for violation of the non-competition agreement, which prohibited Phil's company from importing other products manufactured in Japan and declared the immediate termination of the agreement. They also claimed that Phil owed them 17,500$ in shoe deliveries. In turn, Blue Ribbon argued that the breach was on Onitsuka's part when they had started meeting other potential distributors when the contract was still in force and the business was very positive. The companies were not only severing ties, they were waging a full blown war.

While the heated dispute cast some doubt over the future of Nike, Phil was entirely focused on keeping his company alive. Everyone in the 1970's seemed to be in the market for sports shoes and if he wanted any chance of competing with titans of the industry like Adidas, Puma, Gola, Wilson, Spalding and New

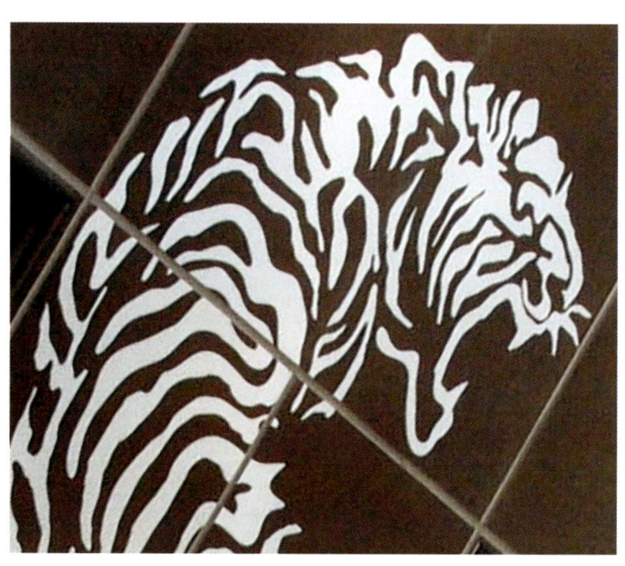

Balance, he was going to have to get creative. Knight quickly decided that athlete endorsements would be the way to do that. He reasoned that if people not only saw world class athletes compete in Nike shoes but actually win in Nike shoes, the brand would go from being just another player in the race to setting the pace as one of the pack leaders. The only problem was that they didn't have enough money to pay top athletes, let alone any knowledge on how to get them to sign on to their cause.

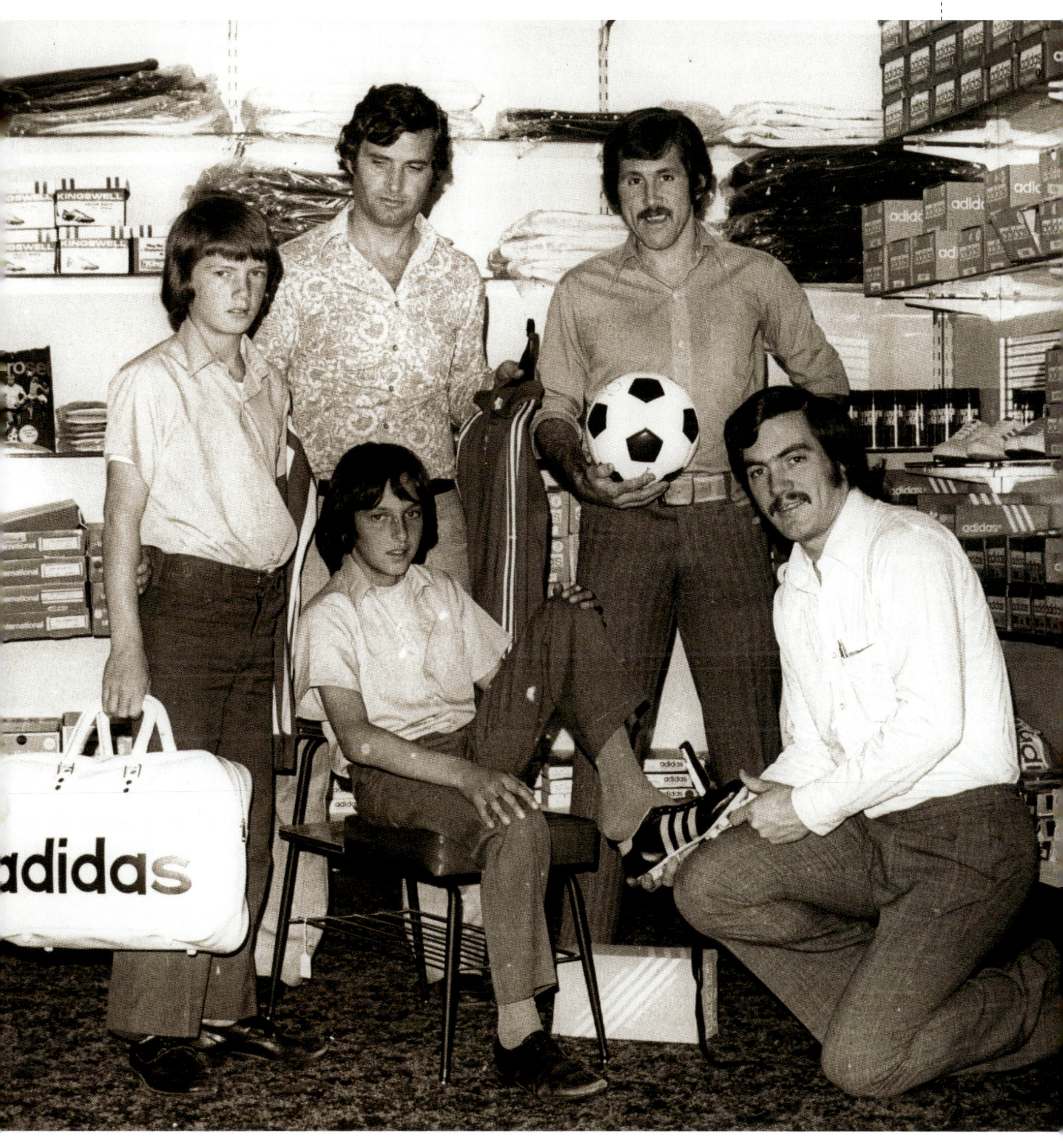
KINGSWELL
KINGSWELL
KINGSWELL
adidas
adidas
adidas
adidas
adidas

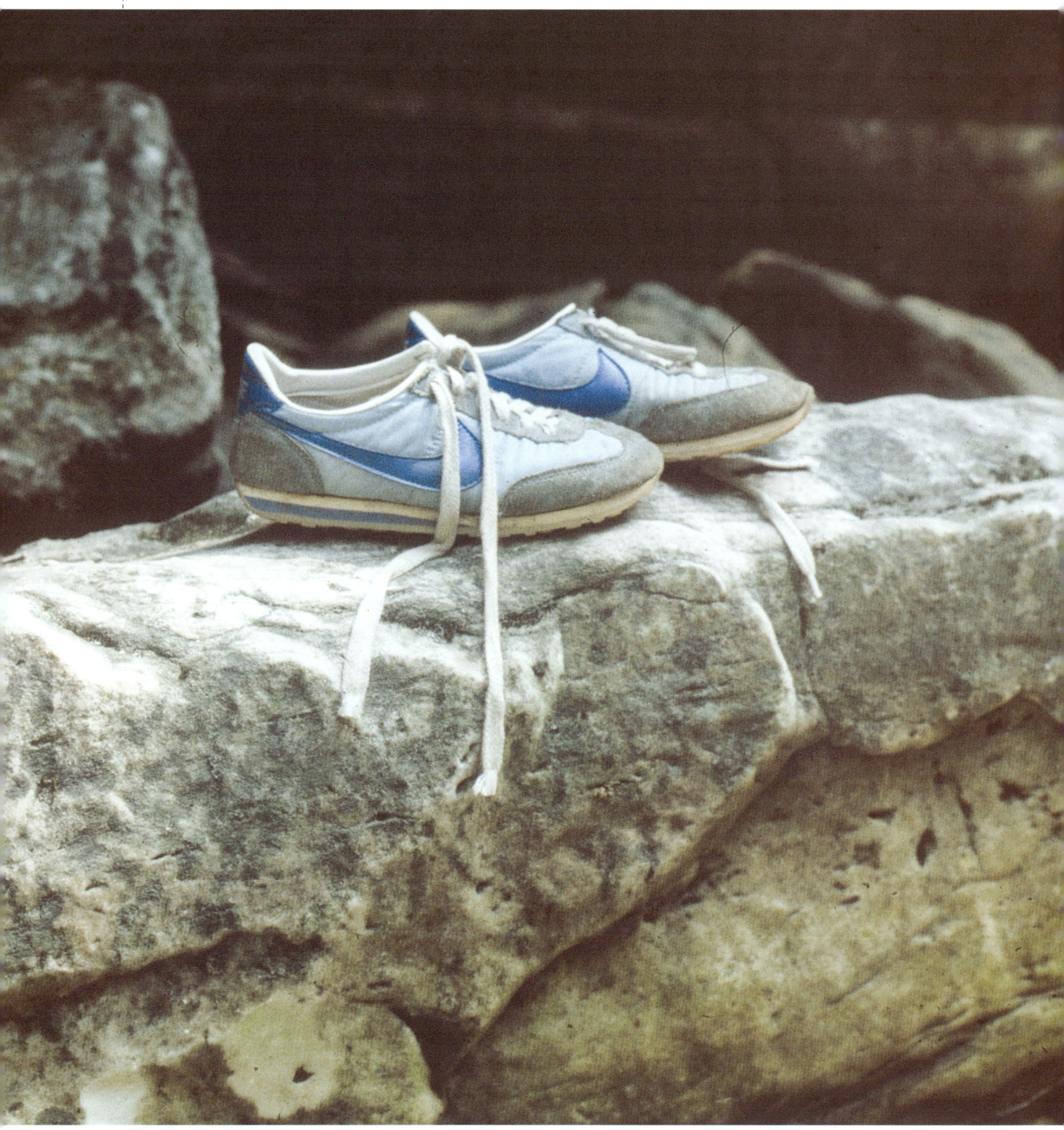

ABOVE: Nike Waffle trainer
OPP PAGE: Ilie Năstase swamped by fans at Wimbledon during the Men's Singles, 2 July, 1973

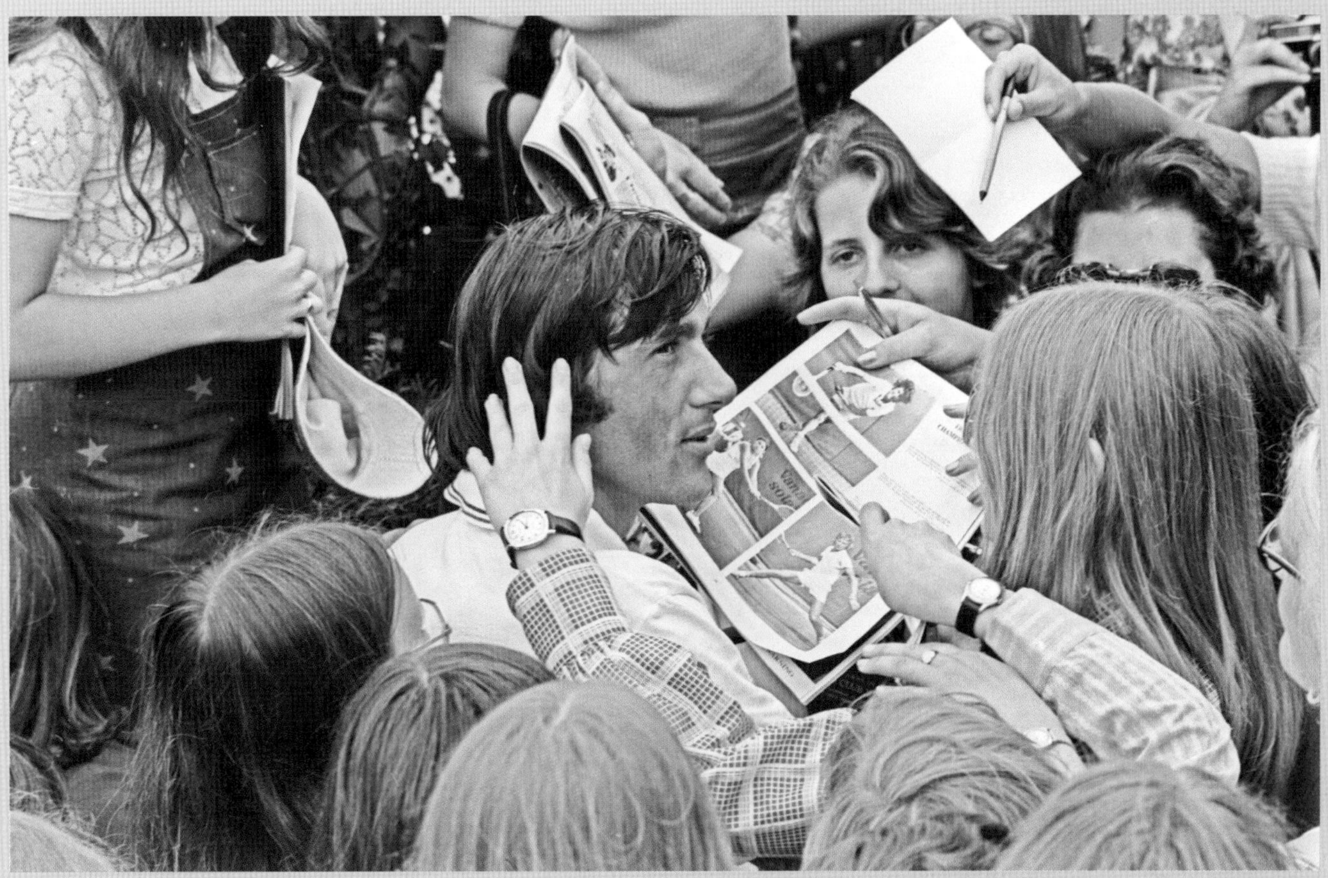

A few weeks later, like in an act of divine intervention, Phil got wind of a young Romanian tennis player completely destroying the competition at the Rainier International Classic tournament; and he was wearing a pair of Nike shoes. The player in question was Ilie Năstase and his success while sporting the Nike Match Points brought significant attention to the brand. Knight knew he needed to capitalise on this moment and offered the up-and-coming tennis star a 5000$ brand deal. Ilie countered with a 15000$ offer but eventually they settled on a 10000$ agreement.

Nike had hired their first celebrity athlete endorser, a deal that would set a precedent for the brand's future marketing strategy, which would heavily rely on athlete endorsements. By associating Nike with successful athletes, it increased product sales but also enhanced the company's visibility and credibility as a top choice for professionals.

After the partnership with Năstase was signed and in full swing, Phil was eager to get a bigger, more recognisable name on board with Nike. He set his sights on Steve Prefontaine, one of Bowerman's long-distance runners, and on track to becoming a once in a generation phenom.

ON TRACK FOR GREATNESS

In the early 1970s, a young, electrifying athlete from Coos Bay, Oregon, was redefining American distance running. Steve Prefontaine, or "Pre" as he came to be affectionately known, captivated the track world with his gutsy racing style, unapologetic personality, and incredible natural talent. By age 22, he was already a household name, gracing the cover of *Sports Illustrated* as "America's Distance Prodigy," and blazing trails on Nike's newly branded shoes.

Prefontaine's love for running was fuelled by an almost mythic competitive spirit. Known for his fearless racing tactics, he saw every track as a battlefield, approaching each race as if his life depended on it. "Some people create with words or with music or with a brush and paints," Prefontaine once reflected. "I like to make something beautiful when I run. I like to make people stop and say, 'I've never seen anyone run like that before.'"

His journey to fame began at Marshfield High School, where he captured his first national record in the two-mile event at just 15, clocking in at 8:41.5. Prefontaine quickly dominated Oregon's

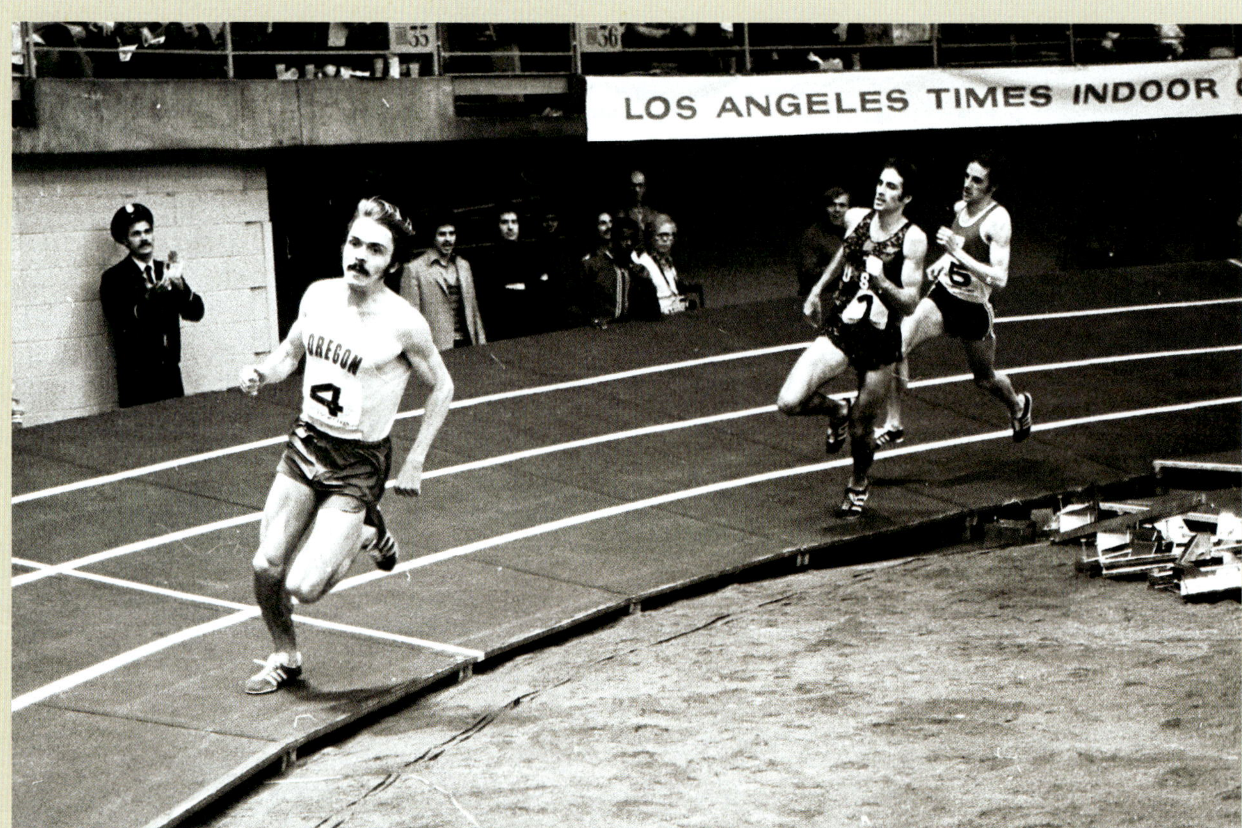

ABOVE: Steve Prefontaine pulls away to win the mile at the 14th annual LA Times Indoor Games in 1973
OPP PAGE: Steve Prefontaine's personal, worn Nike Oregon Waffle shoes

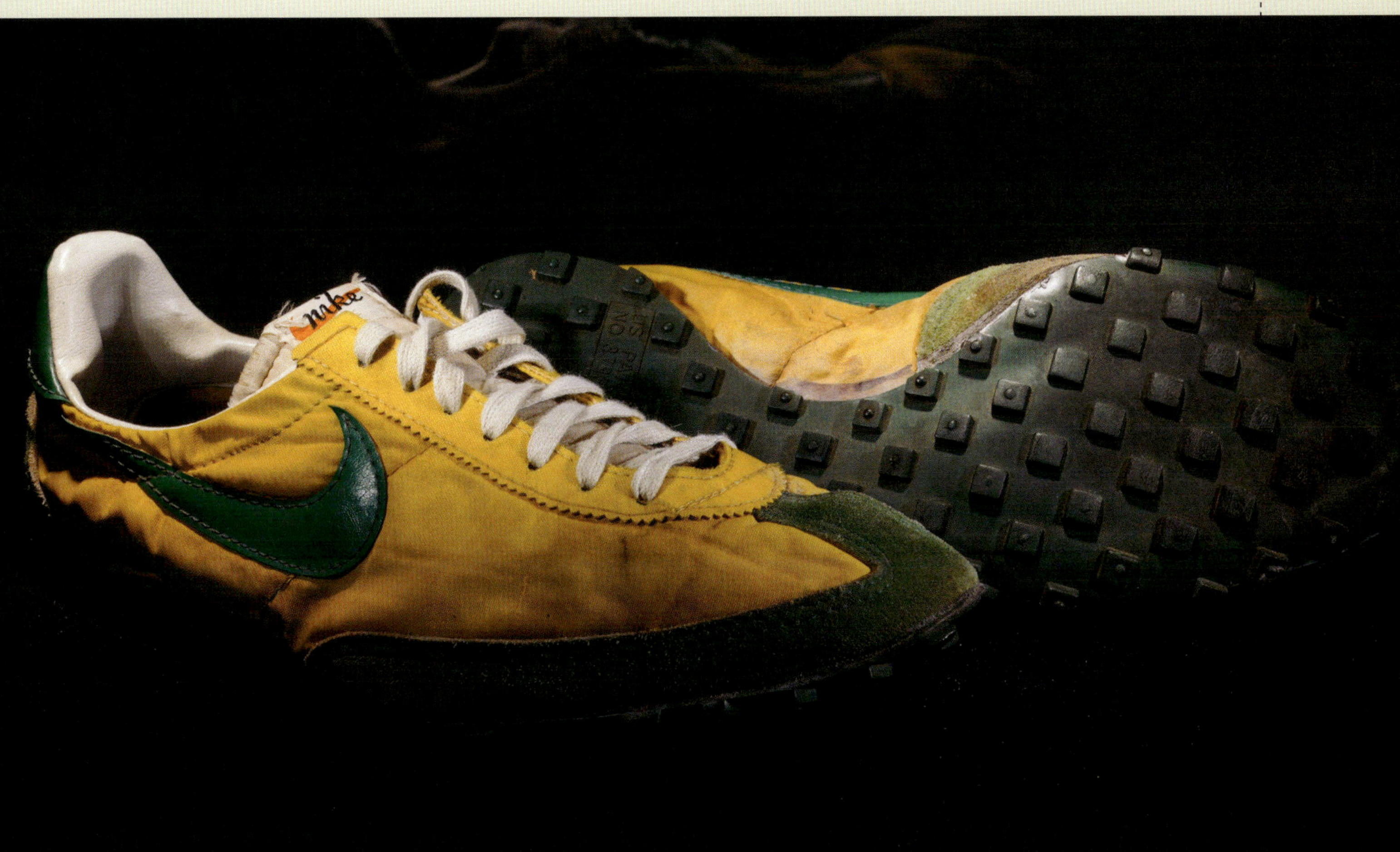

high school running scene, winning back-to-back state cross-country championships in 1968 and 1969. By his senior year, he was undefeated in both cross-country and track, attracting the attention of prestigious running programs across the country.

Among the offers, it was a simple handwritten note from University of Oregon coach Bill Bowerman that sealed the deal. "It said if I came to Oregon, he'd make me into the best distance runner ever," Prefontaine recalled, and that promise led him to Eugene in 1969. Under the guidance of Bowerman

and assistant coach Bill Dellinger, Prefontaine became a dominant force in collegiate running. He won seven NCAA titles—three in cross-country and four in the three-mile track event—becoming a legend at Oregon's Hayward Field, where he claimed 35 out of 38 victories between 1970 and 1975.

To this day, Steve Prefontaine remains a symbol of American distance running, a legend who ran with the heart of a warrior and the soul of an artist. But for now, he was gearing up to participate in the 1972 Munich Olympics.

As the end of summer of 1972 rolled around, so did the 1972 Olympic Games. Bill Bowerman and his team were getting ready to step onto the world stage and compete at the highest level. Among the young athletes representing the United States was Steve Prefontaine, awaiting to make his Olympic debut. Only a few months earlier "Pre" had set the American record of 13:22.8 in the 5,000 meters at the Olympic Trials in Eugene, Oregon and was projected to be the most promising underdog in the tournament. Though the motto of the years games was "Die Heiteren Spiele", meaning "The Cheerful Games", the spectre of the 1968 Mexico City Olympics still loomed over Munich. In addition, these were the first games to take place in Germany since the dark years of World War II, which only further contributed to the profound sense of gravity and intensity in the atmosphere.

As the bell lap rang out, Prefontaine was in contention for a medal. His lungs burned, and his legs felt heavy, yet he was determined not to let up. He moved into first place as the final lap began, pushing himself to the limit. But as they rounded the last bend, Finnish runner Lasse Virén surged forward with astounding strength, followed by Mohammed Gammoudi of Tunisia. In the last 200 meters, British runner Ian Stewart overtook Prefontaine, dashing his hopes of an Olympic medal. Prefontaine crossed the line in fourth, a fraction of a second away from the bronze, heartbroken and exhausted. In the aftermath, he admitted, "That was the most disappointed I have ever been." His performance, though courageous, was shadowed by the realization that he would leave Munich without a medal.

However, this fiercely contested race would not remain the defining story of the Munich Olympics. Just days after Prefontaine's event, an even darker chapter unfolded. On September 5, a Palestinian terrorist group, Black September, infiltrated the Olympic Village and took 11 members of the Israeli Olympic team hostage. The whole world watched as the standoff lasted over 24 hours, ultimately ending in the deaths of all 11 hostages after a failed rescue attempt. The massacre cast a shadow over the Games and reignited feelings of fear and grief.

ABOVE: Artwork from one of the 1972 Munich Olympic Games posters

OPP PAGE: Steve Prefontaine during the Men's 5000M Final at the 1972 Olympic Games in Munich

The two Oregonian men would never be the same after witnessing the tragedy of that day. But when they got home, they had no choice but to keep moving forward, keep moving towards the future. Bowerman got back to training his athletes and tinkering with shoes, and Prefontaine was bartending. At the time, Olympic athletes couldn't collect endorsement money or government money, which meant they often had to take up menial jobs to support themselves while still having enough time to train. Phil and his team had gotten to know and care for "Pre" over the years and were desperate to help him out. In 1973, Knight offered a "job" to the young Steve Prefontaine at Nike. It wasn't much of a salary, but it was better than working at a bar. And just like that, in a roundabout way, Phil found himself his second celebrity endorser.

By the fall of 1973, Nike sales were up 50 percent to $4.3 million, a number that would have seemed so staggering when Phil had initially started his venture. Despite this obvious win, no one was celebrating.

Between the legal battle and the Munich massacre, Phil was solely focused on how to get his company through these trying times.

To make matters worse, the Boston Harbour workers had gone on strike, so no one was receiving any shipments. This strike couldn't have come at a more inopportune time, as public demand for training shoes had never been higher, creating a huge supply and demand problem. Knight spent countless nights trying to figure out a solution to this seemingly impossible situation. He finally landed on this: he would go to the biggest retailers around, the likes of Nordstrom, United Sporting Goods and Athlete's Foot, make them sign ironclad commitments for non-refundable shipments six months in advance, and in return Nike would give them a big discount on their products. It was a long shot, but after some heavy convincing from the Nike team, they all signed on.

The past year had been a rollercoaster of ups and downs, but it also cemented Nike as a genuine competitor to watch out for.

But probably the most memorable moment for Phil was still to come because on his fifth wedding anniversary, his family of three welcomed another member, a little boy called Travis born on the September 13, 1973.

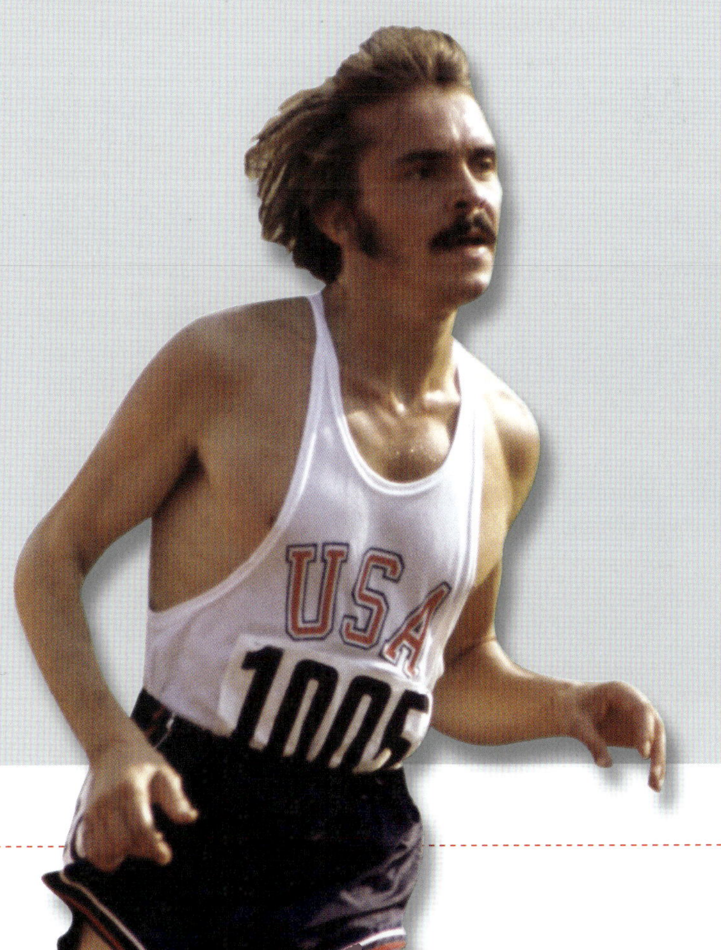

THE PRICE OF AMBITION

1974-1976

"Beating the competition is relatively easy. Beating yourself is a never-ending commitment."

Phil Knight

In the spring of 1974, Phil Knight and his associates found themselves in a courthouse in downtown Portland nose to nose with their rivals at Onitsuka. They would spend the next two months awaiting the outcome of a trial that would determine the future of Nike. After long weeks of deliberation and near misses, the court ruled in Blue Ribbon Sports' favour and Onitsuka was ordered to pay four hundred thousand dollars as a settlement. Over two years of legal back and forth had finally come to a head and Phil Knight came out on the other side the victor. They had done it, they had won. This win was huge for Nike, but Phil couldn't rest on his laurels for too long because no matter how good things got, trouble was always around the corner.

By the mid 1970s, the costs of producing shoes in Japan began to increase sharply. Japan was undergoing an economic boom, driven by rapid industrialization and technological advances, which meant that the cost of labour and materials rose quickly. As labour costs in Japan grew, profit margins on Nike shoes shrank, making it increasingly difficult to maintain the affordability that was essential for their market expansion, especially in the cost-sensitive U.S. market.

ABOVE: The Courthouse in Downtown Portland
OPP PAGE: 1970s USA Nike magazine advert

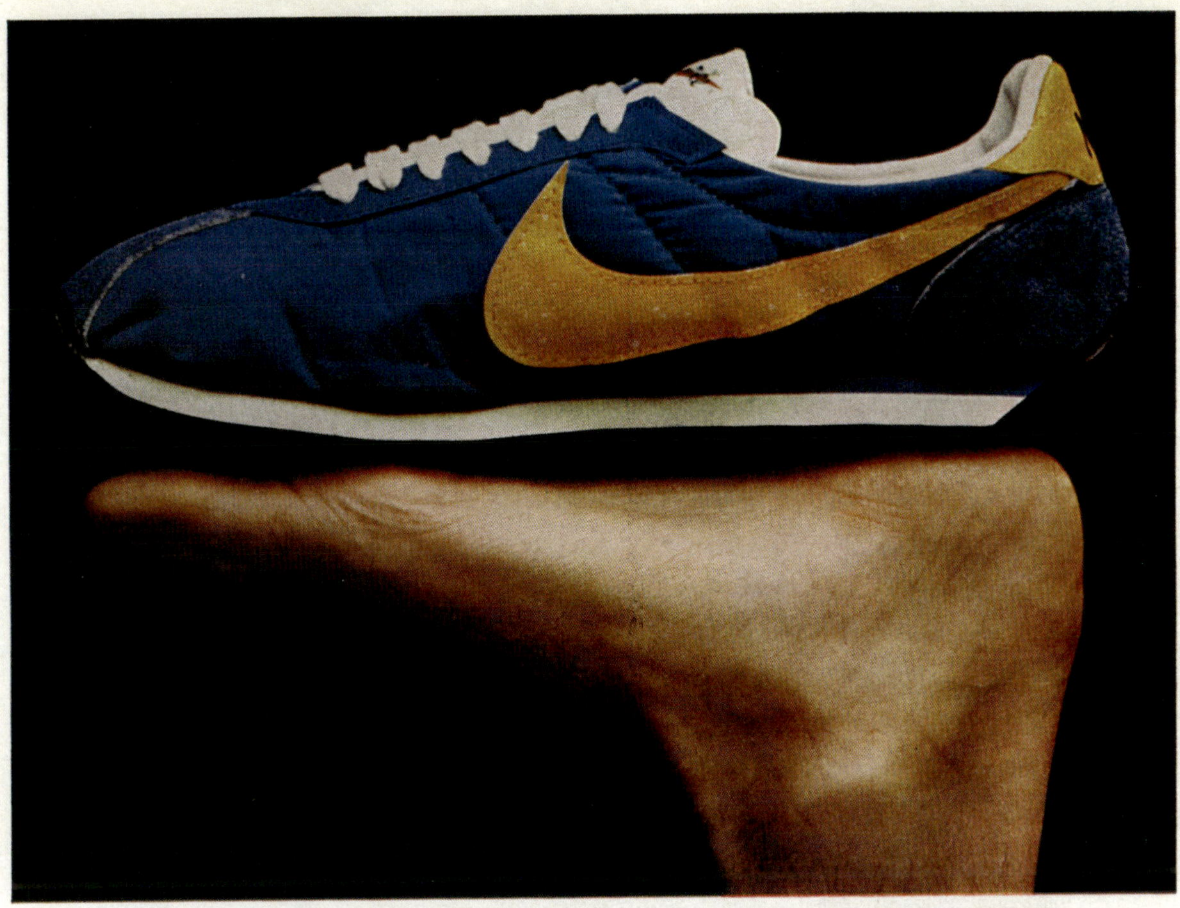
MADE FAMOUS BY WORD OF FOOT ADVERTISING.

The Nike Waffle Trainer is one of the most popular running shoes of all time.
Serious runners started wearing them years ago, for two or three good reasons.
First, the shoe has a patented Waffle sole that's designed for superior traction and cushioning of the foot when you run.
Secondly, the nylon uppers made it an extremely lightweight and comfortable shoe.
Finally, it was word of foot advertising that helped make the Nike Waffle Trainer so popular: Runners seeing other runners wearing them.
Join them.
Bring your athlete's feet to The Athlete's Foot, and tell them you want to start training on Waffles.

No one knows the athlete's foot like
The Athlete's Foot.

NIKE

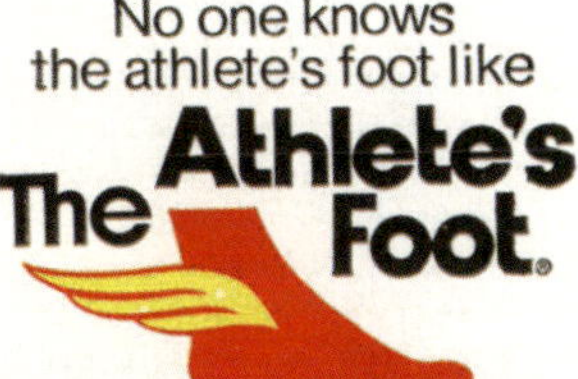

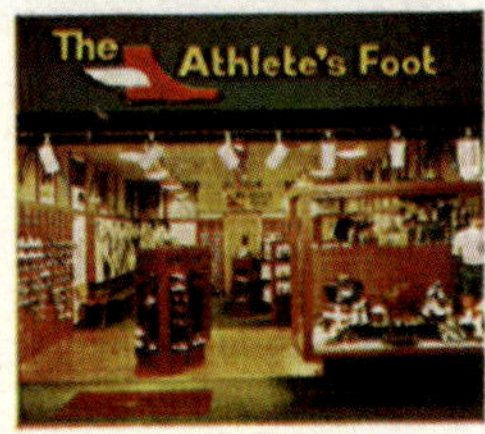
The Athlete's Foot

272 stores...nationwide

IT'S SPREADING — our chain of internationally franchised stores (all locally-owned) in ALABAMA: Birmingham, Gadsden, Montgomery; ARIZONA: Flagstaff, Phoenix, Tempe; ARKANSAS: Little Rock; AUSTRALIA: Adelaide; CALIFORNIA: Arcadia, Canoga Park, Costa Mesa, Cupertino, Modesto, Palo Alto, San Bernardino, San Bruno, San Jose, Thousand Oaks, Torrance, Westminster; COLORADO: Colorado Springs, Denver, Fort Collins, Grand Junction, Lakewood; CONNECTICUT: New Haven, West Hartford; DELAWARE: Newark, Wilmington; FLORIDA: Clearwater, Ft. Lauderdale, Jacksonville, Miami, Orlando, Pensacola, Plantation, Pompano, Sarasota, South Miami, St. Petersburg, Tallahassee, Tampa, West Palm Beach; GEORGIA: Atlanta (Cumberland Mall), (Lenox Square), Augusta, Columbus, Morrow (Southlake Mall); IDAHO: Boise; ILLINOIS: Aurora, Chicago, Decatur, Moline, Northbrook, North Riverside, Peoria, St. Clair, Schaumburg, Skokie, Springfield, Vernon Hills; INDIANA: Columbus, Elkhart, Evansville, Indianapolis, Lafayette, Muncie, South Bend; IOWA: Cedar Rapids, Davenport, Des Moines; KANSAS: Atchison, Kansas City, Overland Park, Topeka, Wichita; KENTUCKY: Florence, Louisville; LOUISIANA: Metairie, New Orleans, Shreveport; MARYLAND: Annapolis, Baltimore, Bethesda, Hillcrest Heights, Lutherville, Randallstown, Wheaton; MASSACHUSETTS: Chestnut Hill, Hyannis, Peabody; MINNESOTA: Minneapolis; MISSISSIPPI: Greenville, Jackson, Tupelo; MISSOURI: Independence, Kansas City, St. Louis, Sikeston; MONTANA: Billings; NEBRASKA: Lincoln, Omaha; NEVADA: Las Vegas, Sparks; NEW HAMPSHIRE: Manchester; NEW JERSEY: Cherry Hill, Deptford, Eatontown, Hackensack, Lawrenceville, Paramus, Rockaway, Voorhees, Woodbridge; NEW MEXICO: Albuquerque; NEW YORK: Brooklyn, Harlem, Hicksville, Ithaca, Johnson City, Manhasset, Manhattan, Massapequa, New York, Poughkeepsie, White Plains; NORTH CAROLINA: Charlotte, Greensboro, Hickory, Winston-Salem; NORTH DAKOTA: Bismarck; OHIO: Akron, Bowling Green, Canton, Cincinnati, Cleveland, Clifton, Columbus, Fairview Park, St. Clairsville, Toledo, Youngstown; OKLAHOMA: Oklahoma City, Stillwater, Tulsa; OREGON: Portland; PENNSYLVANIA: Allentown, Johnstown, Lancaster, Langhorne, Media, Monroeville, Philadelphia, Pittsburgh, Rosemont, Scranton, State College, Washington, Wilkes-Barre, Williamsport, York; PUERTO RICO: San Juan; SOUTH CAROLINA: Charleston, Columbia, North Charleston; SOUTH DAKOTA: Rapid City, Sioux Falls; TENNESSEE: Chattanooga, Jackson, Knoxville, Memphis, Nashville; TEXAS: Abilene, Austin, Dallas, Houston, Mesquite, San Antonio, Sherman; UTAH: Ogden, Orem, Salt Lake City; VIRGINIA: Newport News, Portsmouth, Roanoke, Springfield, Virginia Beach; WASHINGTON: Bellevue, Olympia, Seattle, Spokane, Tacoma, Tukwila, Vancouver; WEST VIRGINIA: Charleston; WISCONSIN: Appleton, Green Bay, La Crosse, Madison, Manitowoc, Milwaukee, Oshkosh, Wausau, Wisconsin Rapids.
The ATHLETE'S FOOT is the registered trademark (in U.S. Patent Office) of The Athlete's Foot Marketing Associates, Inc., 601 Grant Street, Pittsburgh, PA 15219, 412-263-2077

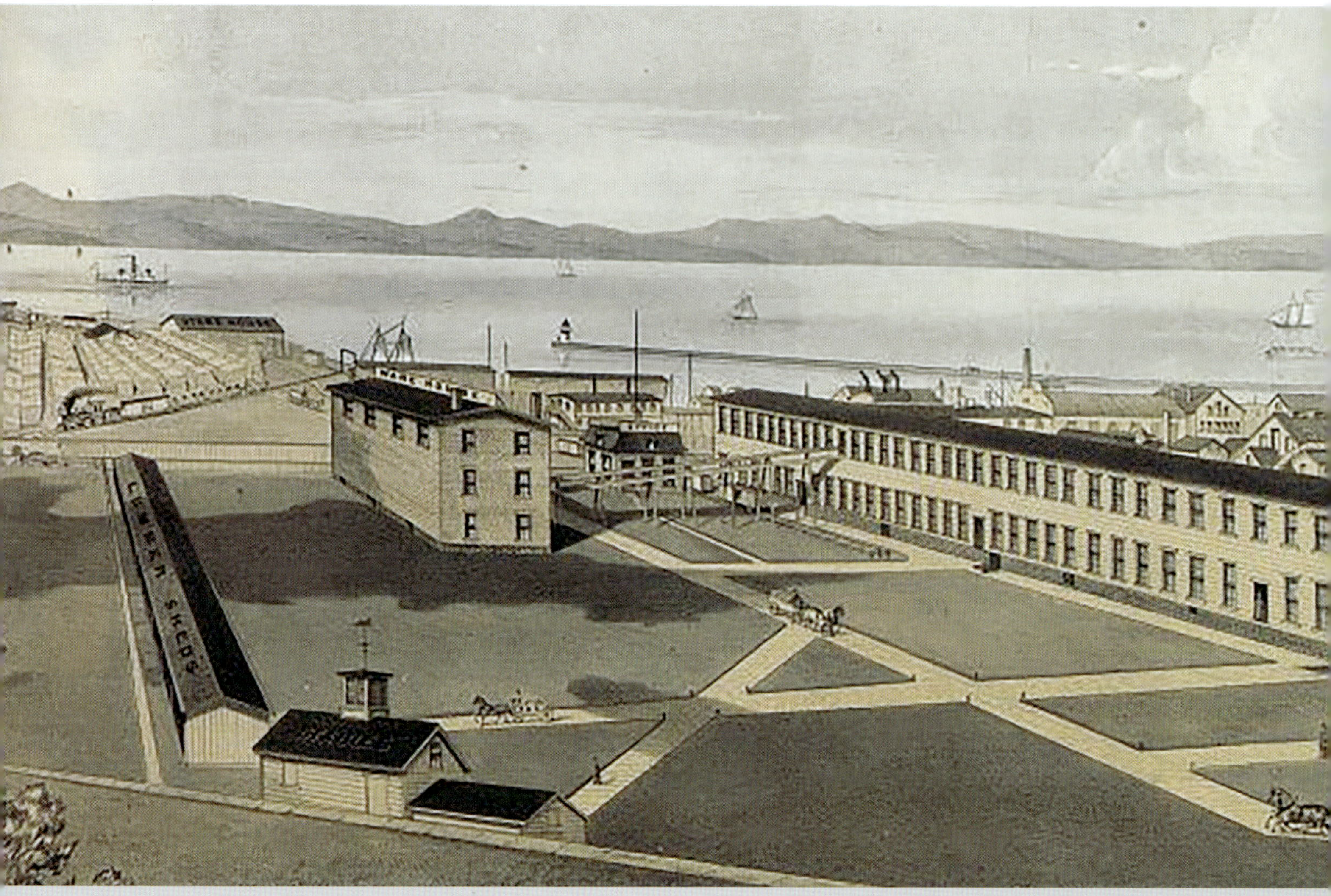

Around this time, currency fluctuations also affected Nike's bottom line. The Japanese yen appreciated against the U.S. dollar, meaning that Nike's costs increased further in dollar terms when manufacturing in Japan. The U.S. government was also pushing for domestic manufacturing as a way to create jobs in America and reduce trade imbalances. Incentives were being introduced to encourage companies to bring production back to the U.S., especially in industries like footwear, where jobs were perceived as more accessible for American workers. Phil was at a crossroads. It no longer made sense to produce Nike products in Japan and so he turned his gaze towards New England. The New England manufacturing sector was historically specialized in textile and footwear production and by tapping into this established expertise, Phil could draw on skilled labour with experience in shoe manufacturing. Additionally, producing shoes domestically offered a clear logistical advantage as turnaround times for production and shipping were significantly shorter than from overseas locations. Moving production

ABOVE: Many manufaturing industries had thrieved in New England for over a century like Kilburn and Gates. Cottage Furniture Manufactory, Burlington, Vt.

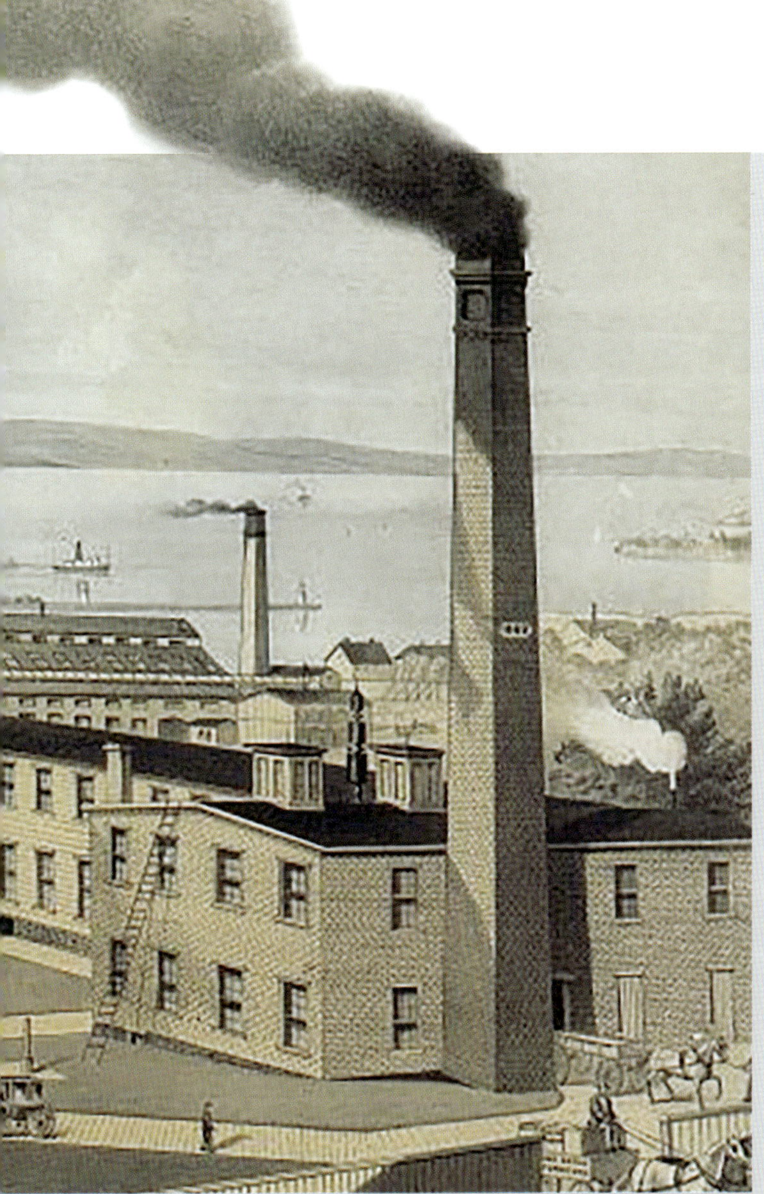

those hopes were just as quickly squashed.

Phil Knight's "grow or die" business strategy had finally caught up with him. For years, he had been operating "on the float"—an accounting technique that leveraged the time lag in check processing to double-count money temporarily, using this brief overlap to cover monthly inventory orders and debt payments. Every month Phil would order as much inventory as he possibly could, maxing his $1 million credit lines with both the bank and the Japanese trading company, Nissho. Each month-end was a high-stakes game of survival, as Knight scrambled to shuffle cash across accounts to meet looming debt deadlines. The bank was already sceptical of his unconventional cash flow tactics but eventually lost patience when he missed the float. His account was frozen, and the bank escalated matters, reporting him to the FBI for what they deemed to be potential fraud. Phil had no bank for the second time in five years, and on top of that the FBI might be getting involved. With his accounts frozen, he not only couldn't pay the $1 million he owed Nissho, but he had to ask for another $1million to pay off his other creditors. Just four years earlier, the Japanese trading company had invested in Phil and his business venture when no one else would extend him more credit. When they heard about Nike's predicament, Nissho did a full audit of their books, which they concluded by telling Knight that there were worse things than ambition. Finally, someone who truly understood debt financing!

closer to its primary customer base meant that Nike could bring new designs to market faster, allowing it to respond more effectively to shifts in consumer demand and athletic trends.

For the first time since the beginning of this adventure, Phil was genuinely hopeful that his "crazy idea" would actually work out.

Though 1974 ended on a positive and almost optimistic note for the future, by the beginning of 1975

A FALLEN STAR

"Pre was a rebel from a working-class background, a guy full of cockiness and guts. Pre's spirit is the cornerstone of this company's soul" – Phil Knight.

On the last weekend of May, Phil and his wife Penny drove down to Eugene to see Steve Prefontaine compete in the 5,000-meter race in front of a roaring home crowd. The onlookers were electrified by his performance. In true Steve Prefontaine fashion, it was only at the very last moment, in the last two hundred yards, that he quickened his pace and won the race. Hayward field was vibrating with the incredible athletic feat they had just witnessed. "Somebody may beat me- but they're going to have to bleed to do it", as "Pre" would say. But the high spirits were soon going to be replaced by tears. That night, after celebrating with friends, Prefontaine was driving home when his car swerved and flipped over a rock wall near Hendricks Park. Trapped beneath the overturned vehicle, the 24-year-old succumbed to his injuries before help could arrive. On May 30, 1975, Steve Prefontaine, the larger-than-life figure in track and field, was killed in a car accident. He was just about to hit his prime, he still had so much to give and prove, but life had something different in store. The shocking loss of Prefontaine sent ripples of grief through the athletic community and deeply affected Knight, who had seen "Pre" not just as a star athlete or friend, but as an emblem of Nike's vision for relentless pursuit and excellence.

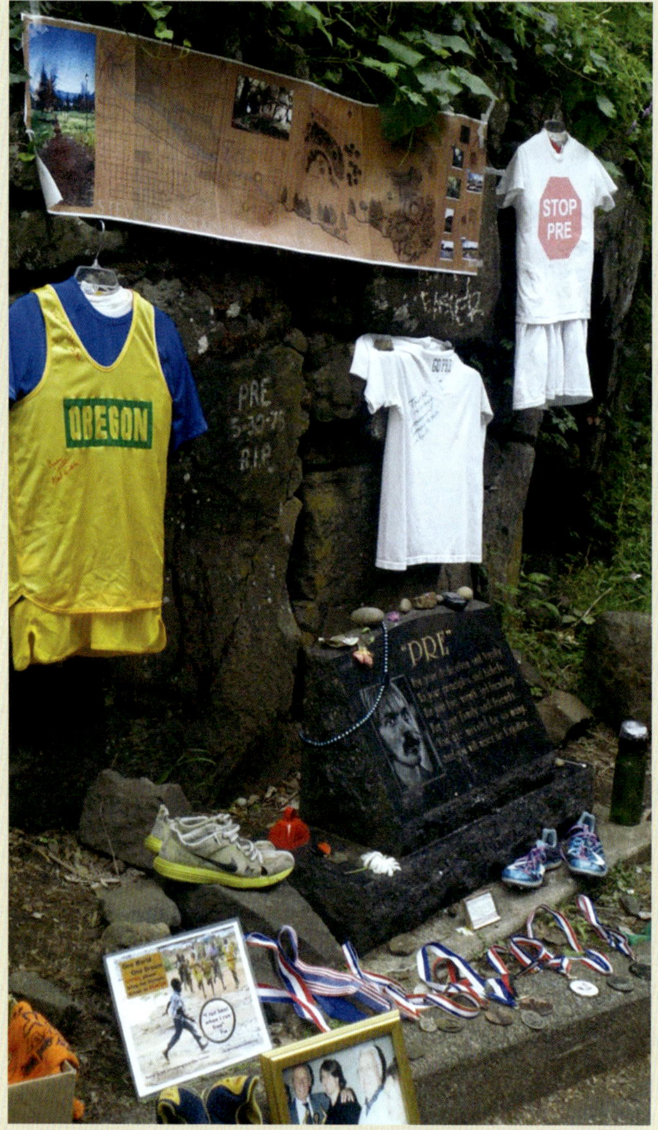

Steve's ascendance came at a time when running was far from mainstream. Prefontaine helped change that attitude from annoyance to admiration through his sheer talent. He was the first person to make running cool. His association with Nike helped establish the Swoosh as a trusted running brand and transform the company from national shoe distributor to worldwide brand.

ABOVE: 'Pre's rock', a memorial marking the place where Steve Prefontain died in Eugene, Oregon
OPP PAGE: A mural depicting Steve Prefontaine, Coos Bay, Oregon

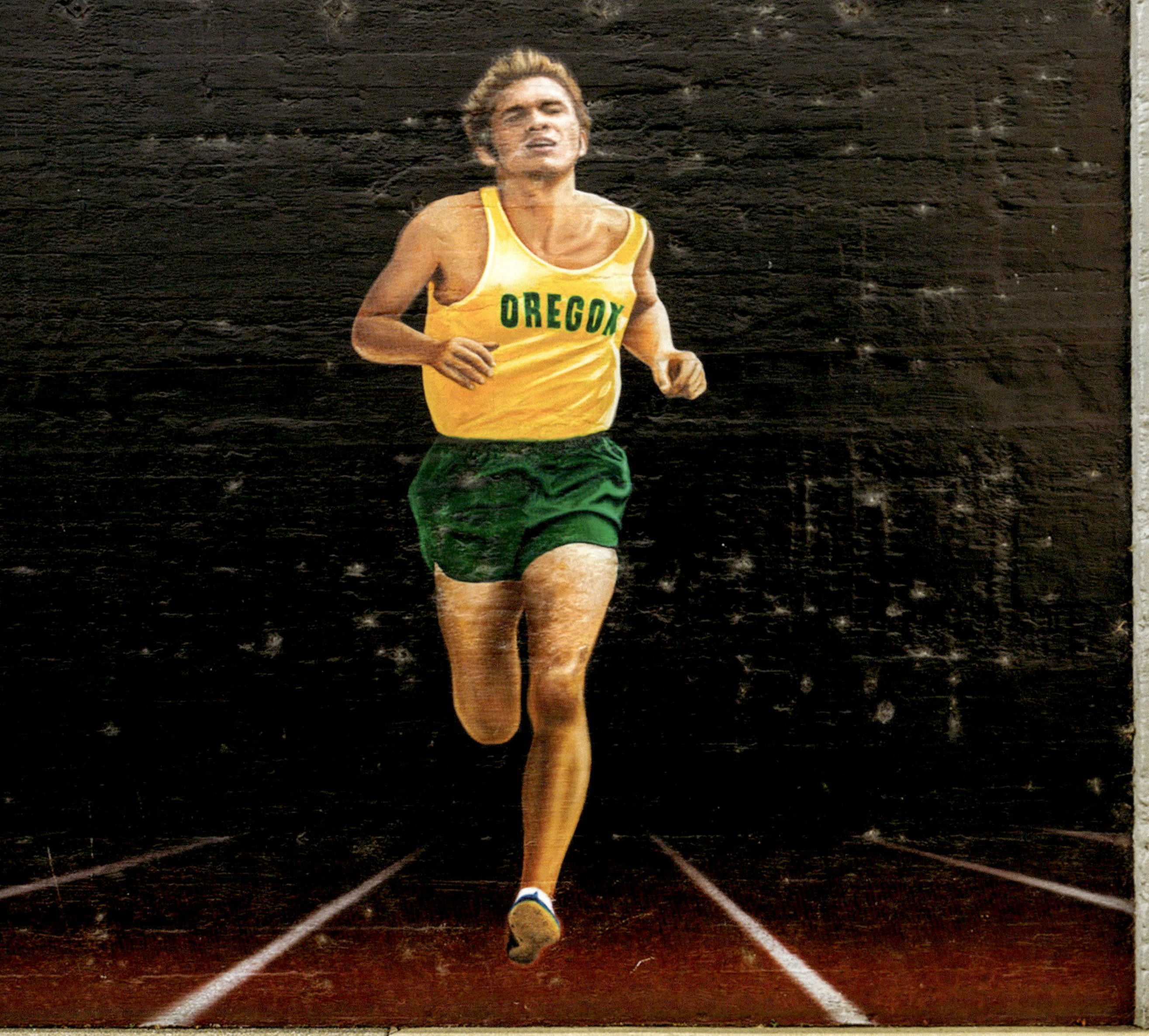

"TO GIVE ANYTHING LESS THAN YOUR BEST IS TO SACRIFICE THE GIFT"
Steve Prefontaine
OREGON

BUBBLES, BURSTS, AND BREAKTHROUGHS

1977-1979

"A pile of rocks ceases to be a rock pile when somebody contemplates it with the idea of a cathedral in mind."

Antoine de Saint-Exupéry

Things were looking a little different at Nike by 1977. Bowerman had stepped down as co-owner of the brand, selling most of his shares to Phil. The events of the last couple of years had worn him down and he craved a simpler life to enjoy retirement with his wife. Phil was undoubtedly a little disappointed by his partner's decision to leave the company, as Nike was just as much his "baby" at it was Bowerman's. But he eventually gave in to his old friend's desires, although not before convincing the coach to stay on as chairman. Bowerman accepted, and so from then on Nike moved forward with Phil Knight as the sole captain of the ship.

With changes to management came changes in business tactics. Nike had a solid and loyal

RIGHT: Actress Farrah Fawcett, wearing Nike shoes, practices skateboarding for an episode of Charlie's Angels in 1977

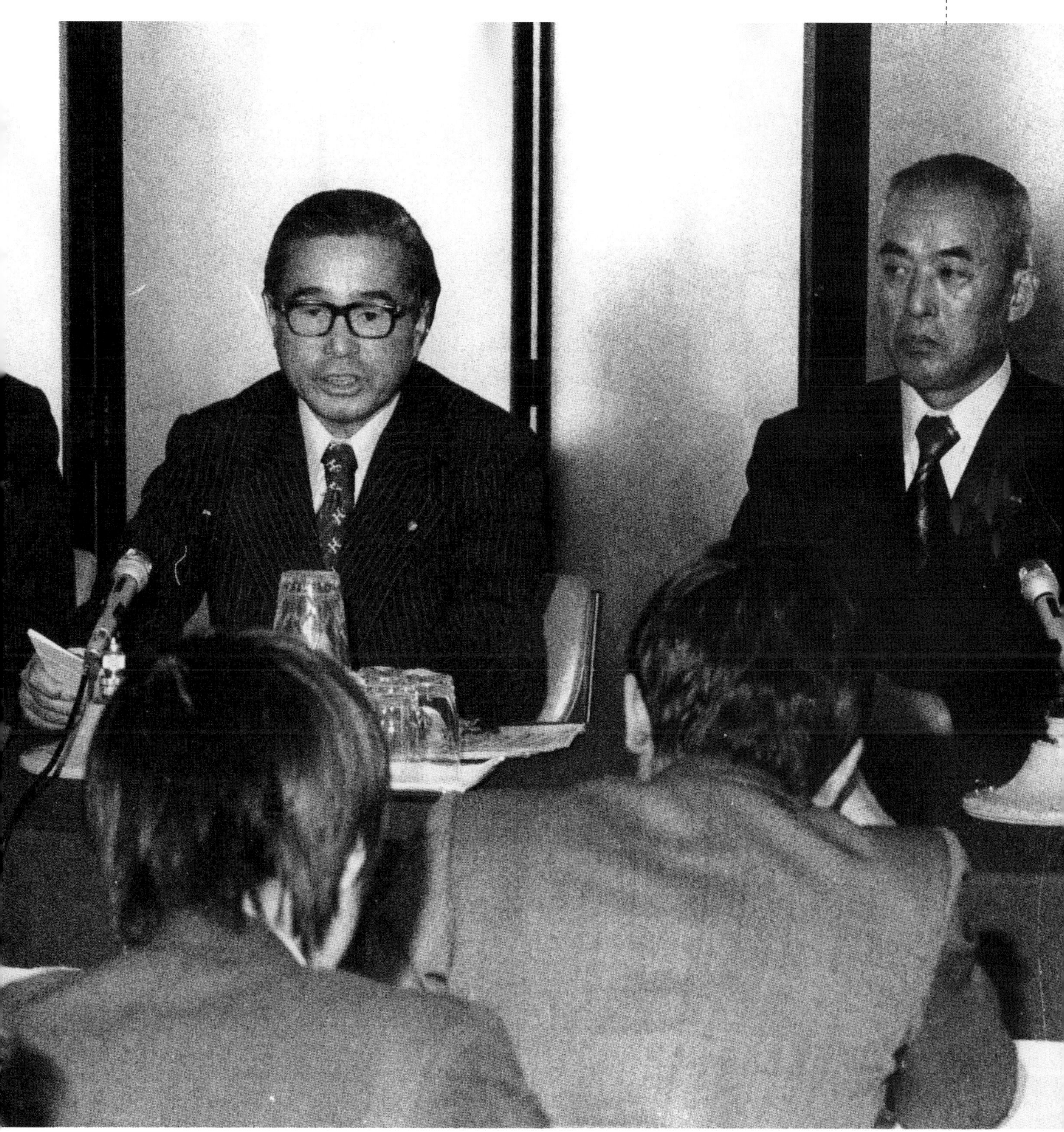

ABOVE: It wasn't just Nike that was seeing change—
January 12, 1977, Onitsuka Tiger President Kihachiro
Onitsuka (centre), GTO president (left) and Jelenk
President (right) announced their merger to form Asics

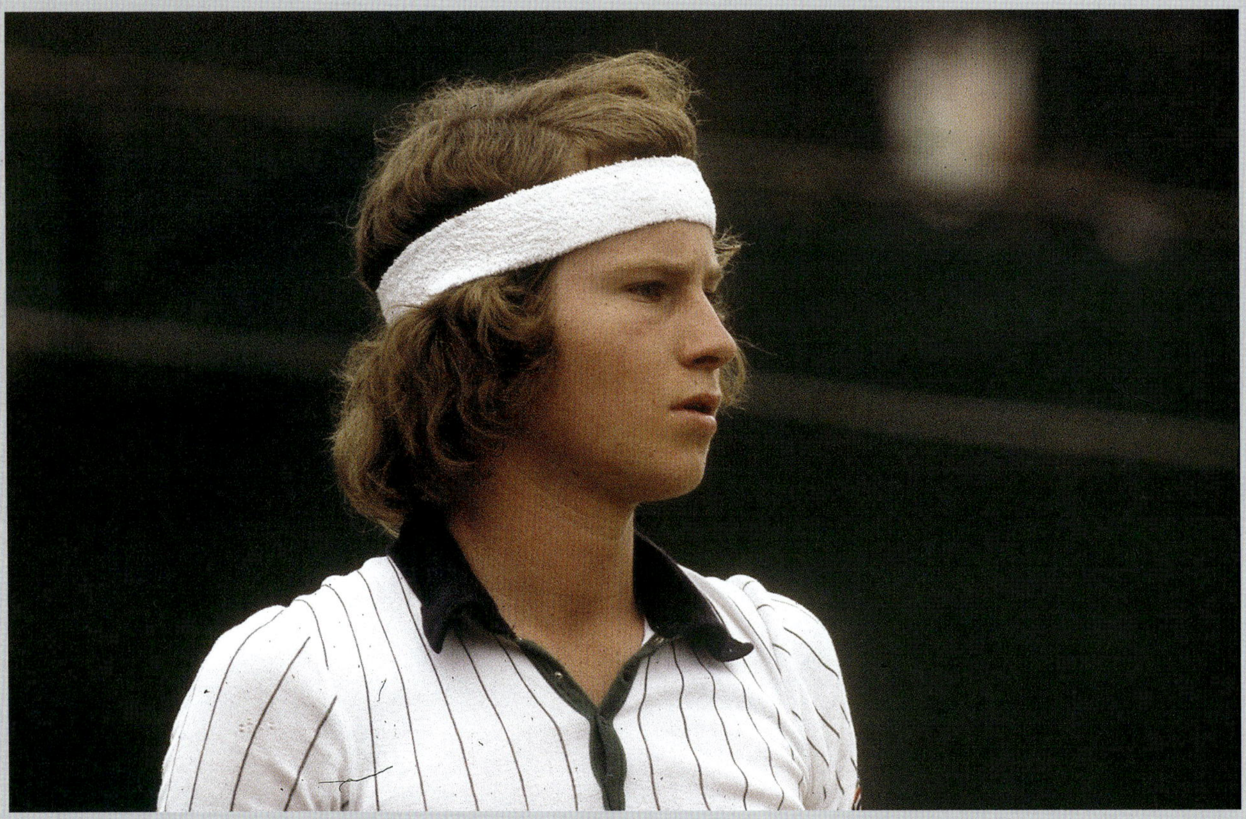

customer base of runners, but to close the gap between companies like them and companies like Adidas, they needed to continue to expand their range of influence.

Nike already had a good stable of NBA players wearing their shoes, but they had yet to sign any college basketball teams. And so, the critical mission was assigned: get college basketball coaches to switch from their longstanding deals with Converse and Adidas, into Nike shoes. Within a few months, the Nike team signed Eddie Sutton, the coach for University of Arkansas, Abe Lemons the head coach at the University of Texas, Frank McGuire from South Carolina. The list continued to grow and so did Nike's grasp on the basketball market.

Knight was determined to reach full domination on sporting goods and to do so he needed to break the tennis market as well. Năstase had since left Nike for a hundred-thousand-dollar endorsement deal with Adidas, leaving Phil with no tennis player on his roster. So, in 1977, Knight and a local tennis pro went to Wimbledon, in London, to find themselves a new horse for the face of Nike tennis. It was at that tournament that Phil fell hopelessly in love with the hot-headed and frizzy haired highschooler from New York City, John McEnroe.

ABOVE: John McEnroe during a match in the Men's singles tournament at the Wimbledon, 1977
OPP PAGE: A pair of the original 1979 Nike Air Tailwind shoes

IN SEARCH FOR AIR

By the late 1970s, Nike had established itself as a rising star in the athletic shoe market, but Phil Knight and his team were determined to push the boundaries of innovation further. Their first groundbreaking step into a new era of footwear technology came with the Nike Tailwind, a shoe that marked the beginning of the company's revolutionary "Air Sole" venture.

The idea of incorporating air into the cushioning of running shoes was the brainchild of aerospace engineer Frank Rudy. Rudy approached Nike with an unconventional pitch: tiny pockets of air, sealed in durable plastic, could be embedded into shoe soles to improve cushioning and performance. Sceptical but intrigued, Phil and his team saw potential in Rudy's concept. They agreed to experiment with the technology, testing its durability and performance under the rigorous demands of running.

The Tailwind debuted in 1978 as a prototype at the Honolulu Marathon, Nike's testing ground for the unorthodox idea. Runners were intrigued by its lightweight design and the promise of a smoother, more cushioned stride, thanks to the air-filled midsole. Feedback from the marathon confirmed what Rudy had claimed: the air technology reduced impact stress on runners, making each stride feel lighter and less jarring. So, Nike prepared for a mass-market release. The Tailwind debuted in 1979 as the first commercial shoe with Air Sole technology, a bold gamble on a futuristic design.

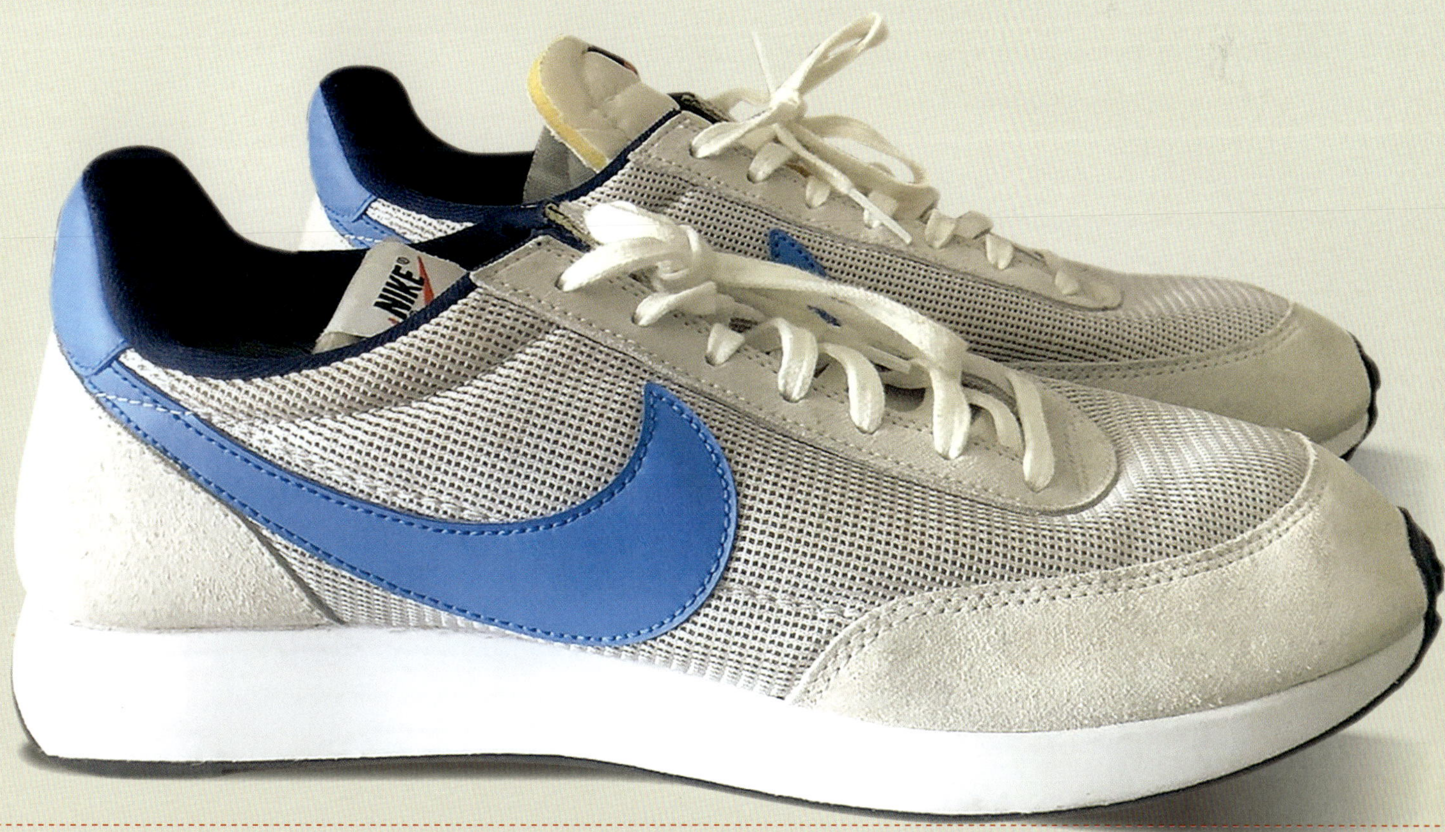

Yet, not all gambles pay off smoothly. Shortly after its launch, Nike began receiving complaints from customers. The Tailwind's air pockets were prone to bursting under stress, leaving runners with shoes that were deflated and unusable. Some customers even joked that their "air shoes" had literally blown up. Despite these issues, the initial enthusiasm for the Tailwind's concept didn't waver. Customers weren't just buying shoes—they were buying into Nike's vision of pushing boundaries.

Acknowledging the problem, Nike issued a recall, pulling faulty Tailwinds from shelves. They worked quickly to improve the durability of the air pockets, reengineering the design to ensure that future iterations could handle the demands of performance athletes. Surprisingly, the backlash Nike feared never materialized. Many customers expressed support, admiring the company's willingness to take risks and try something entirely new. In a way, the mishap underscored Nike's ethos of innovation:

bold, sometimes messy, but always forward-thinking.

The Tailwind's shaky debut became a valuable lesson for Nike. It underscored the challenges of launching cutting-edge products but also proved that customers were willing to give the company room to experiment. Far from tarnishing its reputation, the incident reinforced Nike's identity as a brand unafraid to break the mould.

Ultimately, the Tailwind laid the foundation for a revolution in footwear. Its improved versions paved the way for the iconic Air Max line, cementing Air technology as a hallmark of Nike's identity.

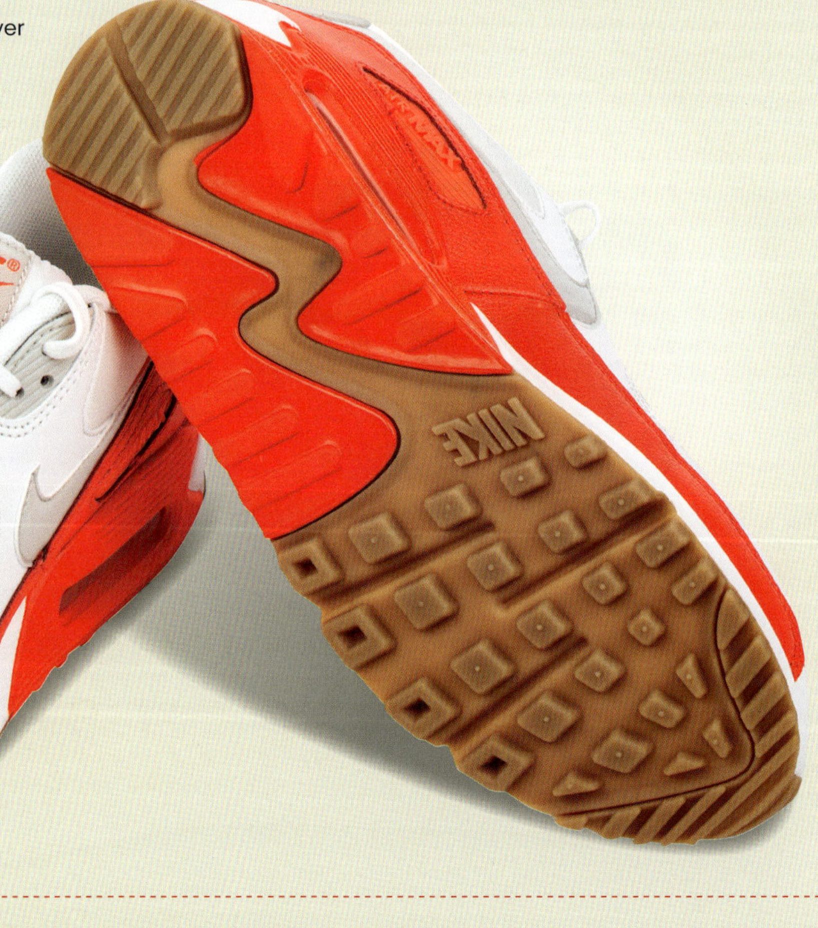

Around the Christmas season of 1977, a small, unassuming white envelope with a return address to the US Customs Service, Washington DC was delivered to Phil. He opened it with unsteady hands. The letter stated that Nike owed custom duties dating back three years by virtue of something called "the American selling price". By using this archaic and protectionist law, rival brands like Converse, Keds, and other competitors successfully lobbied the U.S. Customs office to invoke A.S.P. or American Selling Price, sticking Nike with a $25 Million dollar bill. This couldn't be real; Phil had just gotten his company through the Onitsuka trial and now he was yet again facing annihilation. Even though Nike was finishing the year with over 70 million dollars in revenue, Knight couldn't afford to pay that colossal amount of money… at least not without ruining his years of hard work.

By the time the new year came along, a lot of things had changed. Phil and his growing family moved out of their quaint family home in Beavertown, into a bigger house. Nike had also acquired a few new factories in Taiwan, Korea, England and Ireland to keep up with the ever-rising consumer demands. Clearly, there wasn't enough change, because the looming debt continued to cast a shadow over Knight and his company. He was going to fight the government with everything he had. In 1979, Phil's colleague brought in a lawyer, Rich Werschkul, to head to Washington and mount a counter-offensive. Werschkul spent months in Washington, lobbying against A.S.P. to anyone who would listen. He penned and bound *Werschkul on American Selling Price* and languished in D.C., seemingly unable to break through.

It wasn't until Phil intervened that he and Werschkul were able to get a meeting with Senator Mark Hatfield from Oregon. When Knight and Werschkul sat down in Hatfield's office, the Senator had already been briefed on their predicament by his aides. Though Hatfield couldn't make their problem disappear, he could come pull a few strings to placate the feds and buy Nike more time to come up with a solution.

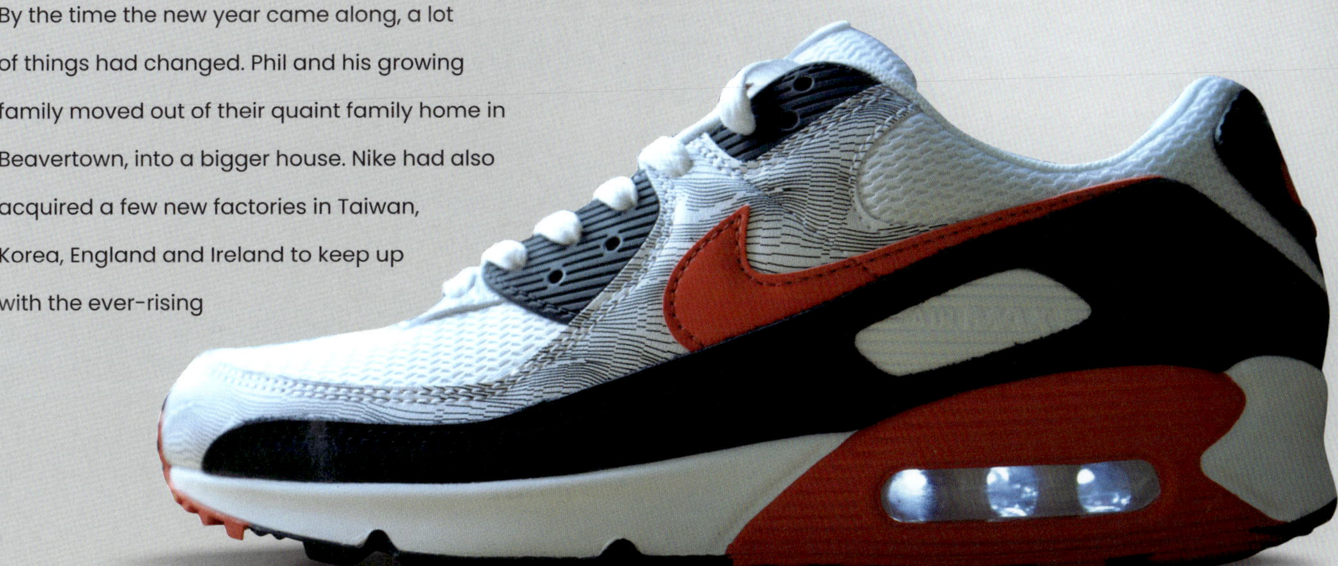

OPP PAGE: The later Nike Air Max 90 featuring visable air bubbles

ABOVE: The iconic Nike Air Max III made its debut a decade later in 1990

RISK, REWARD, AND REINVENTION

1980

"Greatness is not born, it is made"

Nike

At the beginning of 1980, while brainstorming ideas for how to solve their issues with the US customs department, Phil came up with a rather brilliant idea. What if they made their own American Selling Price? The entire team initially said it couldn't be done but the more they thought about it, the more plausible the crazy idea seemed. So, they gave it a try. They launched a pair of dirt-cheap shoes called One Line and priced it low, just above the cost of production. Based on the principle of ASP, customs laws would have to use this "competitor" shoe as the new reference point for deciding Nike's import taxes. To further prove their point, Nike came out with a TV ad recounting their story of a homegrown Oregonian company getting bullied by the government and infringing upon the "American Dream", the very idea on which the United States is built. Lastly, as a final act of defiance, Phil Knight and Nike filed for a 25-million-dollar antitrust suit against the US District Court for the Southern District of New York, alleging that their competitors, through underhanded business tactics, had conspired to take them out. Almost immediately, calls from the government came through with settlement offers. Phil eventually relented and agreed to pay 9 million dollars to finally put the case to bed.

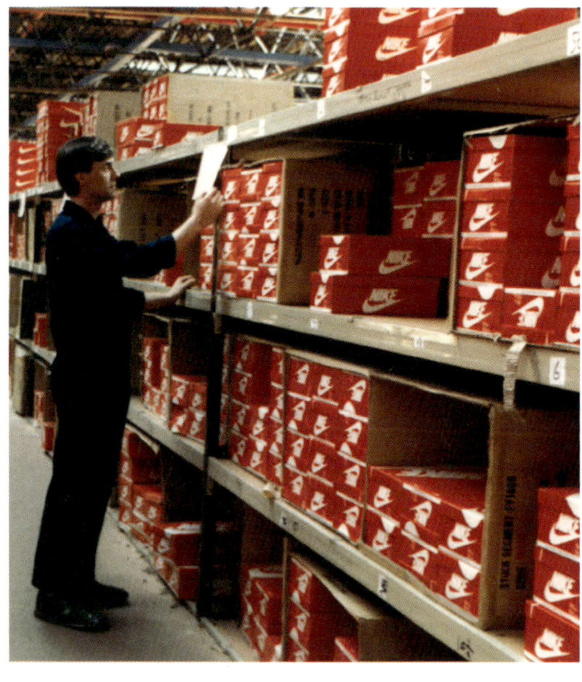

ABOVE: Nike's import taxes were an issue in 1980
OPP PAGE: 'Prosperity at Home, Prestige Abroad' poster from 1896

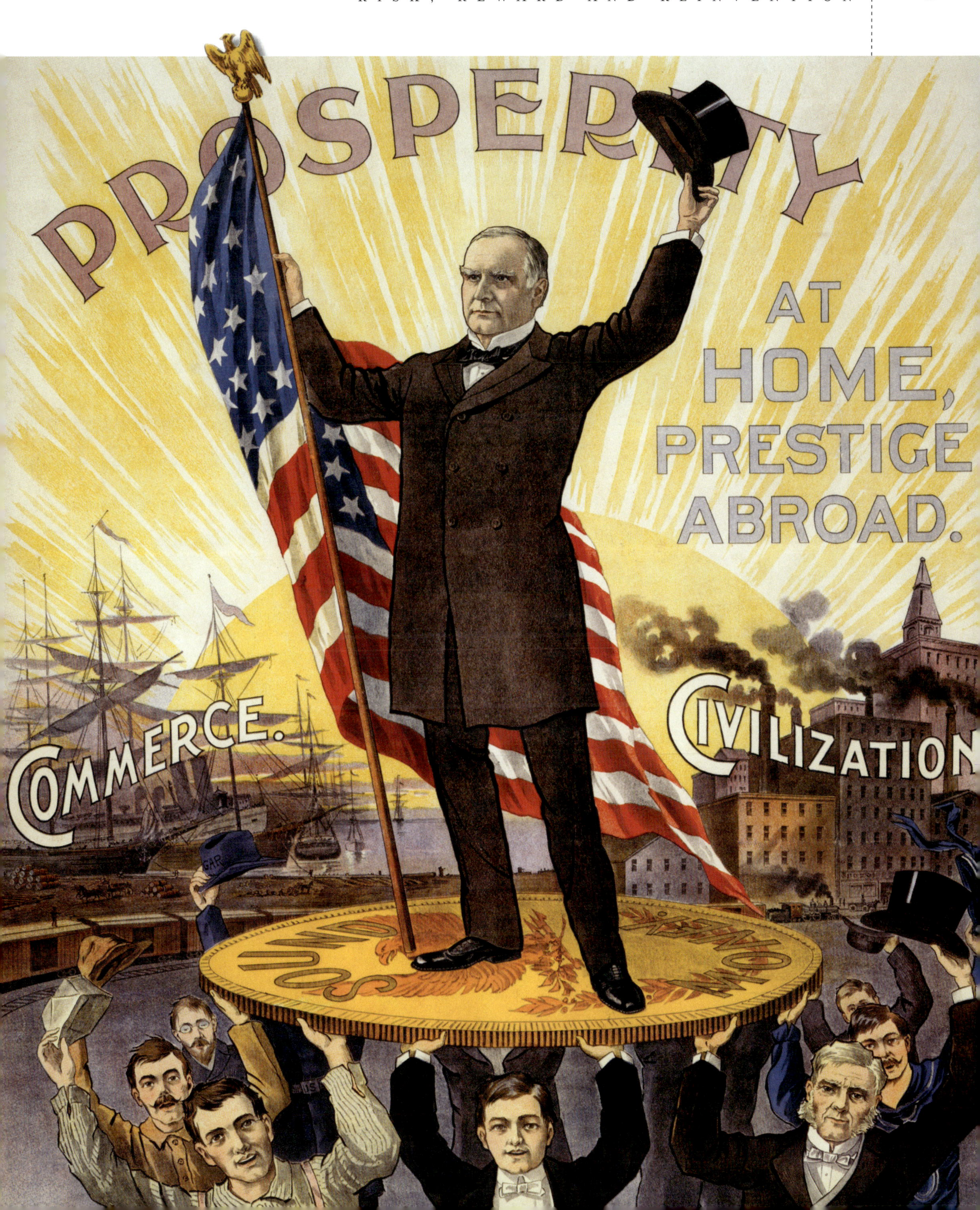
PROSPERITY
AT HOME, PRESTIGE ABROAD.
COMMERCE.
CIVILIZATION
SOUND MONEY

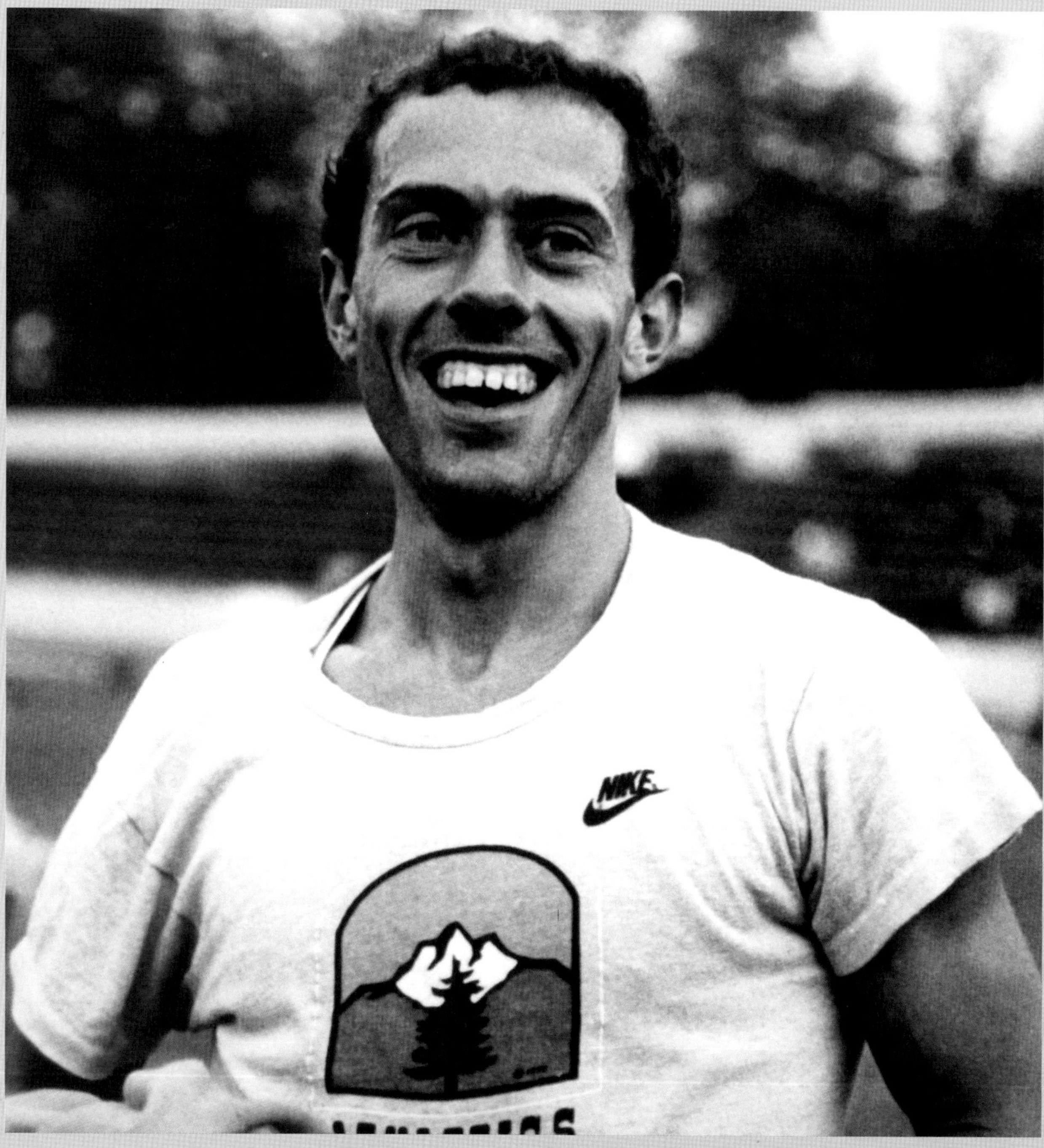

While Phil was busy clearing his company of detrimental debt, the Nike team were strategizing on the brand's next move. They realised that many of the Nike shoes being sold weren't just used for training; people were starting to wear sneakers as part of their daily lives. The next step seemed obvious: Apparel.

ABOVE: The first sub-4-minute mile runner, England's Roger Bannister, wearing a Nike T-shirt on May 21, 1980
OPP PAGE: Tom Cruise wore Nike trainers in the 1983 film *All The Right Moves*

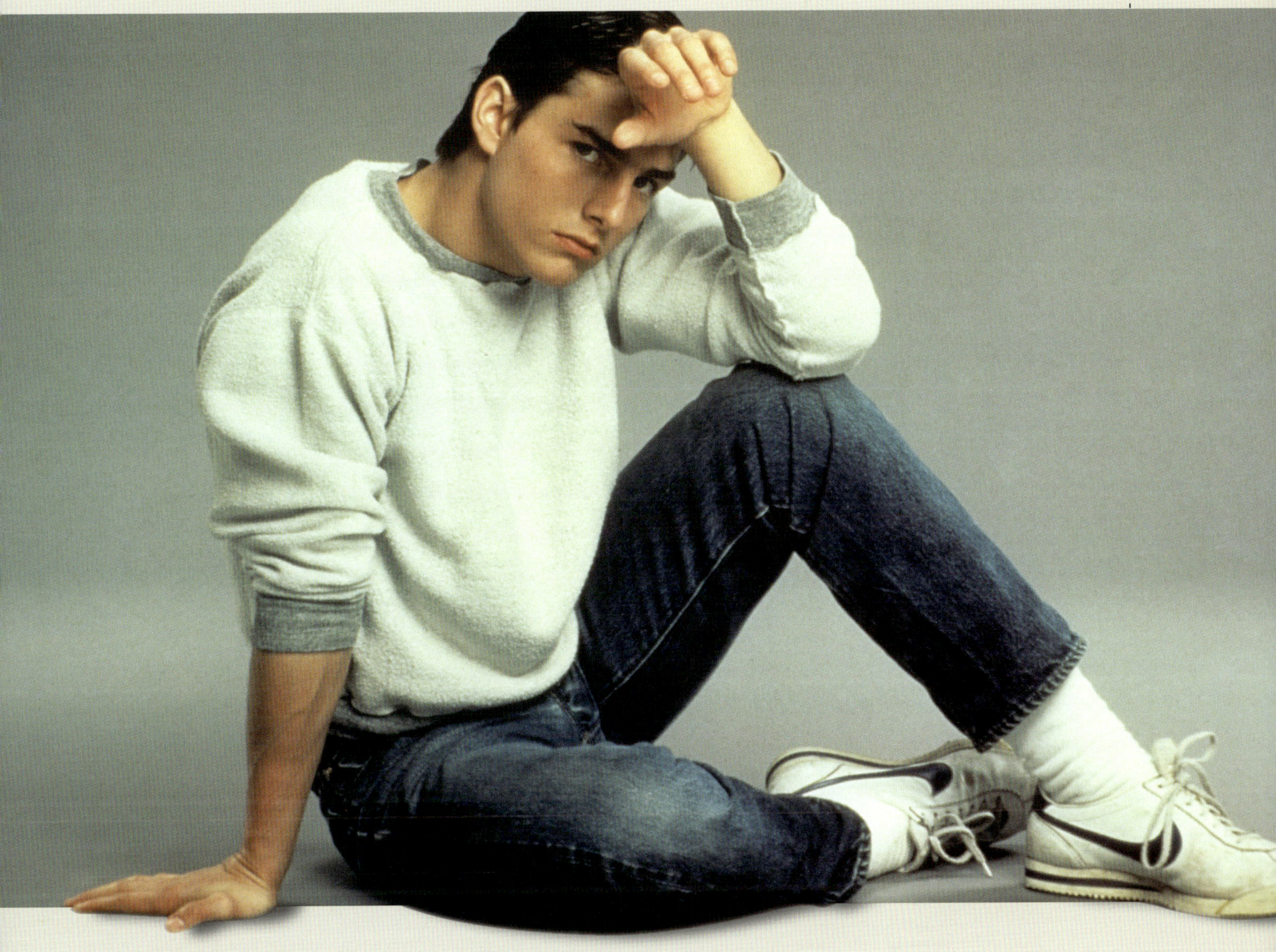

FROM TRACKS TO SIDEWALKS

By the late 1970s, the Nike team began noticing a curious trend. The running shoes they'd poured so much effort into designing for athletes weren't just gracing tracks or pounding treadmills—they were showing up on sidewalks, in schools, and supermarkets. People weren't just running in Nikes; they were living in them. What had started as a mission to craft the ultimate performance shoe was evolving into something bigger: Nike was becoming a lifestyle.

Phil and his team were both intrigued and energized by this discovery. If their shoes could transition from the track to everyday life, why couldn't Nike itself expand its horizons? The opportunity was clear. The time had come to think beyond footwear and step into the world of apparel. They envisioned Nike-branded hoodies, jackets, and tracksuits to complement their footwear and resonate with customers who wanted more than just shoes—they wanted the Nike ethos in every aspect of their wardrobe. But turning this vision into reality posed a whole new host of challenges.

Nike's expansion into apparel required finding the right manufacturing partner—someone who could produce high-quality garments at a scale and cost that fit their business model. The natural choice was to look beyond the United States. Japan, which had been integral to Nike's early success in shoe manufacturing, was no longer an affordable option.

China emerged as the next frontier. It was a rapidly industrializing nation with a massive labour force, and its government was just starting to open its doors to foreign businesses. This wasn't just an opportunity—it was a race. Phil realised that if they didn't establish a foothold in China soon, another competitor would. Getting in first could offer Nike a significant advantage.

But working with China was uncharted territory, fraught with risks. Negotiating contracts, ensuring consistent product quality, and navigating international trade laws would all be new challenges. Yet, the potential rewards were undeniable. If they were going to succeed, Knight would have to assemble an A team to go to China and make turn their vision onto reality.

In the summer of 1980, Phil and his team's visa requests were approved and so in July of that year they hopped on a plane and spent twelve days touring factories and building relationships with head of production and government officials across mainland China. This was unfamiliar ground, but Knight was no stranger to risk. The team prepared meticulously, knowing that their success in this endeavour could shape Nike's future.

Before heading back to Oregon, Phil made a pitstop in Shanghai. He wanted to secure a deal with the government's Ministry of Sports and within two hours he did just that. His hard work paid off because four years later, at the Los Angeles Olympics, the entire Chinese track and field team would be wearing Nike shoes. China was no longer just a manufacturing partner—it became the symbol of Nike's willingness to adapt, innovate, and chase the future at any cost. And as customers began sporting Nike shirts and jackets alongside their iconic sneakers, it became clear: Nike was no longer just making products. They were making a statement.

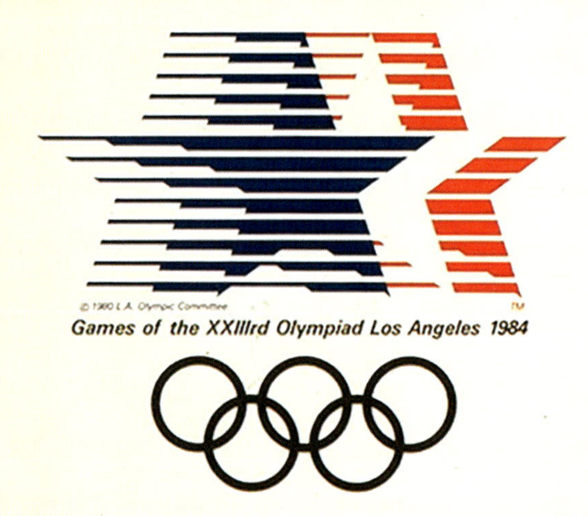

ABOVE: Los Angeles 1984 Olympic Games poster
OPP PAGE: 1980s UK Nike billboard advert

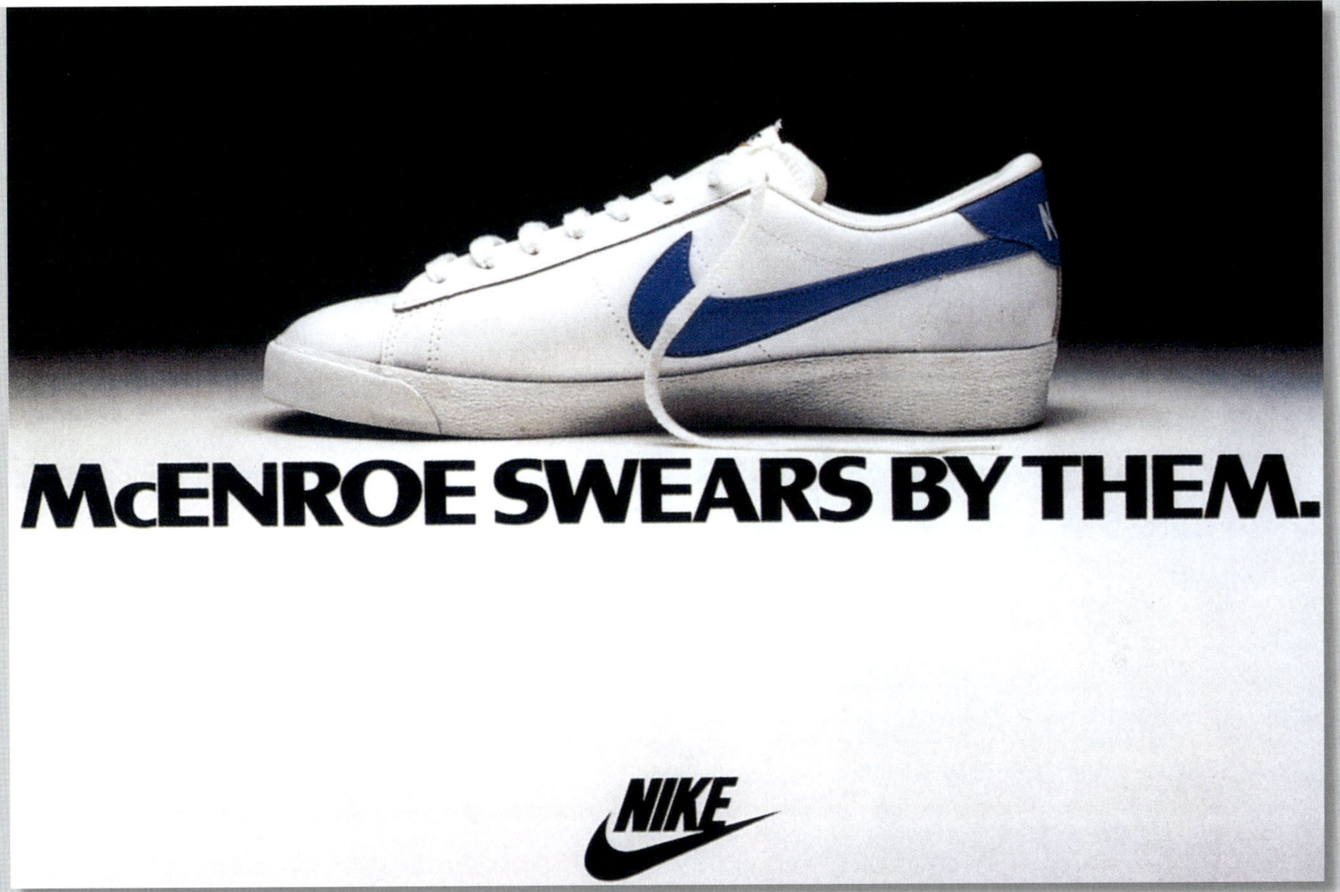

1980 was truly a big year for Nike because it was the year they decided to finally go public. The decision to go public wasn't made lightly. Phil had always been wary of external control. For years, he had resisted the idea of taking the company public, fearing that shareholders might interfere with Nike's unique, risk-taking culture. But as demand for Nike products skyrocketed and the costs of scaling production increased, Phil had no choice but to recognize the need for a more substantial and stable source of capital and the timing couldn't have been more ideal. By 1980, Nike controlled roughly 50% of the U.S. running shoe market and was rapidly gaining ground in basketball and tennis. Endorsements from star athletes like Steve Prefontaine and John McEnroe, combined with cutting-edge designs like the Air Tailwind and the innovative waffle sole, had cemented Nike's reputation as a leader in sportswear. The brand was riding high, but to maintain its momentum, it needed the resources to invest in marketing, product development, and global expansion.

Nike filed for its initial public offering (IPO) in December 1980. Influenced by the company Apple, who had also gone public that same month, Nike's offering was priced at $22 per share, valuing the company at $178 million—a significant figure for a business that had started with Phil selling shoes from the trunk of his car just over a decade earlier.

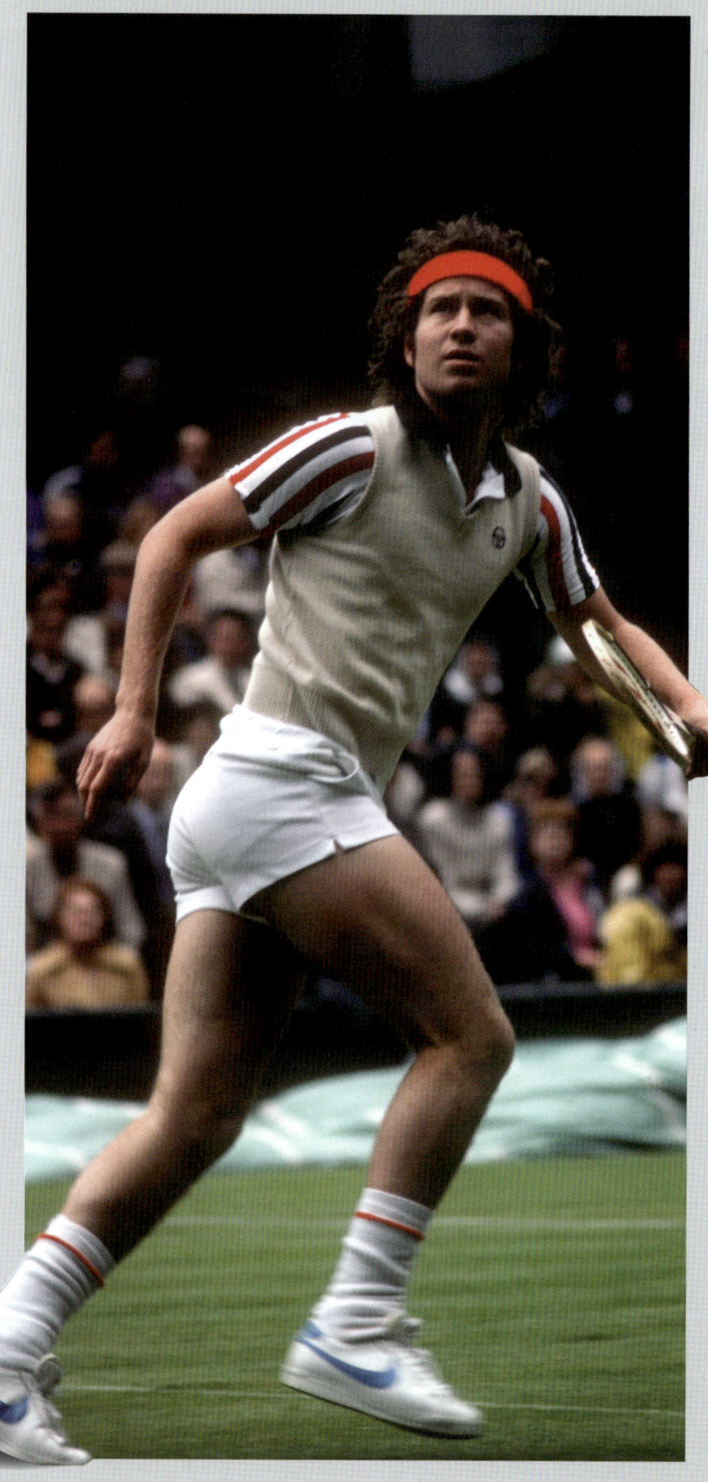

The move was meticulously planned. Nike's main objective in the proceedings was to maintain its independent spirit and to do so, it was imperative to ensure that Knight and his core team retained majority control over the brand. They also structured the IPO to prioritize long-term growth over short-term gains, emphasizing that Nike's mission extended beyond mere profitability.

On the day of the IPO, excitement ran high. Nike's offering was well-received, raising $51.2 million, another reminder of the public's confidence in the brand's future. It also made Phil and his team immensely wealthy, though Knight remained focused on the company's mission rather than personal gain. "Going public wasn't about cashing out", Phil later remarked, "It was about securing the resources we needed to keep growing".

Their newfound funds allowed Nike to double down on its strengths. The company expanded its marketing campaigns, refined its supply chain, and further invested in groundbreaking technologies including their air-cushioned soles. With their increase in capital, Nike could also accelerate its global expansion, targeting emerging markets in Europe and Asia. Going public was the biggest turning point for Nike. Phil's crazy idea was no longer just a scrappy startup—it was a major player on the world stage. Yet, despite its newfound status as a publicly traded company, Nike retained its entrepreneurial spirit. Knight and his team remained committed to innovation, pushing boundaries in both design and branding.

ABOVE: John McEnroe wearing Nikes at Wimbledon, 1980

OPP PAGE: Nike Air Force white sneakers

THE LOGO LADY

Since the creation of the Swoosh, over fifty years ago now, the iconic symbol representing motion and energy modelled after the wings of the Greek goddess of victory, has evolved into one of the world's most recognisable brand logos, not to mention a key ingredient in Nike's success story.

However, despite this unprecedented triumph of design, the mastermind behind the emblem, Carolyn Davidson, was famously paid the modest sum of $35 (equivalent to $272 in 2025) for her services. Over the years, that small paycheck became something of company lore, sparking debates about whether she was ever properly compensated for her work. In response, Davidson eventually revealed that wasn't the only payment she ever received from the Nike team. "First of all, they gave me my start. I learned the design world. I got referrals and I became known as the 'Logo Lady'". She also recounted how in September 1983, nearly three years after the company went public, Phil Knight invited Carolyn to a company reception where him and his team presented her with a surprise gift as a gesture of their gratitude. She received chocolate swooshes, a diamond ring made of gold and engraved with the Swoosh, and crucially, an envelope filled with 500 shares of Nike stock, then worth about seventeen cents per share or $85, now worth about $3 million. While the exact number of shares and their ultimate value remain private, Davidson's recollection of Knight's generosity helped dispel the notion that she was shortchanged for her now iconic design and allowed her to share in the brand's explosive success.

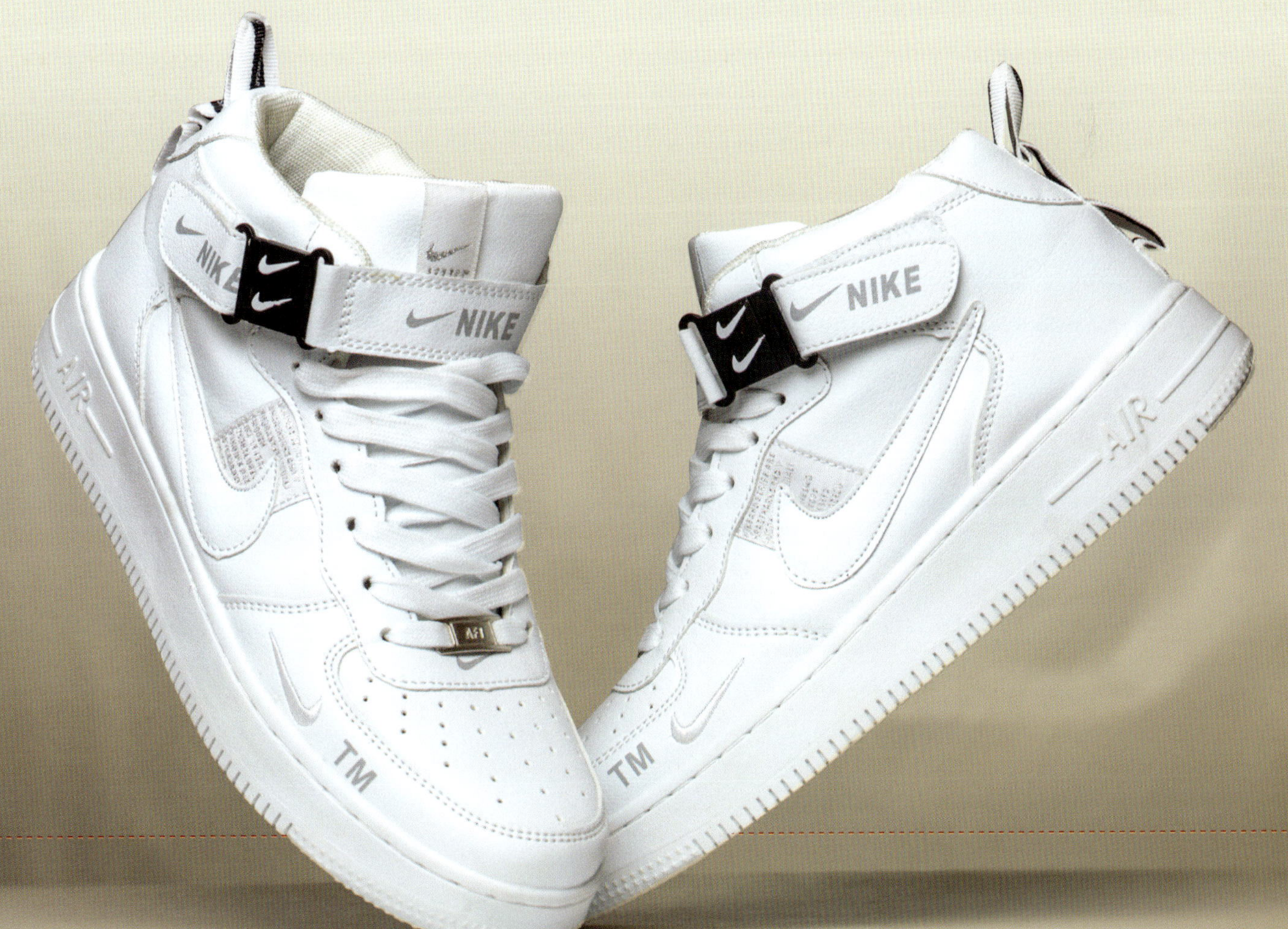

THE GAME CHANGER
1984

"I've missed more than 9,000 shots in my career. I've lost almost 300 games. Twenty-six times, I've been trusted to take the game-winning shot and missed. I've failed over and over and over again in my life. And that is why I succeed."
Michael Jordan

In the years following the IPO, Nike achieved dizzying levels of success. The brand was now the undisputed titan of the running industry, completely dominating the competition with its innovative designs and loyal customer base. However, despite the company's growing popularity, there were still a few areas of sport and sportswear that remained elusive to Nike. Most apparently, the multi-billion-dollar basketball market. When it came to the basketball world, Nike was actually lagging behind its main rivals, Converse and Adidas. Converse had dominated the courts for years, with endorsements from the NBA's biggest stars, including Larry Bird and Magic Johnson, while Adidas had a strong foothold thanks to its streetwear appeal. For Phil Knight, Nike's inability to crack the basketball market was a glaring gap in the company's quest for all-around dominance. A breakthrough wasn't just desirable—it was essential.

Enter Sonny Vaccaro, a brash, unorthodox consultant who had joined the Nike team back in 1977 but quickly became instrumental in the company's push in penetrating the basketball space. Vaccaro had an

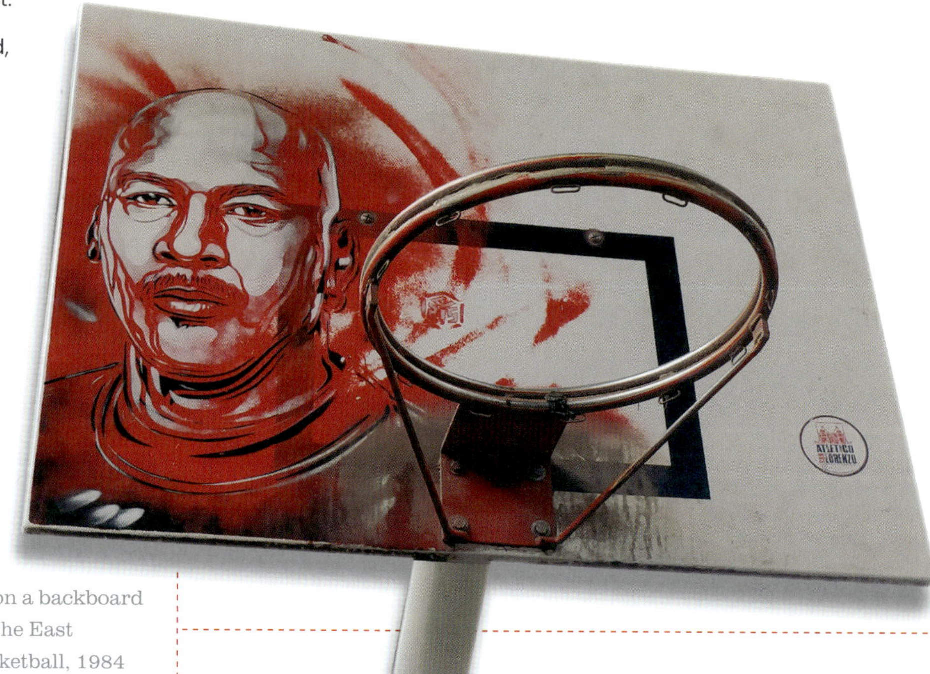

RIGHT: Michael Jordan graffiti image on a backboard
OPP PAGE: Jordan of North Carolina in the East Regional Semi Finals of the NCAA Basketball, 1984

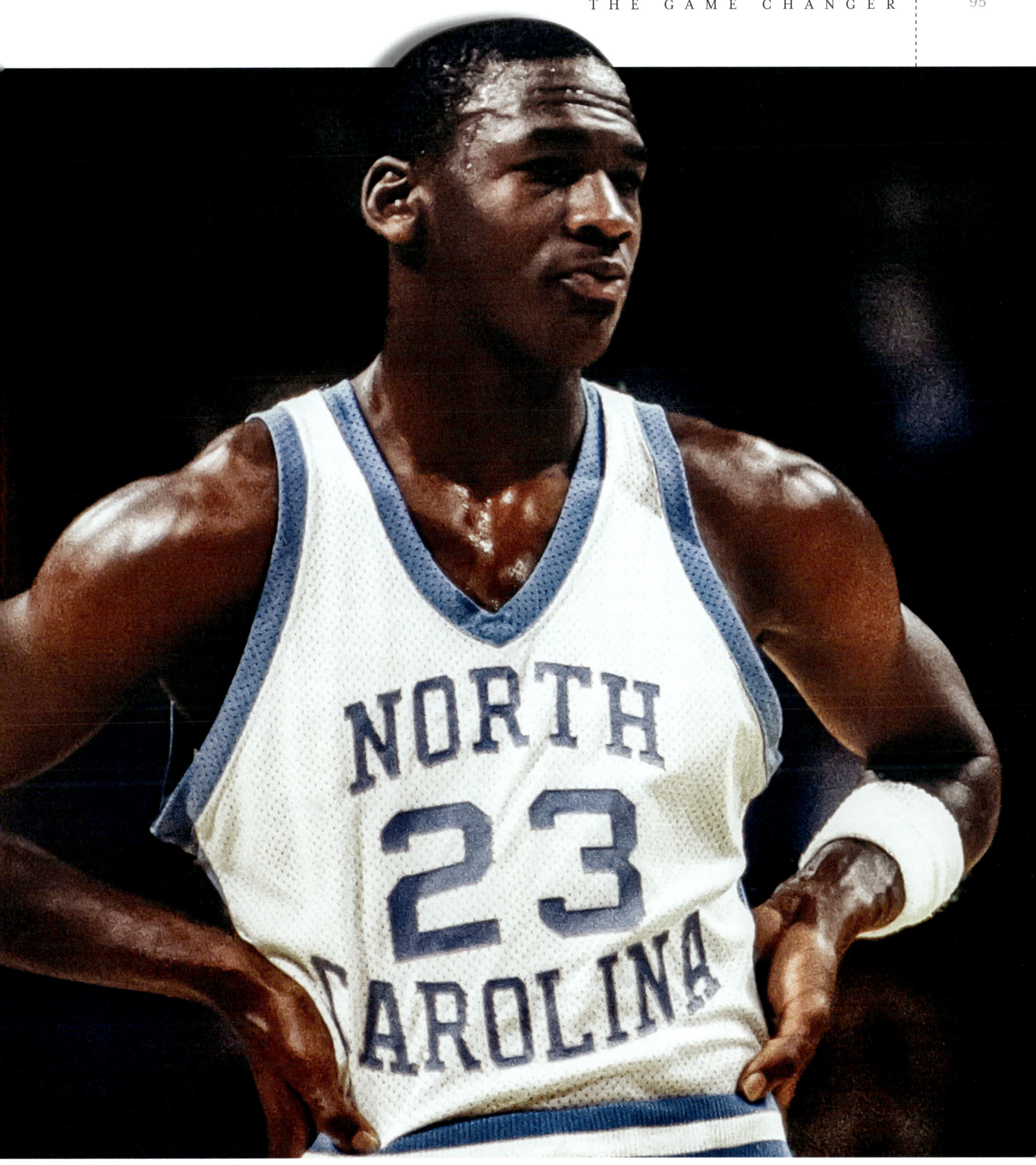

uncanny knack for understanding basketball culture and spotting talent before anyone else and so he was tasked with the job of helping Nike not only gain visibility in the sport but also to overcome its rivals. His strategy proposal to Phil was far from conventional: instead of spreading Nike's limited basketball budget across multiple players or teams, Vaccaro believed in focusing all efforts onto one transcendent athlete—a single, generational star who could embody the brand and redefine the game. The challenge, however, was finding the player in question. And so began the hunt for the next big thing in basketball.

It wasn't until 1982, when Vaccaro attended the NCAA championship game between the University of North Carolina and Georgetown, that he finally found the athlete he had long been searching for. In a tense, closely contested matchup, a then 19-year-old freshman sank a game-winning 16ft jump shot with just 15 seconds left on the clock. Watching the young player's poise, athleticism, and competitive spirit, Vaccaro felt certain that the athlete standing in front of him would not only transform Nike, but the game of basketball itself. All Vaccaro needed to do now was find out who in the world was that kid. His name: Michael Jordan.

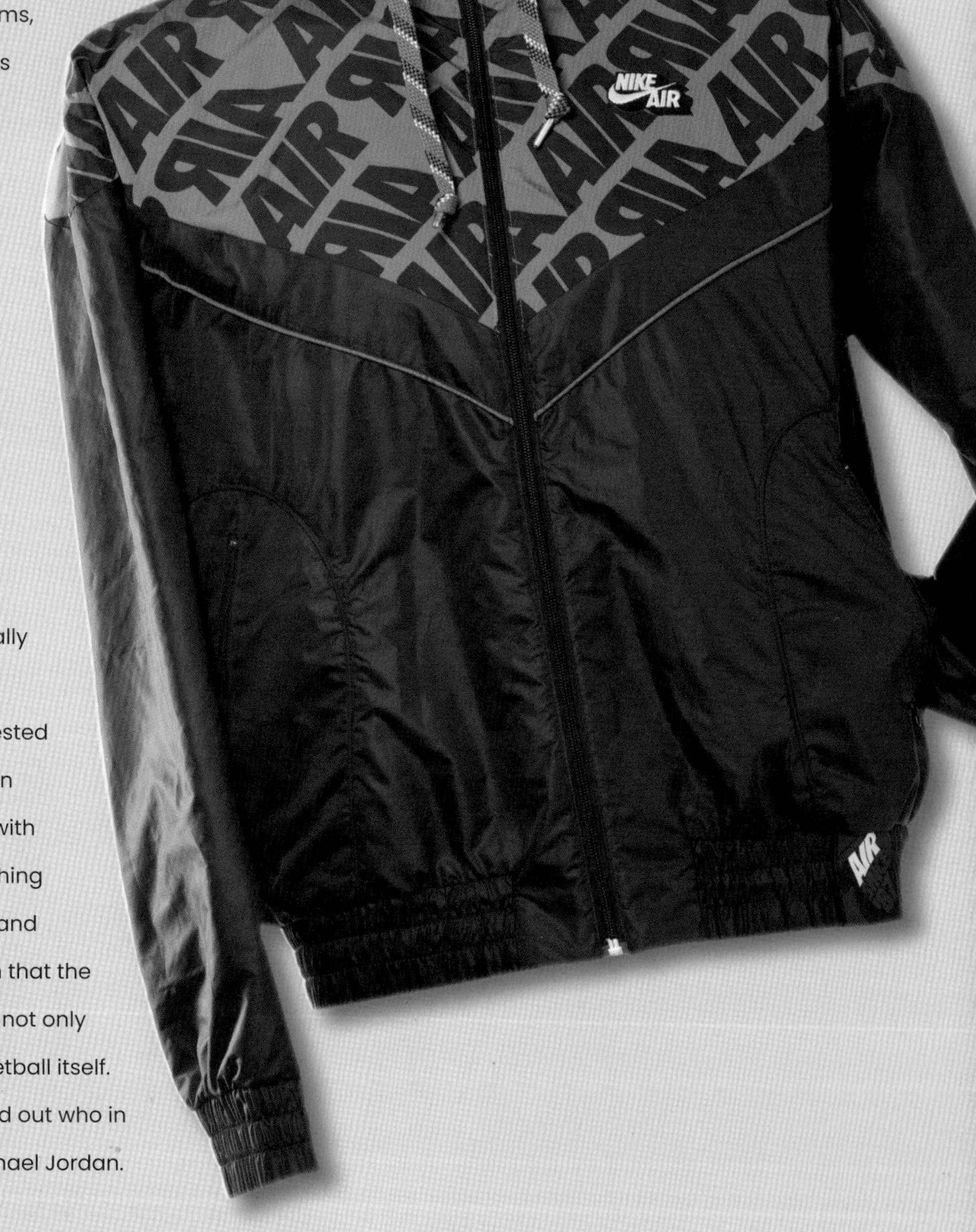

ABOVE: Vintage Nike Air windbreaker jacket
OPP PAGE: Michael Jordan making waves in the local press

MICHAEL JORDAN, THE ROOKIE

"If you do the work, you get rewarded. There are no shortcuts in life."

Born Michael Jeffrey Jordan on February 17, 1963, in Brooklyn, New York, he was the fourth of five children to James and Deloris Jordan. The family moved to Wilmington, North Carolina, when Michael was still a toddler, and it was there, amidst the salt air of the coastal city, that he began his journey toward basketball immortality.

As a young boy, Jordan was a natural athlete, excelling in a wide range of different sports. Baseball was his first love, and football was another one of his passions. Basketball, however, was a slower burn. He was first introduced to the game by his older brother Larry, but by the time he got to high school, Jordan had fully developed an obsession for the sport.

Jordan famously failed to make the varsity basketball team during his sophomore year at Laney High School. Standing at just 5'11" at the time, he was considered undersized. This setback, though disappointing, could have discouraged many, but for Jordan, that moment only fuelled his competitive fire.

Determined to prove himself, Jordan trained relentlessly. By the time he returned as a junior, he had grown four inches and was now playing

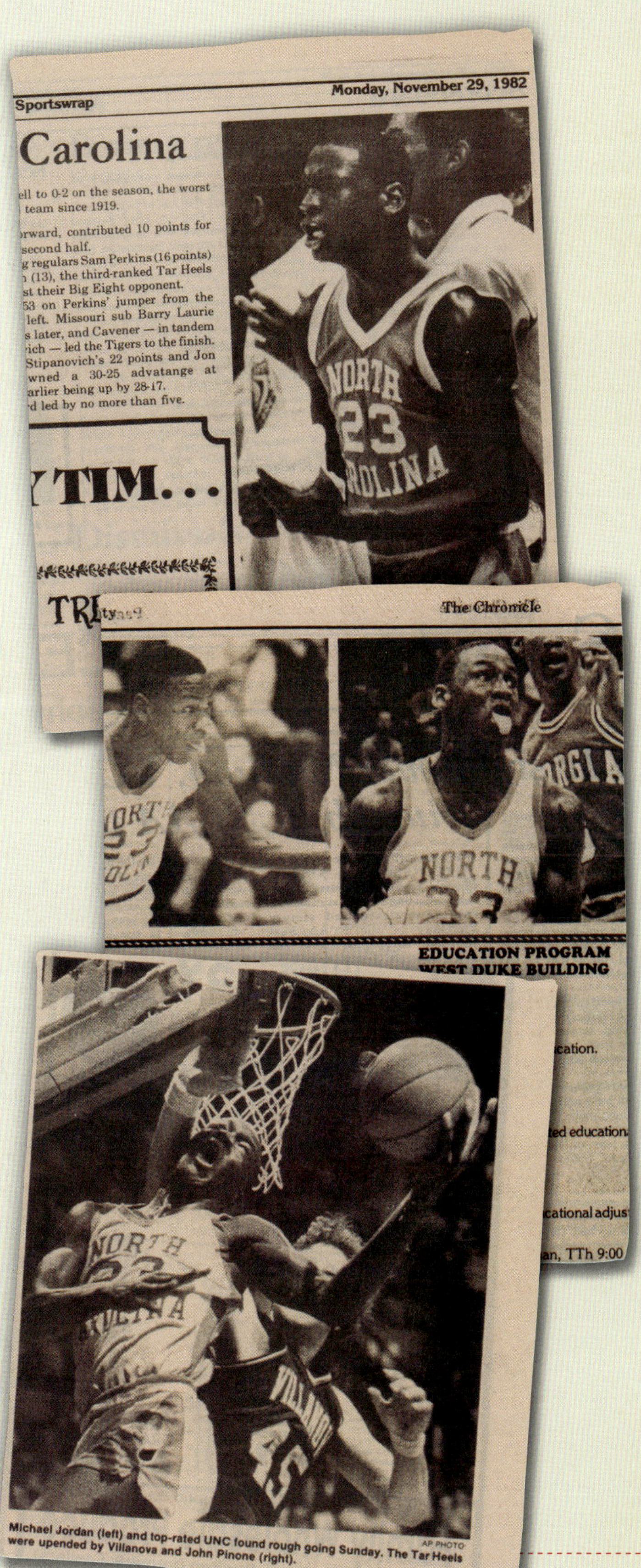

Michael Jordan (left) and top-rated UNC found rough going Sunday. The Tar Heels were upended by Villanova and John Pinone (right).

with a chip on his shoulder. His senior season saw him average a near triple-double, and his series of electrifying performances earned him a spot in the prestigious McDonald's All-American Game. His dominance caught the attention of colleges nationwide, and in 1981, he accepted a scholarship to play basketball at the University of North Carolina at Chapel Hill under the legendary coach Dean Smith.

At UNC, Jordan quickly established himself as a star among stars. But his defining moment came in the 1982 NCAA Championship game against Georgetown, where he hit the game-winning jump shot, securing a title for the Tar Heels. This iconic moment catapulted Jordan into the national spotlight, and more importantly caught the attention of Sonny Vaccaro.

Though he continued to hone his skills and excel as an athlete during his time at North Carolina, Jordan would eventually leave college after his junior year to join the NBA in 1984.

The 1984 NBA Draft was a historic one. The Houston Rockets selected Hakeem Olajuwon with the first overall pick, and the Portland Trail Blazers, needing a centre, chose Sam Bowie second. The Chicago Bulls, picking third, happily took Michael Jordan—a decision that would change the fortunes of the franchise and basketball forever.

Jordan soon proved his worth out on the court in a dynamic first season. He helped the Bulls make the playoffs and scored an average of 28.2 points per game. For his efforts, Jordan received the NBA Rookie of the Year Award and was selected for the All-Star Game. After just a few short months on the big stage, Michael Jordan seemed to be the name on everybody's lips.

Jordan would go on to have one of the most prestigious careers in basketball over the course of his 15 seasons in the NBA between the years 1984 and 2003. His profile on the NBA website even states, "By acclamation, Michael Jordan is the greatest basketball player of all time". Known for his slam dunks from the free-throw line, earning him the nicknames "Air Jordan" and "His Airness", he's also a six-time NBA champion with the Chicago Bulls, as well as a six-time winner of the NBA Finals MVP awards. In April 2009, Jordan received one of basketball's greatest honour's: He was inducted into the Naismith Memorial Basketball Hall of Fame. Attending the induction ceremony was a bittersweet affair for Jordan because being at the event meant "your basketball career is completely over," he explained. Though Jordan achieved an unparalleled legacy in his career, his influence extended far beyond the basketball court. He was a cultural icon. Jordan elevated the NBA to unprecedented heights and setting new standards for athletic excellence and marketability. That shift from legend to cultural icon was largely in part to the brilliance and creativity of the people at Nike.

Vaccaro wasted no time pushing Nike to pursue him. It was a hard sell. Jordan was a rookie with no guarantee of NBA success, hell, he hadn't even set foot on an NBA court yet. The idea of staking so much on an unproven player made Phil Knight and his team of misfits uneasy.

To add more fuel to the fire, Jordan's brand of choice was Adidas, having worn them since college, and Converse was the league's official shoe sponsor. Both companies seemed to have the upper hand.

Vaccaro, however, was relentless. He argued that Jordan wasn't just an athlete—he was a phenomenon waiting to happen. As the rookie started making waves in the basketball world, Phil finally let himself be convinced that the kid was worth taking a chance on. Nike, then a smaller player in basketball, saw an opportunity and went all in. Despite Jordan's initial reluctance—he famously told his agent, "Just get a deal with Adidas"—Nike persisted. The pitch to Jordan was simple: "We don't want you to fit into the Nike brand; we want Nike to fit around you". Nike wanted to come out with a Michael Jordan signature shoe line that he would help create and rather originally, have a stake in its success. The proposed contract was groundbreaking: $500,000 annually for five years, plus bonuses and a 5% royalty of each Air Jordan pair sold. This offer was unprecedented, as the top players at the time didn't earn more than $100,000 a year. For comparison, the top deal at the time was New Balance's $150,000-a-year deal with James Worthy. Despite this generous offer, getting Jordan on board wasn't an easy feat. The Nike team had their work cut out for them.

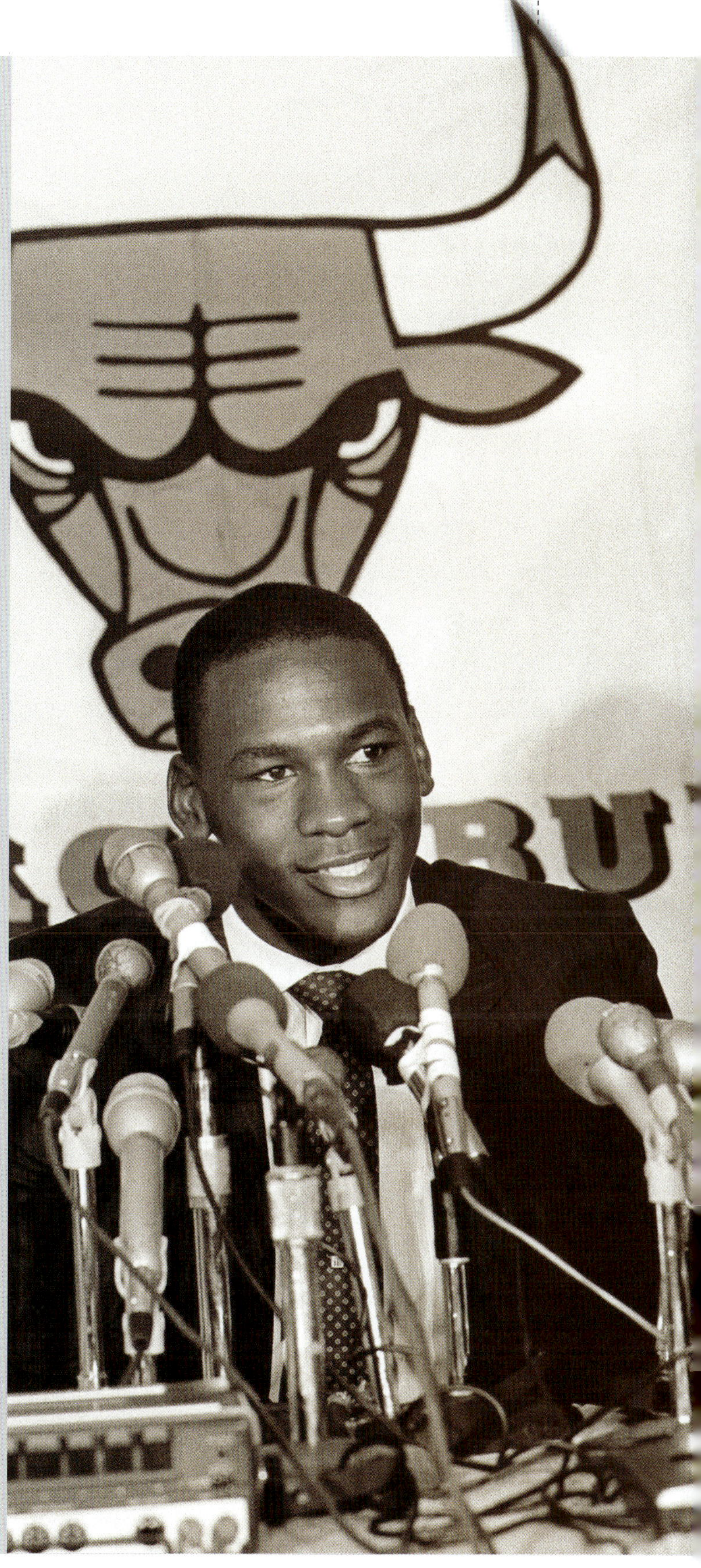

ABOVE: Michael Jordan at a news conference after signing a seven-year contract with the Chicago Bulls, 12 September, 1984

AIR (2023)

In 2023, the movie Air brought the story of Nike's groundbreaking deal with Michael Jordan to the big screen, dramatizing the partnership that revolutionized basketball, sports marketing, and sneaker culture. Directed by Ben Affleck, *Air* follows Sonny Vaccaro (played by Matt Damon) and his relentless pursuit to convince Michael Jordan to believe in Nike's vision, by pitching an innovative idea: a signature shoe built entirely around Michael's identity. This pitch ultimately leads to the creation of the Air Jordan line, a gamble that paid off beyond anyone's wildest expectations.

But first came the extensive negotiations. One of the most poignant scenes depicted in the film was Vaccaro's heartfelt meeting with Deloris Jordan. Played with quiet strength by Viola Davis, Deloris becomes the linchpin of the negotiations. Vaccaro appeals to her belief in Michael's potential and her desire for him to have more than just a typical endorsement deal. It was upon Deloris's insistence and protectiveness over her son, that Michael was offered a percentage of every Air Jordan sold—a clause that was unheard of at the time. This revolutionary contract not only secured financial security for Jordan but also set a precedent for athletes' participation in the success of the products they endorse.

Air received widespread acclaim from critics and audiences alike. It was praised for its sharp script, compelling performances, and nostalgic 1980s setting. Basketball fans and sneaker enthusiasts appreciated the insider look at the origins of the Air Jordan line, while casual viewers enjoyed the underdog story and dynamic character interactions.

Air not only celebrated the groundbreaking Nike-Jordan deal, but also highlighted its cultural significance. The Air Jordan line redefined how sports endorsements were structured, putting athletes at the centre of branding and marketing. It also cemented Nike's dominance in the basketball world and transformed sneakers from functional footwear into coveted fashion statements.

ABOVE: *Air* (2023) film poster
OPP PAGE TOP: Young breakdancers dressed in Nike tracksuits and trainers, Brooklyn, New York, 1984
OPP PAGE BOTTOM: Nike SB Dunk Low 'What the Dunk, part of the iconic Nike Dunks style first released in 1985

Ultimately, it was the unique, player-centric deal that swayed Michael Jordan into signing the deal with Nike. In 1984, the young player was unaware of just how much this endorsement was going to change his life and ultimately go down in sport history, pushing boundaries in both design and branding.

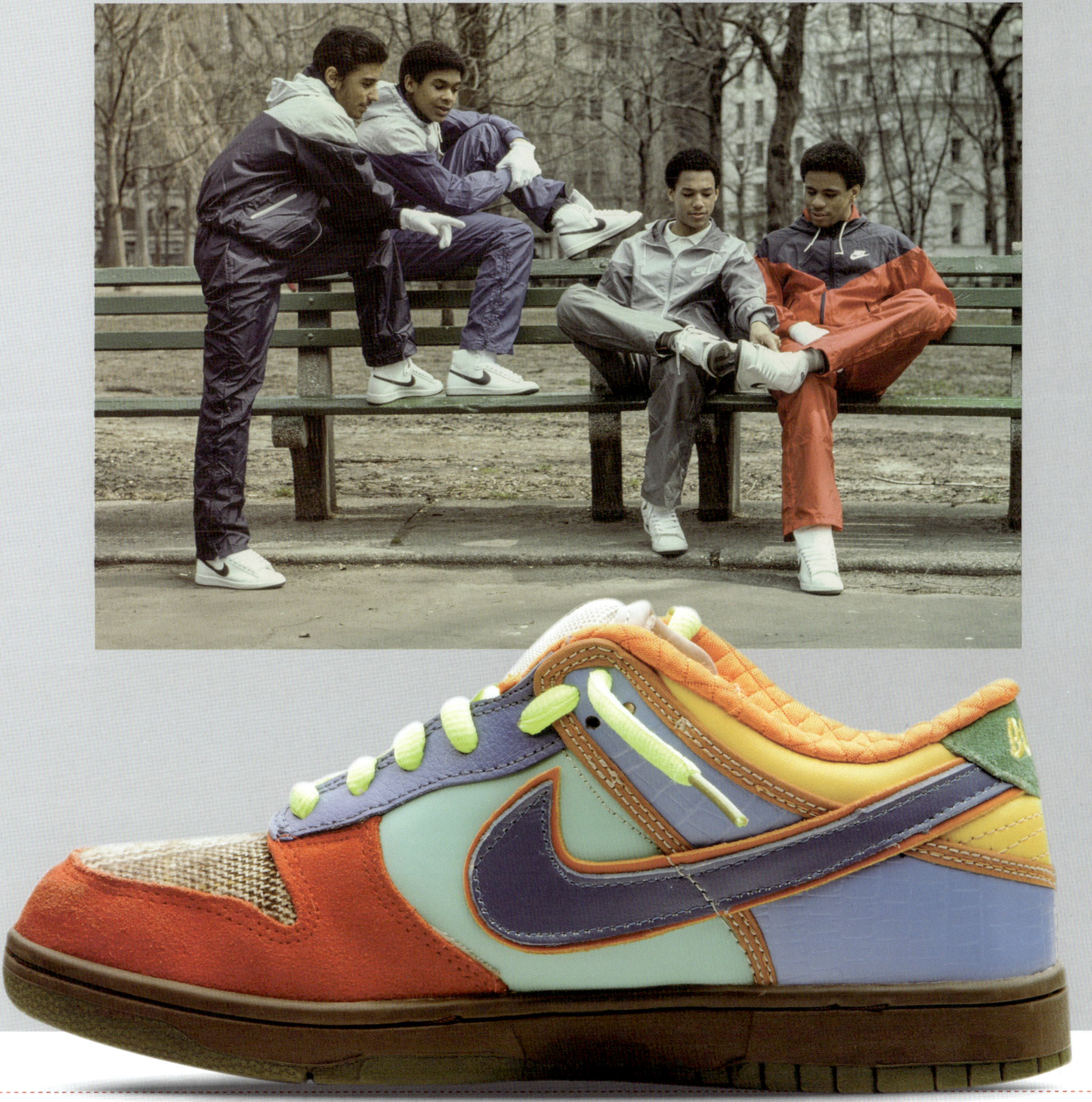

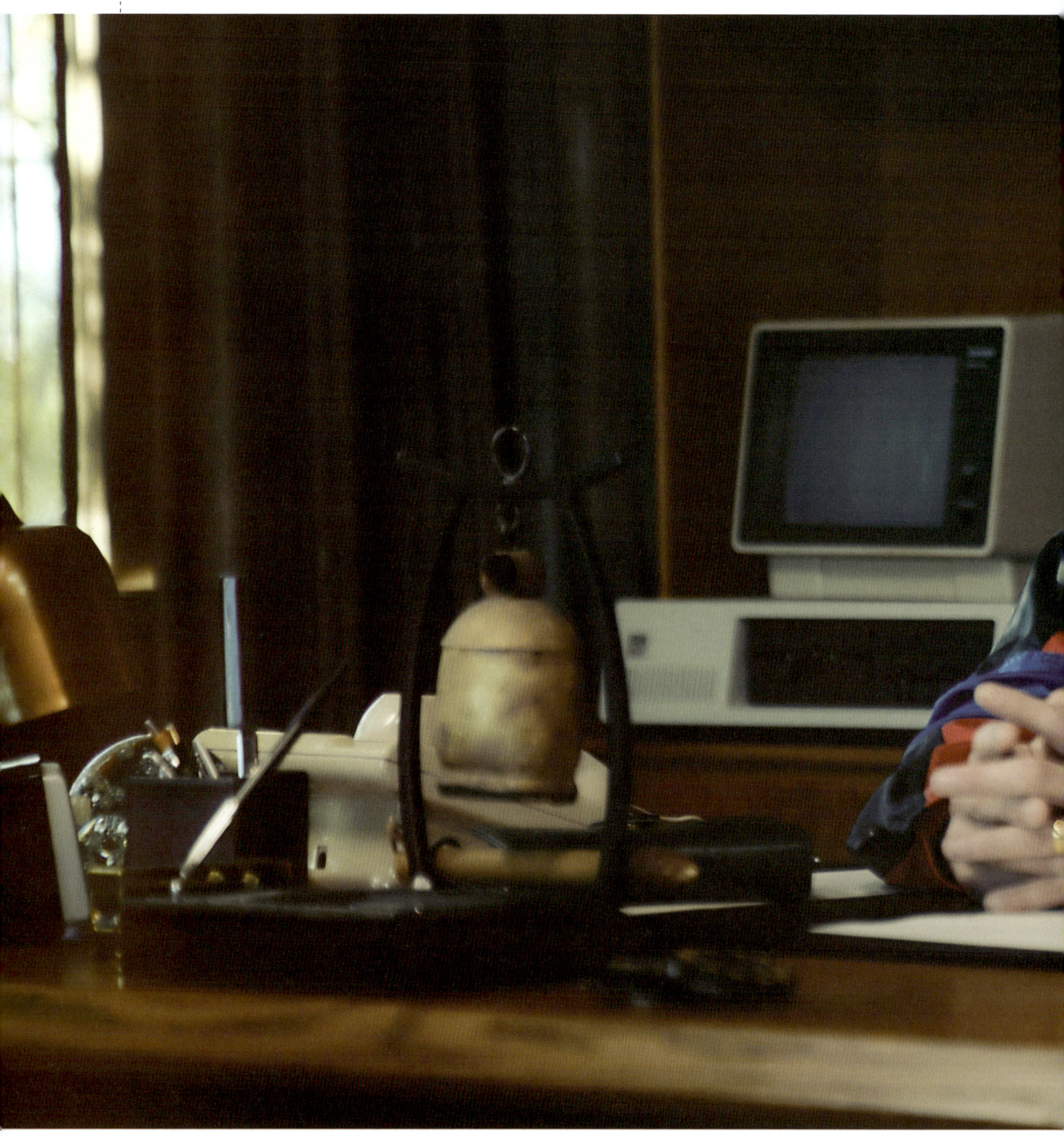

ABOVE: *Air* (2023), directed by Ben Affleck, who also stars as Nike co-founder Phil Knight, tells the story behind the creation of the legendary Air Jordan basketball shoe

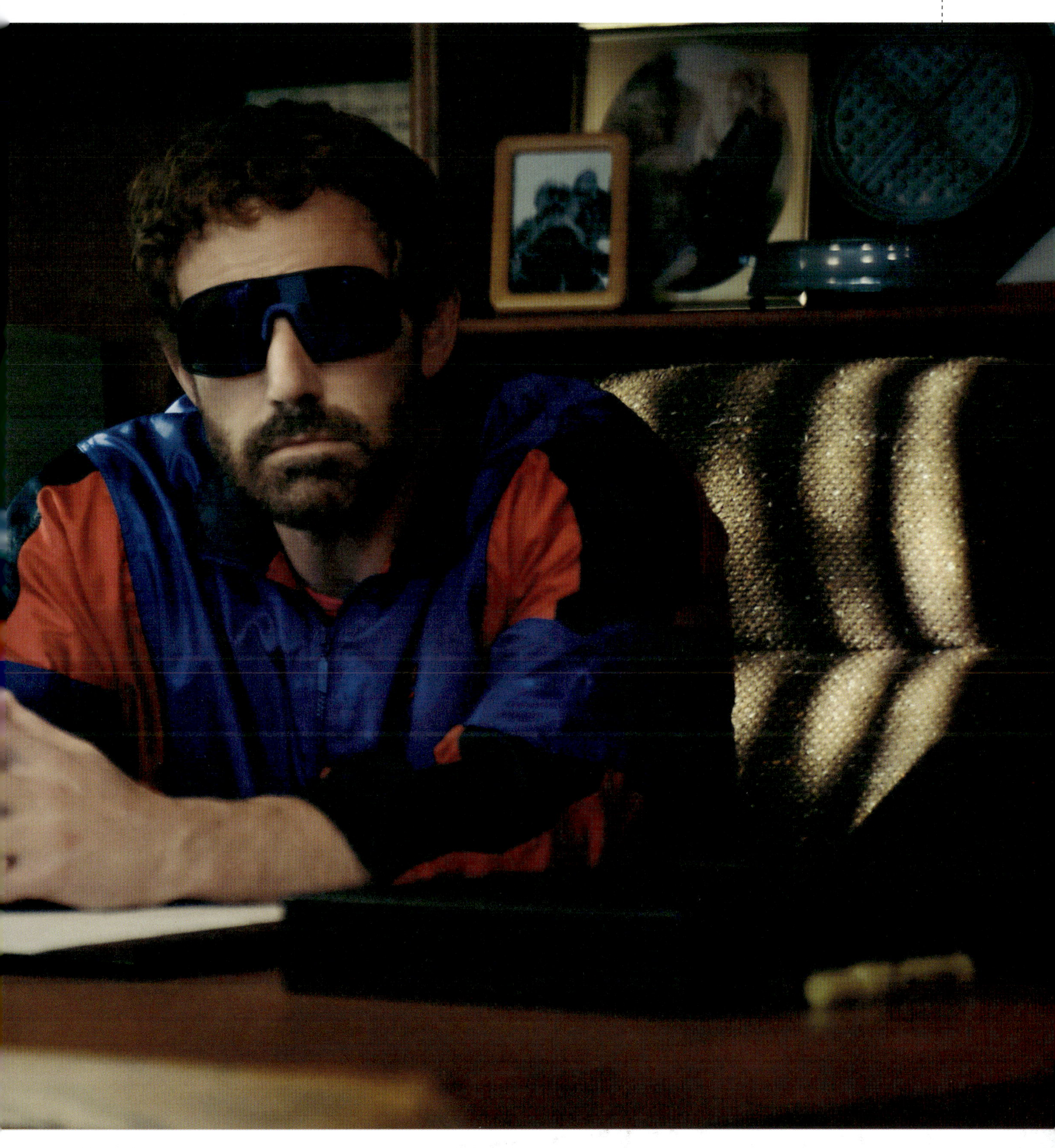

WALKING ON AIR (JORDANS)

1985

"We all fly. Once you leave the ground, you fly. Some people fly longer than others."

Michael Jordan

In 1985, Nike launched the groundbreaking Air Jordan 1. Retailing at $65—an unprecedented price at the time—the Air Jordan 1 was more than just a shoe; it was a statement. The design, featuring bold red, black, and white colour blocking inspired by Michael Jordan's Chicago Bulls team, stood out sharply from the muted tones of traditional basketball shoes. It was a rebellious, daring choice that matched Jordan's dynamic presence on the court. The reception was electric. Air Jordans sparked a frenzy, particularly among younger basketball fans who wanted to emulate the rising star. Within the first year, the shoe generated over $126 million in sales—a staggering figure that cemented its place in sneaker and sports history. The allure was fuelled not just by the shoe's aesthetic appeal and Jordan's on-court heroics, but also by Nike's innovative and provocative marketing strategies.

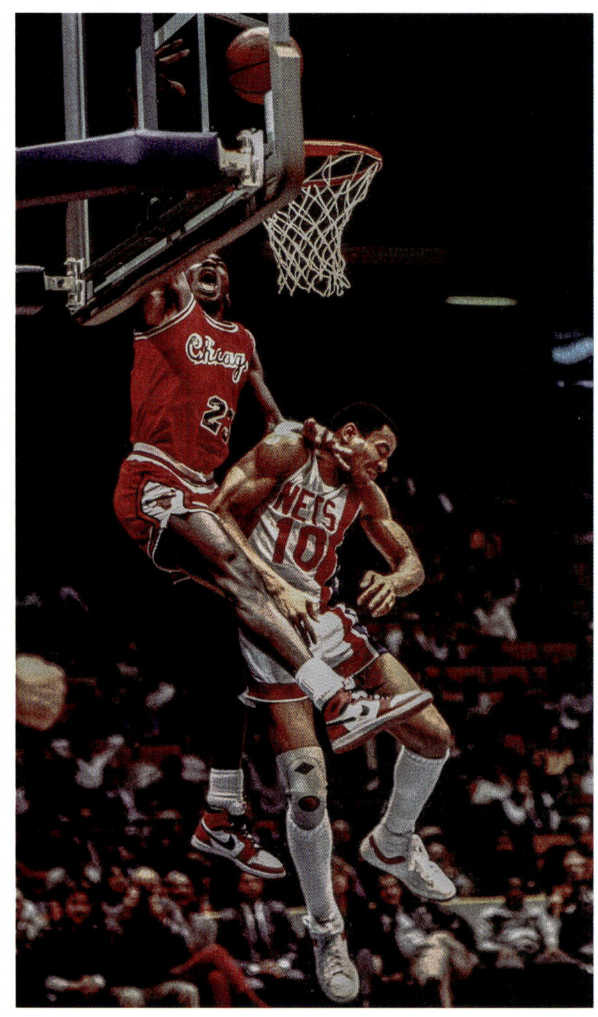

RIGHT: Michael Jordan flying high for Chicago Bulls against New Jersey Nets in 1985

OPP PAGE: Air Jordan 1s worn by former NBA basketball player Michael Jordan in 1985

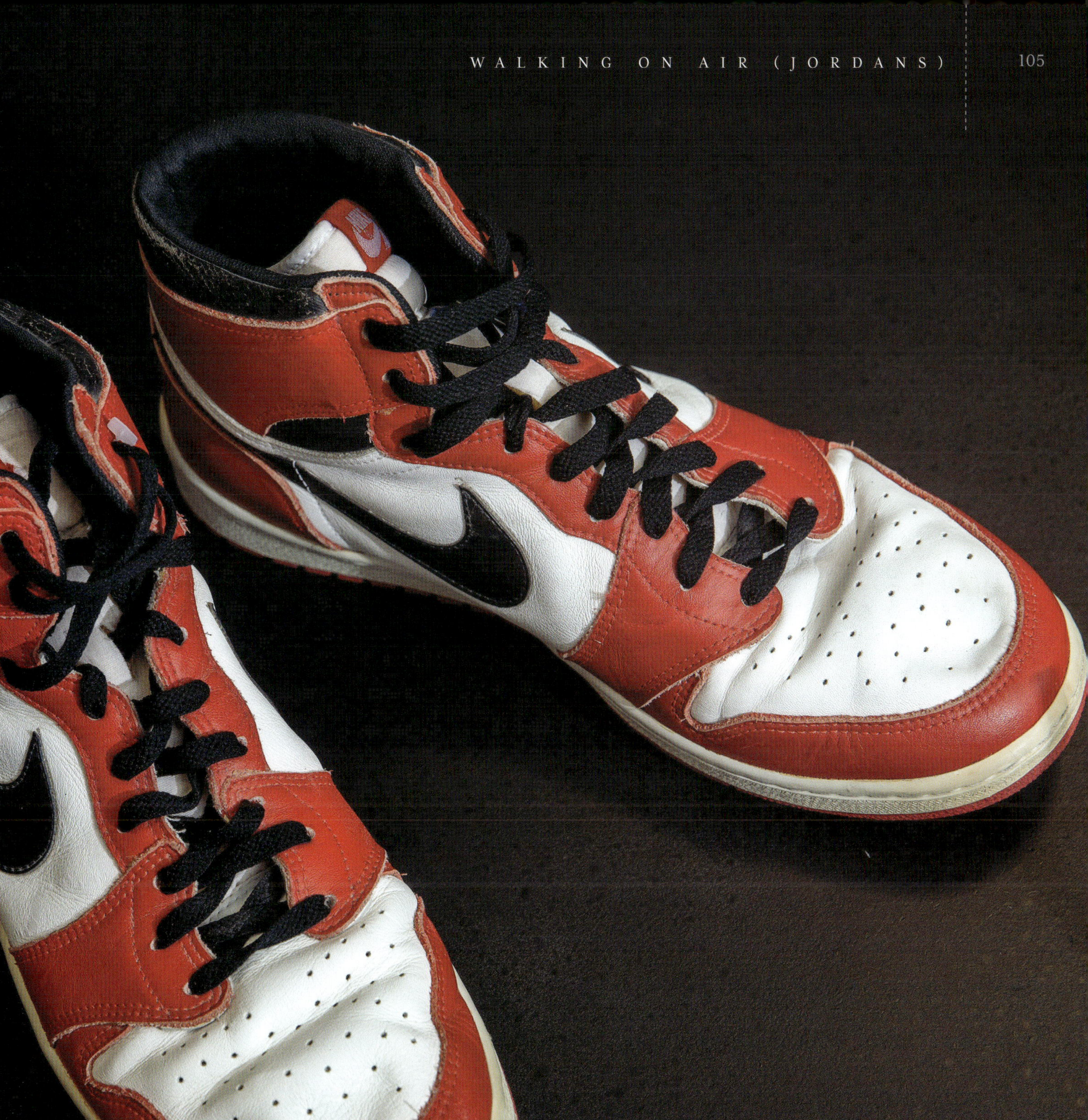

BANNED BY THE NBA

Nike's marketing campaign for the Air Jordans was a masterstroke, blending bold advertising with a touch of controversy. The NBA famously banned the original Air Jordan 1 for not meeting the league's uniform guidelines stating that "the red and black Nike basketball shoes" violated league policy, incurring a $5,000 per game fine. The NBA policy was that "shoes had to be 51% white and in accordance with what the rest of the team was wearing". For any other company, this situation would have spelled disaster for the new product, but for Nike this was the perfect scenario.

The fines were a drop in the ocean compared with the money that Nike was making, so Phil Knight agreed to pay each fine to ensure his Air Jordans were tearing up the court.

Nike turned the controversy into a marketing goldmine. Ad campaigns boldly proclaimed: "Banned. By the NBA" with a voice over saying "On Sept. 15, Nike created a revolutionary new basketball shoe. On Oct. 18, the NBA threw them out of the game. Fortunately, the NBA can't keep you from wearing them. Air Jordans. From Nike".

The message was clear—wearing Air Jordans was an act of rebellion, a way to channel the defiant spirit of Michael Jordan himself.

The campaign introduced the idea that Air Jordans were not just for professional athletes but also for anyone with the determination to "fly".

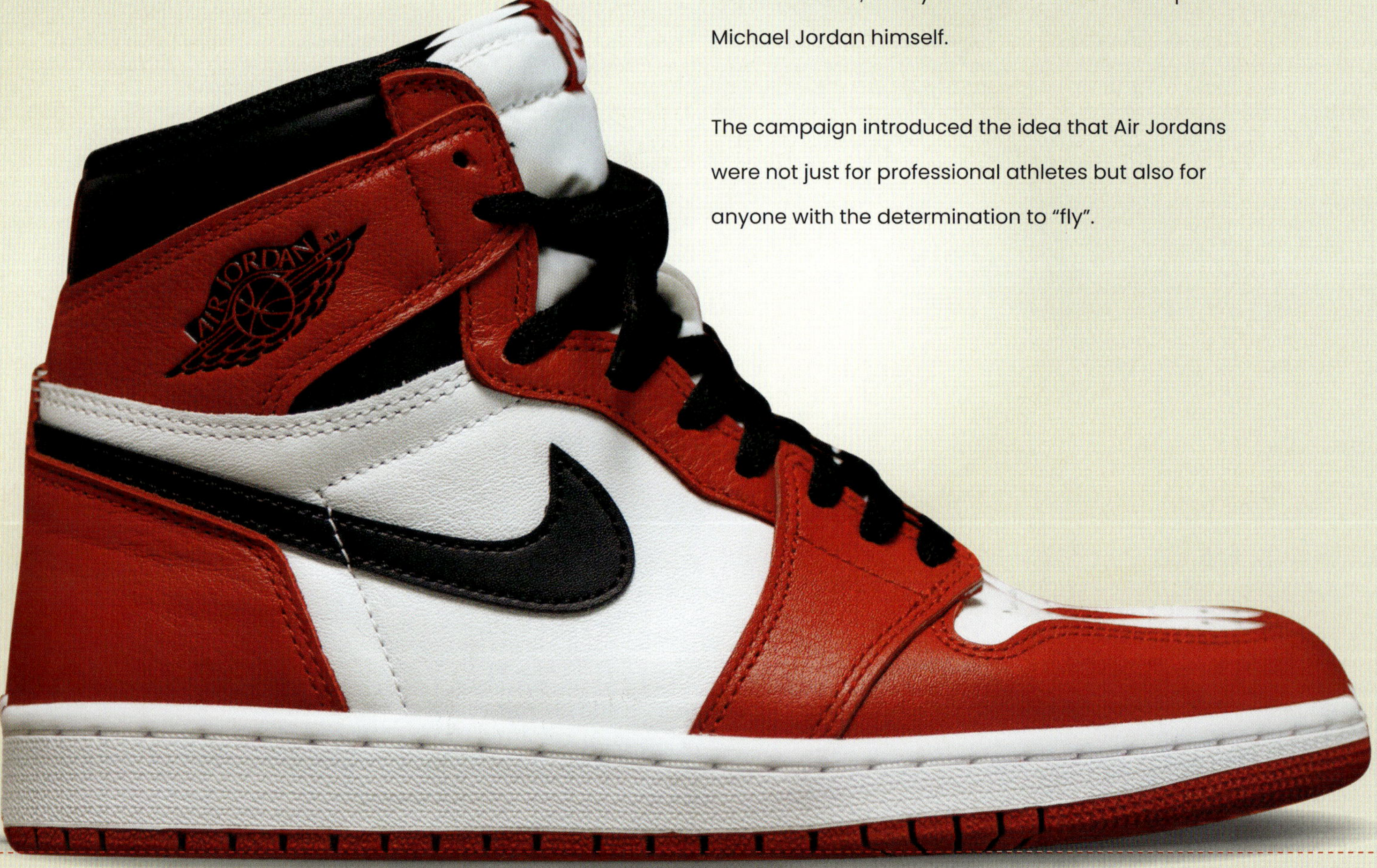

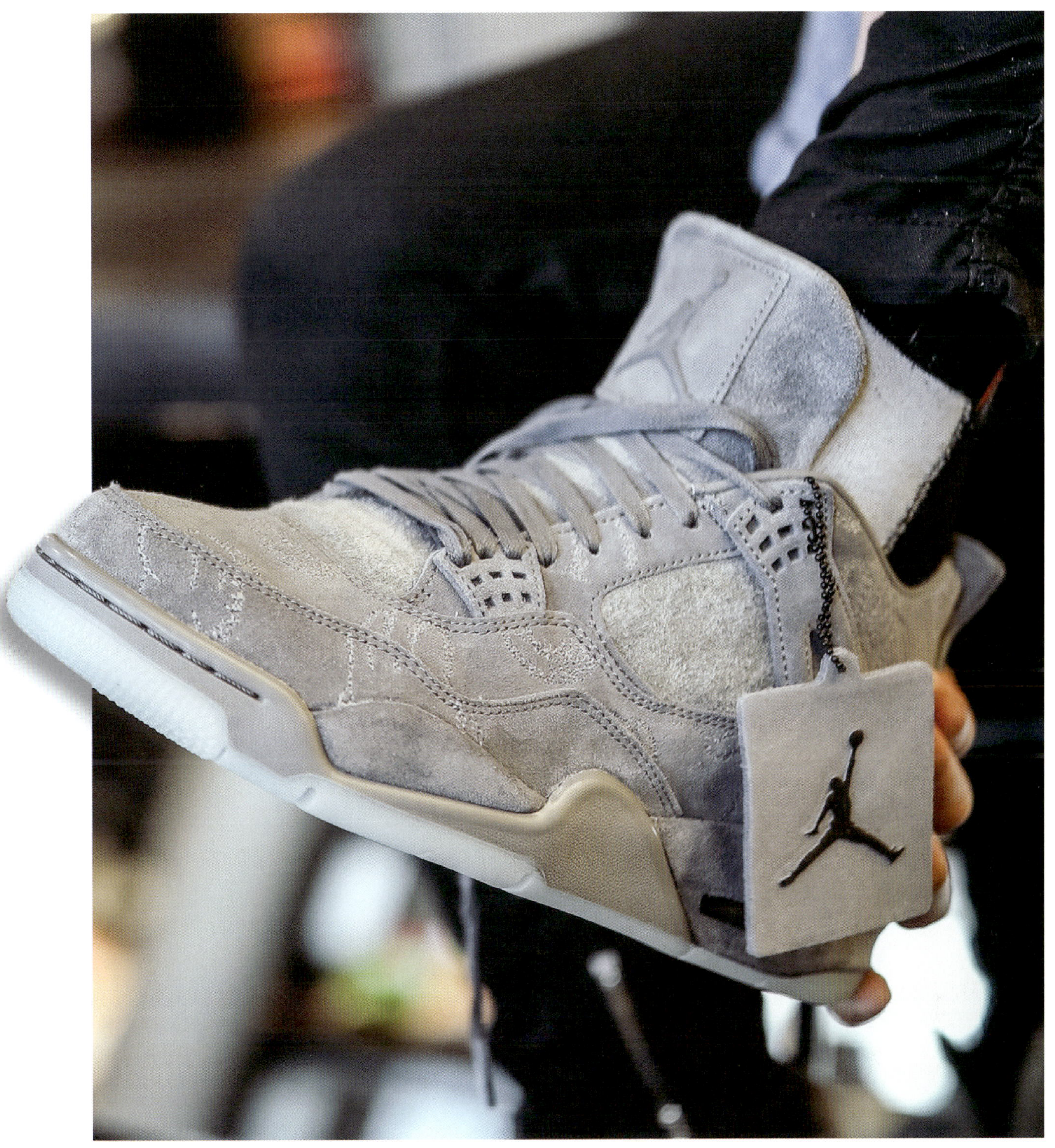

OPP PAGE: Jordan 1 Retro High Chicago
ABOVE: KAWS x Air Jordan IV sneakers, which saw fans camping outside Overkill for 5 days in Berlin to get their hands on one of the 50 pairs available, 31 March 2017

When Nike first released the Air Jordan 1 collection, they had the goal of making three million dollars within the first three years. What they definitely weren't expecting were sales exceeded $126 million in just one year of the shoes being on the market. Phil Knight called this unprecedented moment "the perfect combination of quality product, marketing, and athlete endorsement".

The Air Jordan 1 was just the beginning. Its success launched an entire line of signature sneakers, each iteration accompanied by innovative designs, cutting-edge technology, and boundary-pushing marketing. During Jordan's playing career (1984–2003), a new Air Jordan sneaker was released every season. If you want to play like Mike, you must buy his sneakers, was the message in Nike's marketing strategy. Consumers believed buying his shoes could improve their game.

The Air Jordan not only became a cultural icon, but it also proved to be one of the most lucrative partnerships in sports and business history. Today, Nike's Jordan Brand generates approximately $5 billion annually, making it a cornerstone of the company's revenue. Meanwhile, Michael Jordan personally earns around $300 million annually from his endorsement deal, with lifetime earnings from the partnership exceeding $2 billion. This makes him one of the highest-paid athletes in history, even years after his retirement.

Though it had a rocky start, the relationship between Jordan and Nike was and continues to be a slam dunk.

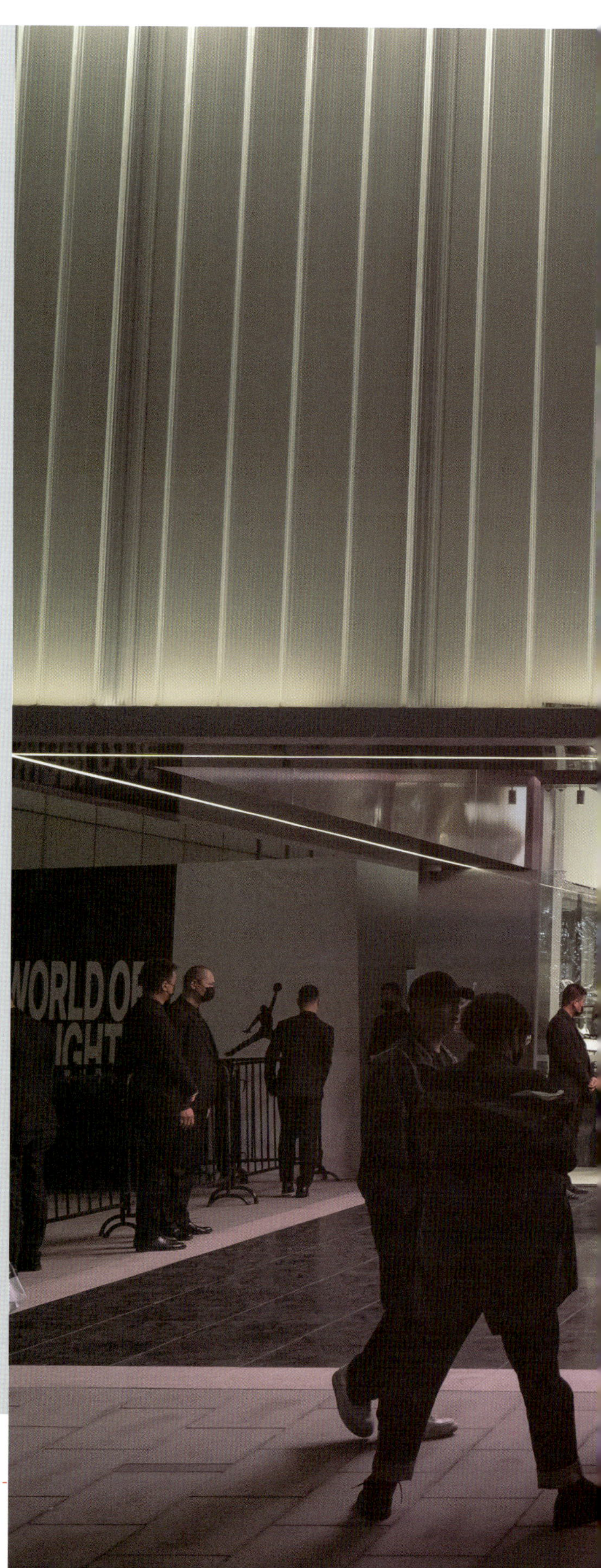

RIGHT: The Opening of the Jordan World of Flight Store in Beijing, 22 March, 2024

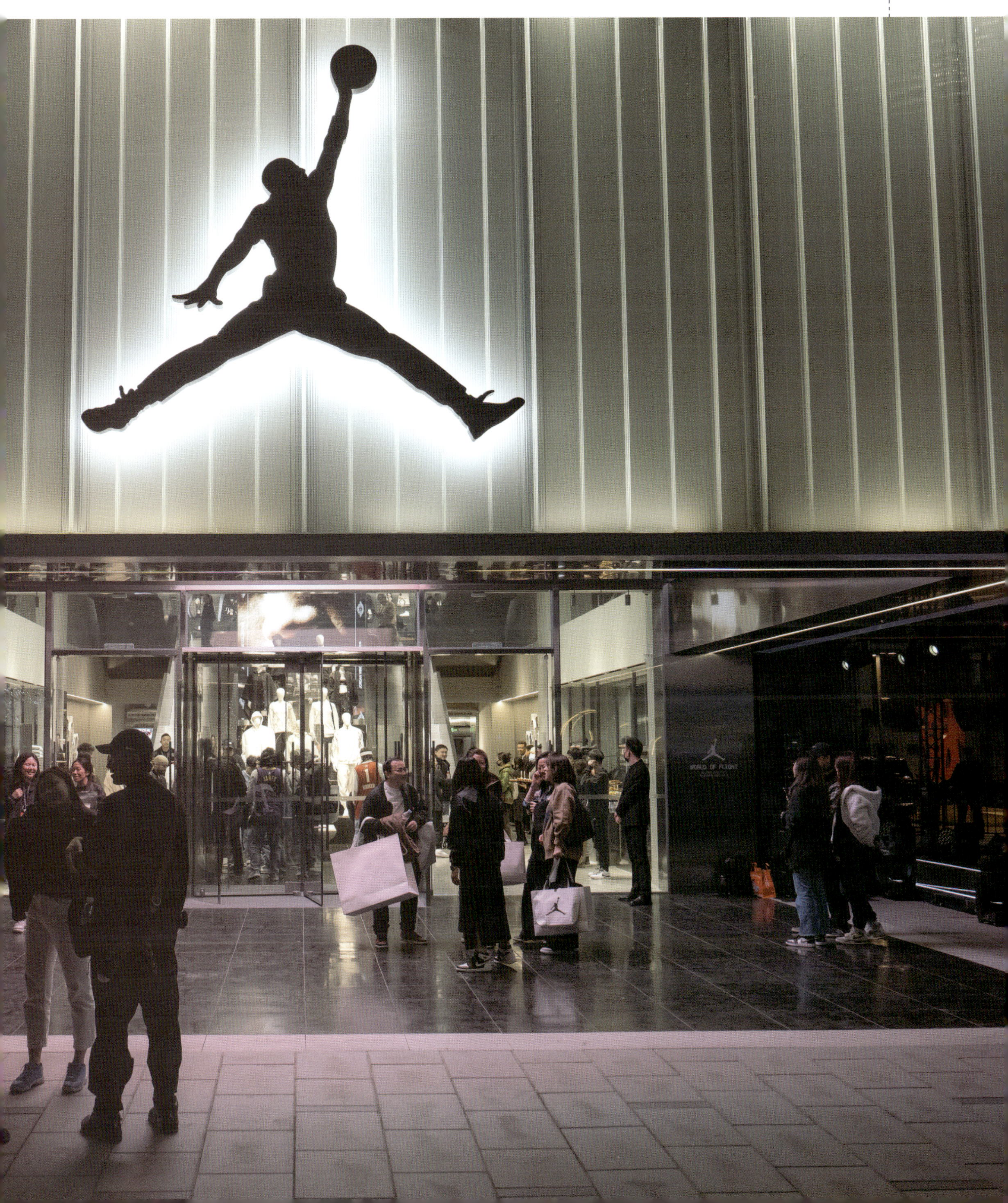

"JUST DO IT."
1987-1988

"Everybody is different. Everybody has different styles. Just do it the best way you know how."

Vince Carter

On March 26, 1987, during *The Cosby Show*, Nike first aired "Revolution," a black-and-white, punch-in-the-face kind of commercial. Part music video, part sports ad, this one-of-a-kind clip truly changed the world of advertising for good. The concept for "Revolution" originated at the offices of Wieden+Kennedy, the advertising agency that had already begun to carve a reputation for itself as a creative powerhouse. The idea to pair sports visuals with the Beatles' iconic song, "Revolution", was audacious. Until then, almost all the songs used in adverts were either jingles or covers of pop tunes. By using the Beatles' "Revolution," Nike paved the way for real songs, by the real artists, to be the soundtrack for everything from cars to computers, fashion to phones, and everything in between.

Soon after the ad hit the airwaves, however, the Beatles' record label, Apple Records, sued Nike for $15 million, claiming that the band hadn't given their "authorization or permission". George Harrison went on to say that that advert opened the door for the band's songs to be used to promote anything from "women's underwear" to "sausages." Yet Yoko Ono – who held shares in the Beatles' record company – had helped broker the original deal. She thought the commercial would help introduce a whole new generation of people to her late husband's music. Though there was no clear

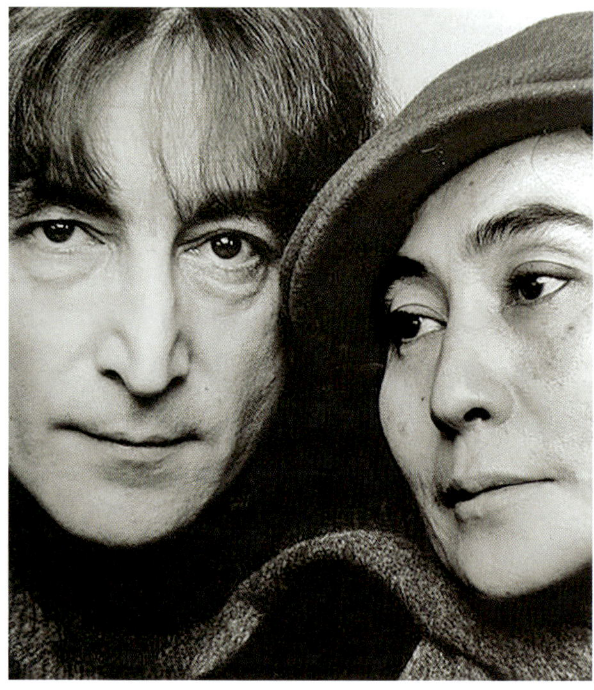

ABOVE: John Lennon and Yoko Ono in 1980

OPP PAGE: Just Do It sweatshirt

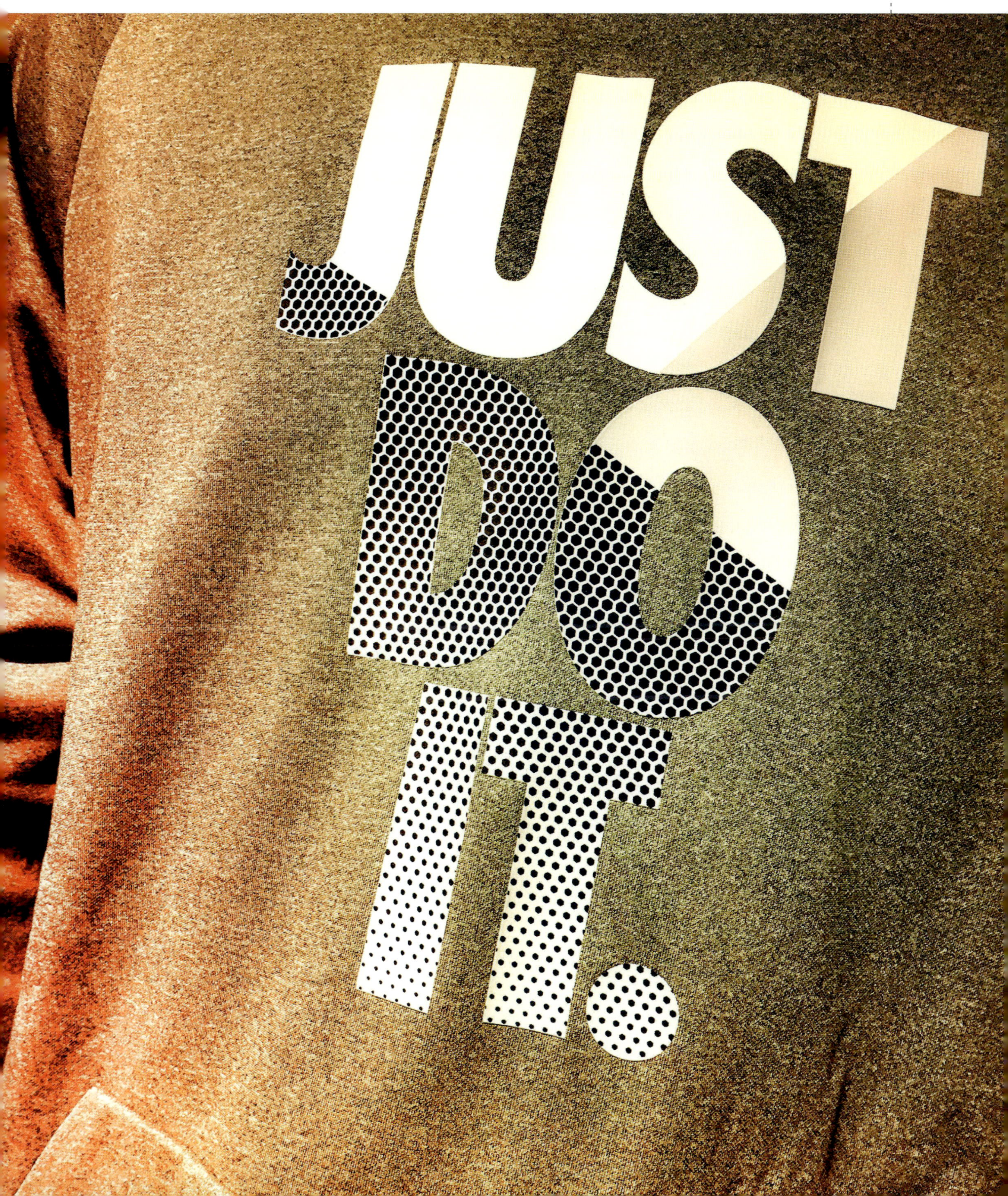

JUST
DO
IT.

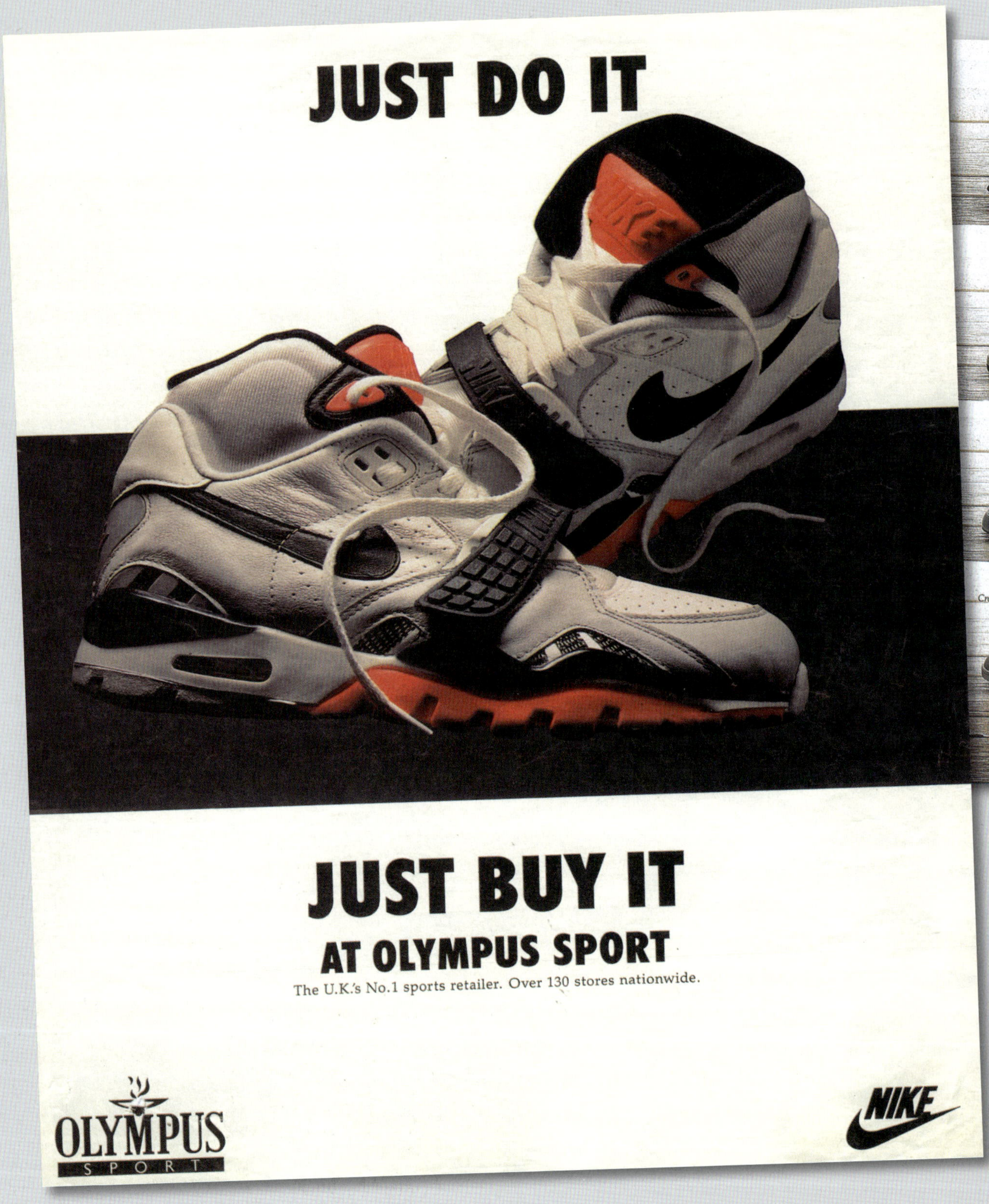

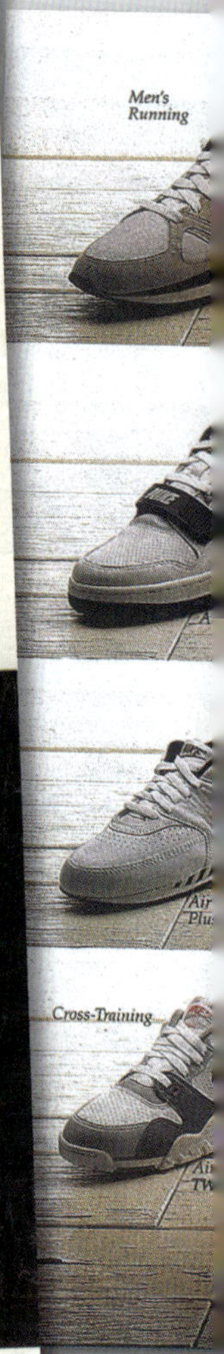

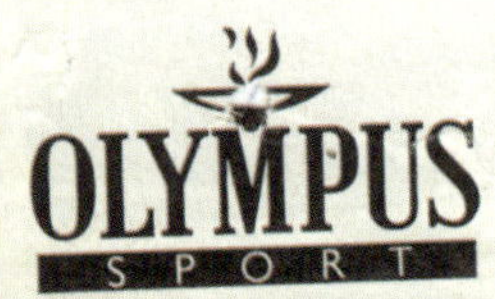

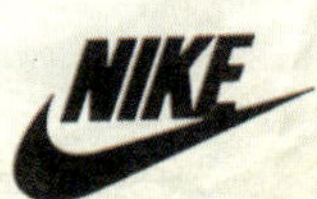

ABOVE: 1980s UK Nike 'Just Do It' magazine advert
OPP PAGE: 1988 Nike Air athletic shoes advert

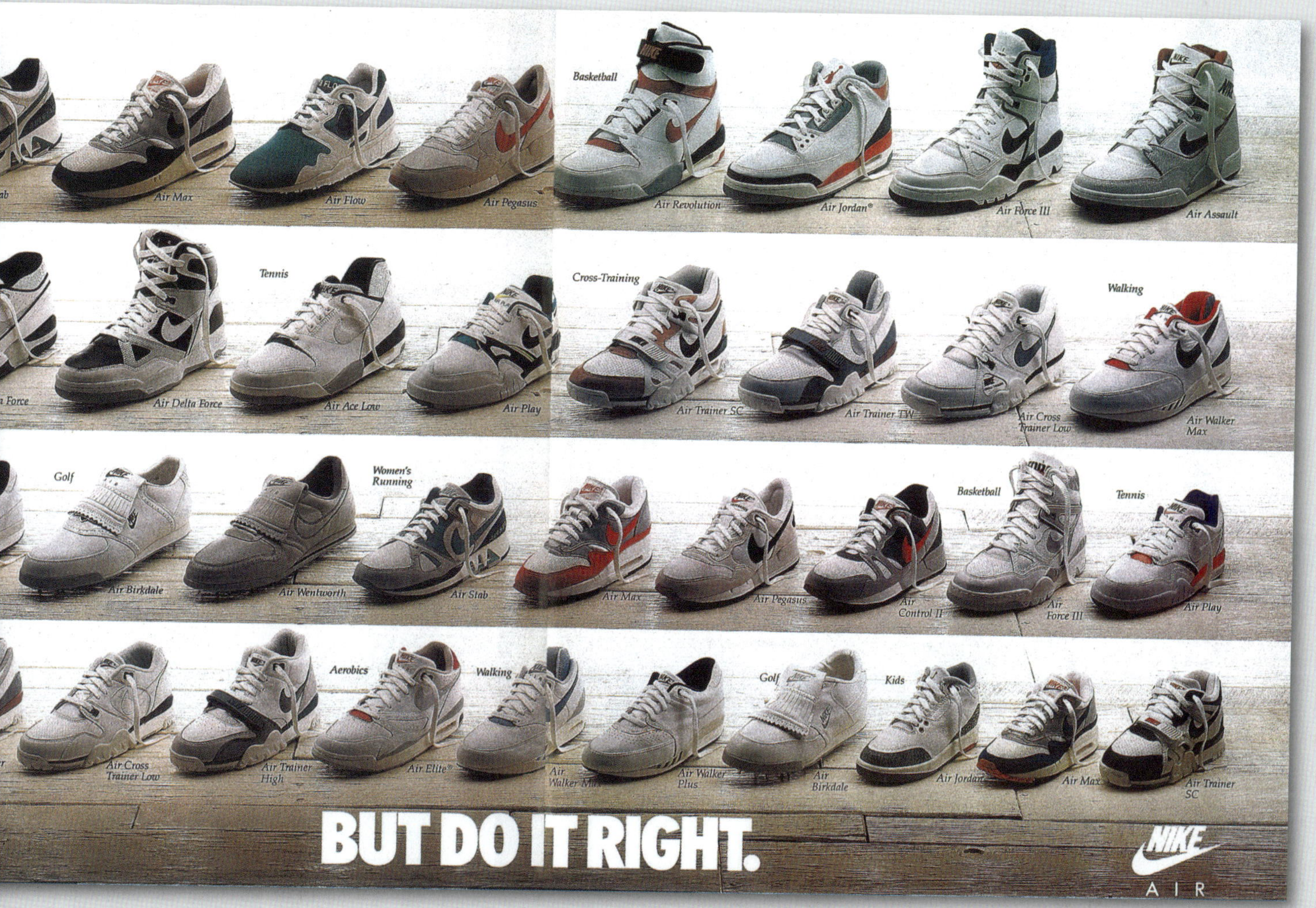

conclusion to this legal battle, Nike did stop running the ad in early 1988, and the case was eventually settled out-of-court the following year on terms that have been kept secret since.

But the commercial didn't recede into video history. After the spot ran and it worked, Phil Knight decided to research it in hopes of gaining a better insight on marketing trends and improve his own promotional strategies. Much to his surprise, the ad tested poorly despite its real-world impact. From that moment on, Nike has never put their advertising into research, deciding instead to be trendsetters rather than followers. The Air Revolution, as it has come to be known as, broke the mould on what advertising could and should be, and inspired very different approaches to what makes a good idea. This wouldn't be the last enduring impact of Wieden + Kennedy on Nike. In fact, their biggest contribution to the brand was yet to come.

JUST DO IT.

Given the global phenomenon that this campaign was to become, it's hard to imagine that the tagline was no more than a rushed addition to a TV advert. It was created in 1987 by Wieden + Kennedy to accompany Nike's first major television campaign, which included commercials for running, walking, cross-training, basketball and women's fitness. While Reebok was directing their campaign at aerobics during the fitness craze of the 1980s, Nike responded with "a tough, take no prisoners ad campaign". "Each spot was developed by a different creative team and was markedly different from the others," remembers Dan Wieden, founder of the agency and author of the Nike line. It's even harder to believe that the words themselves were inspired by the final words of Gary Gilmore, a convicted murderer. Facing execution by firing squad in Utah, Gilmore's final statement was, "Let's do it." Wieden, reflecting on the phrase, found it hauntingly simple and adaptable. He slightly rephrased it to "Just Do It," infusing it with a sense of urgency and determination that resonated far beyond its grim origins. This may not

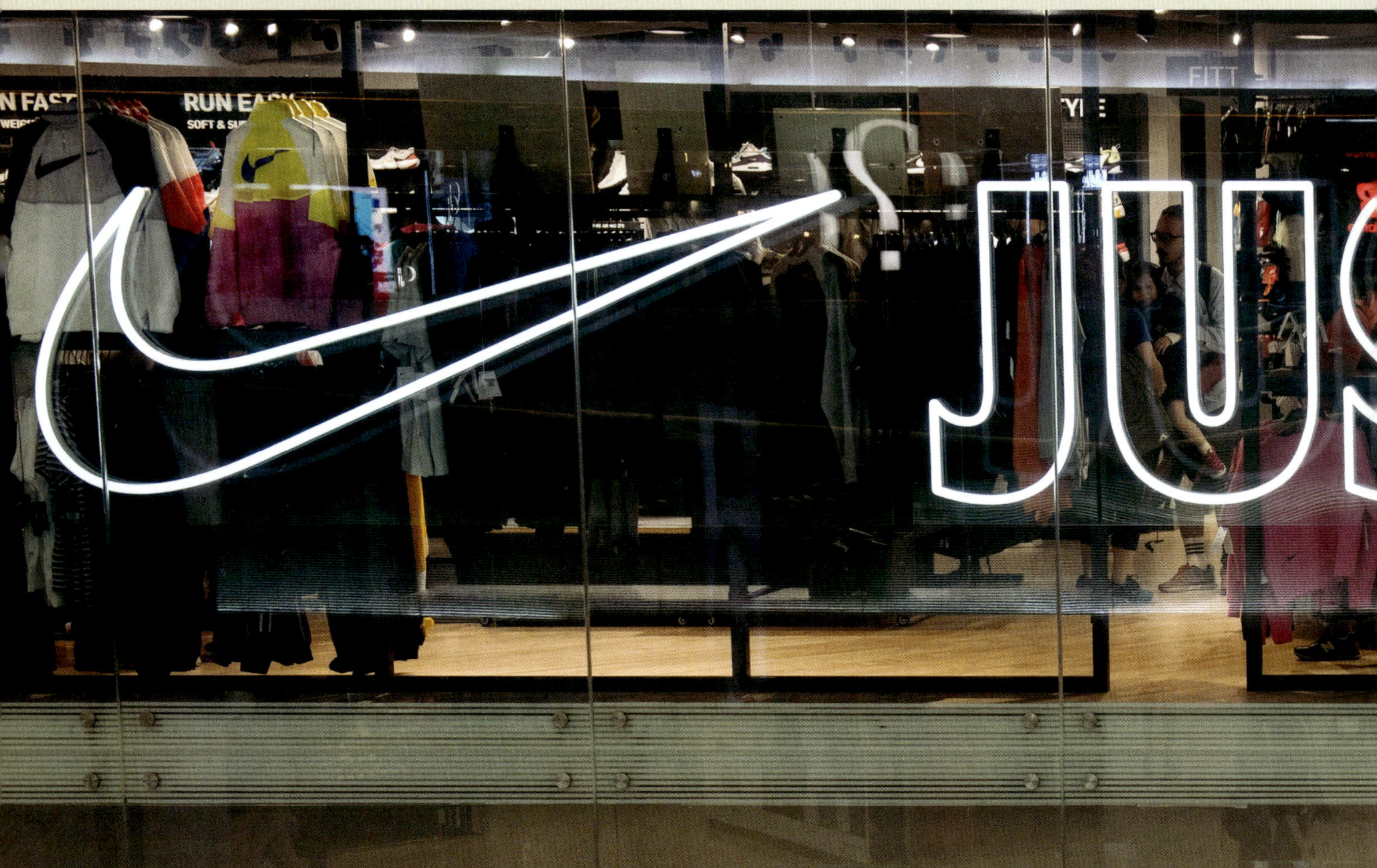

ABOVE: Nike store in Hong Kong displaying the 'Just Do It' logo in the window

have been the brand heritage that Nike would ideally have chosen, yet at the time such matters were largely irrelevant, as nobody was convinced that the tagline was even necessary, let alone had any inkling of the impact it would have. How wrong they would be.

From professional athletes to everyday people, the ads celebrated all who dared to challenge themselves. The unifying message was clear: whether you're running marathons, lifting weights, or simply starting your fitness journey, you can "Just Do It." In many ways, the campaign's enduring success lies in its versatility, in the fact that it doesn't just refer to sports. "Just Do It" speaks to something innate in everyone—a drive to overcome doubt, silence excuses, and take action. Whether it's running that first mile, launching a new business, or standing up for a cause, the phrase invites the world to push its limits and then go even further.

And in doing so, it became a reminder that greatness isn't reserved for the extraordinary—it's waiting for anyone brave enough to "Just Do It."

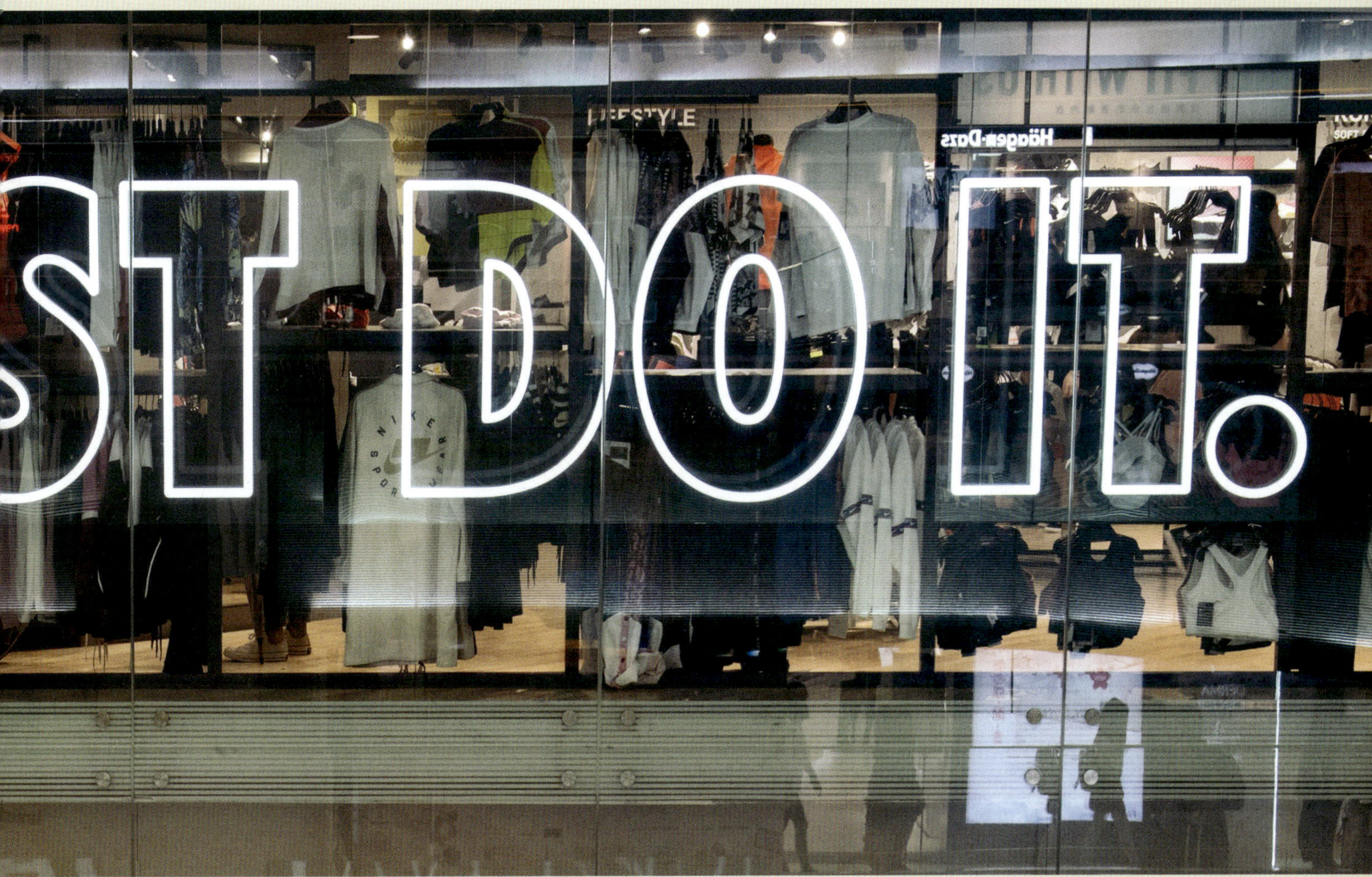

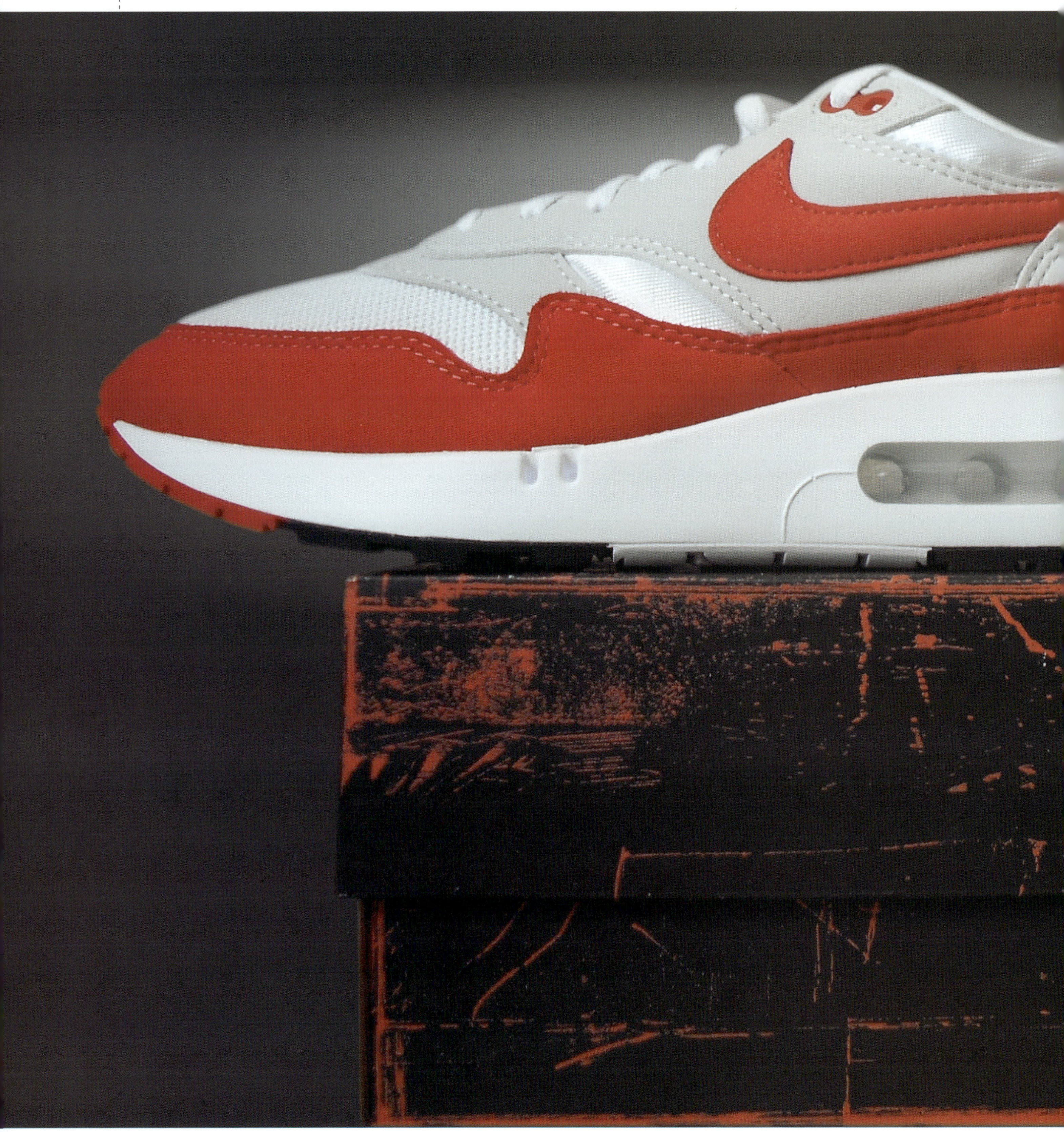

ABOVE: Nike Air Max 1 '86 Big Bubble, a retro shoe
staying true to the design of the OG Air Max 1 made
in 1986 and released in 1987

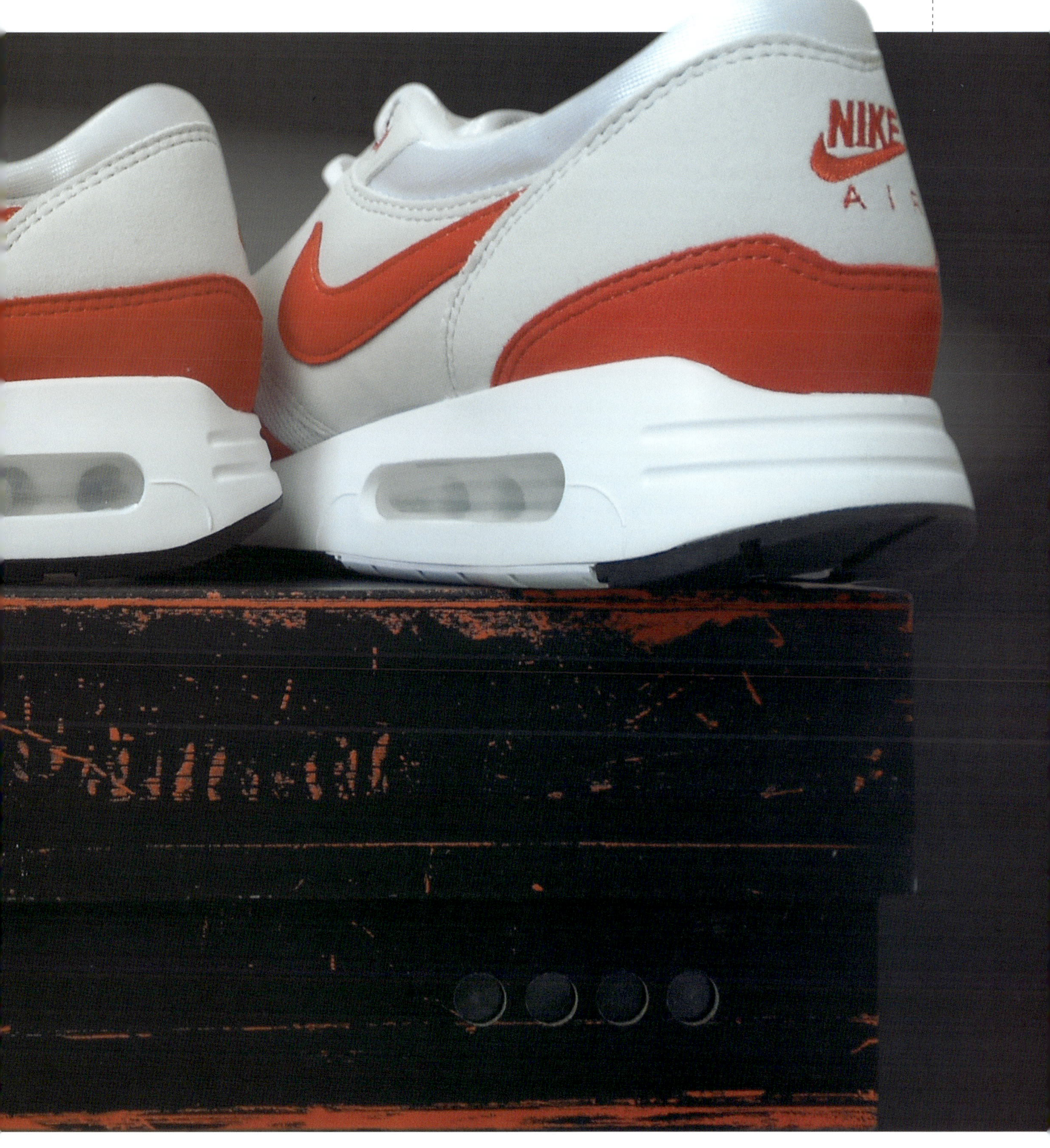

WINNING AT ALL COSTS
1991-1998

"I think everyone born in Oregon is an environmentalist by birth"

Phil Knight

As the turn of the 21st century started to approach, Nike's grasp on the world only seemed to tighten. Wearing Nike branded sneakers and sportswear had spread to all walks of life, all sports disciplines and all generations. With the success of its iconic *Just Do It* campaign, endorsements from global sports superstars like Michael Jordan and their move towards apparel, the company had truly cemented its place as a cultural juggernaut. The dazzling performance of the American basketball Dream Team at the 1992 Barcelona Olympics, followed by sprinter Michael Johnson's unforgettable victory in Atlanta four years later—complete with his iconic golden Nike shoes— were just two shining moments among many for the brand. Adidas, their once-formidable rival, had finally been outpaced, and both the public and investors couldn't get enough of the swoosh. The chaos and struggles of Nike's early days felt like a distant memory as Phil Knight and his team basked in their hard-

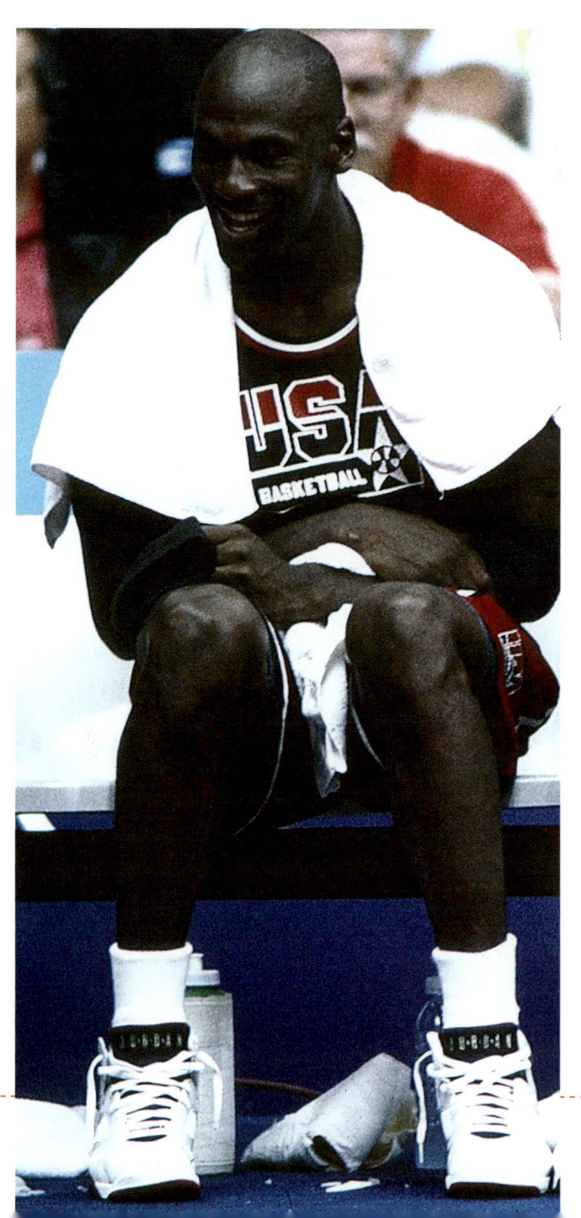

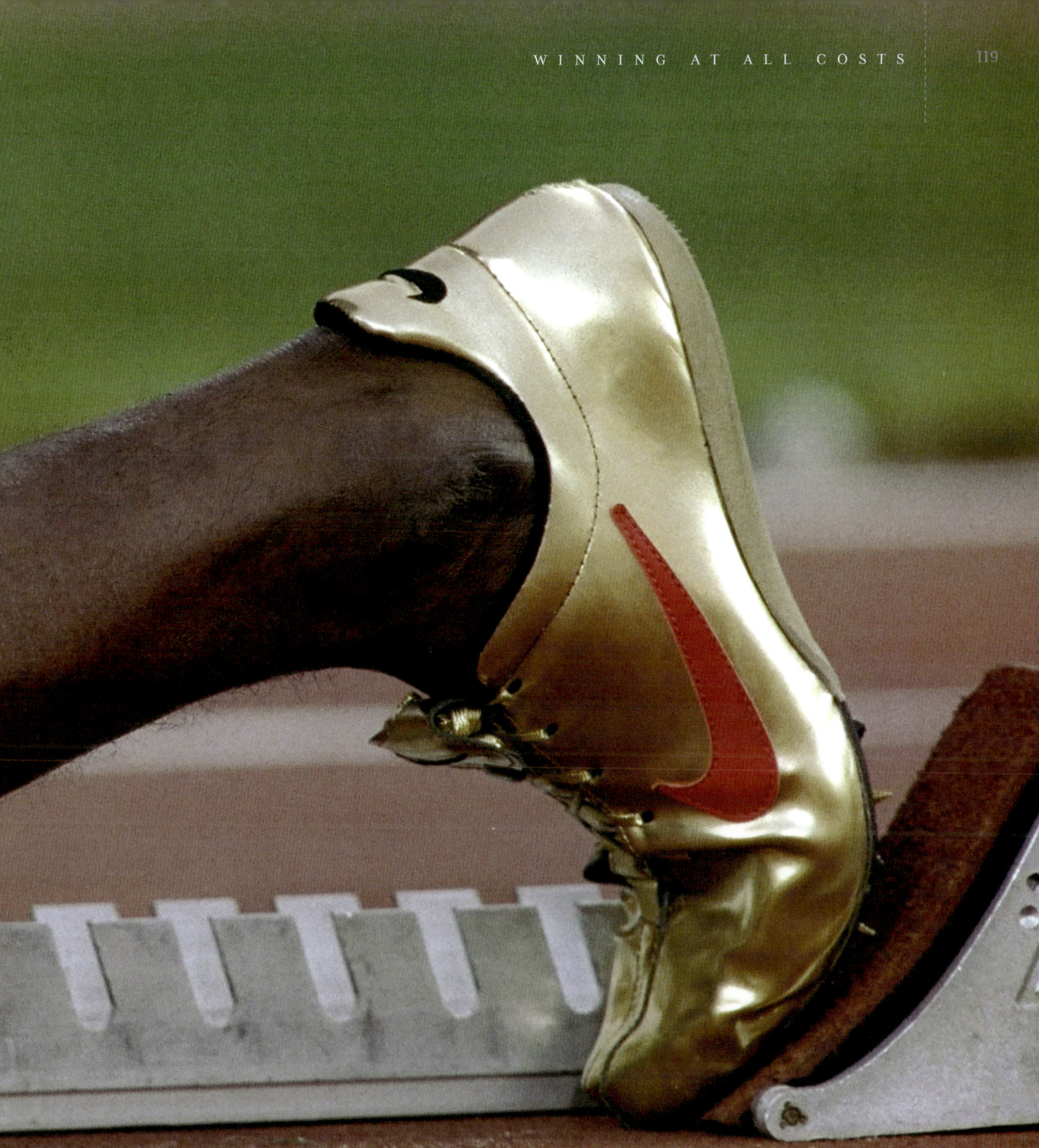

OPP PAGE: Michael Jordan during the 1992 Summer Olympics in Barcelona

ABOVE: The Nike gold running shoes of Michael Johnson at the 1996 Summer Olympics

earned triumph. However, in life—just like in business—good times can only last for so long. Phil, usually one to anticipate the rainy days, could not have expected the sudden fall from grace in store for Nike, as well as the damage it would cause to the young and cool image the brand had so carefully built since its inception in 1972.

Nike faced its first major public reckoning in 1991 when activist Jeff Ballinger, director of Press for Change, published a scathing report detailing the harsh realities of life inside Indonesian factories producing Nike goods. His investigation uncovered workers earning a mere 14 cents an hour—wages that were nowhere near enough to survive on—while enduring gruelling shifts and frequent abuse. Though many major brands at the time relied on similar labour practices, and even shared factories with Nike, it was the Swoosh that became the poster child for unethical manufacturing.

Ballinger's findings hit a nerve, exposing a jarring contradiction: the brand synonymous with aspiration and excellence was thriving on the backs of exploited workers. The report quickly gained media traction, igniting widespread outrage and thrusting Nike into the uncomfortable spotlight of global scrutiny. Phil hoped that the wave of bad press would eventually subside as it does for most news stories—but that wouldn't be the case.

While revelations about working conditions at the company's subcontractors had been spreading for some time, it wasn't until March 1996, when the American magazine *Life* published a shocking exposé on child labour in Pakistan, that Nike was forced to confront the backlash that had been simmering for years. The article featured a harrowing photo of young boys tying together pieces of leather to make soccer balls marked with Nike's famous logo. The production lines, where adults and, sometimes children, worked in deplorable conditions, earned the derogatory nickname "sweatshops", creating a global scandal.

Activists organized boycotts, staged protests outside Nike stores, and campaigned on college campuses to sever ties with the brand. Celebrities and athletes were questioned about their association with Nike, and the company became a symbol of corporate greed and exploitation. In several major cities in the United States, demonstrations brought together public figures, NGOs and unions to denounce the exploitation of workers at the subcontractors of some major Western brands.

Nike's corporate ethos of "winning at all costs" now seemed uncomfortably literal, with critics arguing that the company was willing to overlook ethical considerations to maintain its dominance in the market.

Despite all the controversy, Nike was still laser focused on asserting their dominance in every sports market. This time, they were looking at breaking into the golf world and they had just the athlete to do it with.

OPP PAGE: Indonesian workers from PT. Doson Indonesia, a sub-contracting factory of US shoe giant Nike, protest

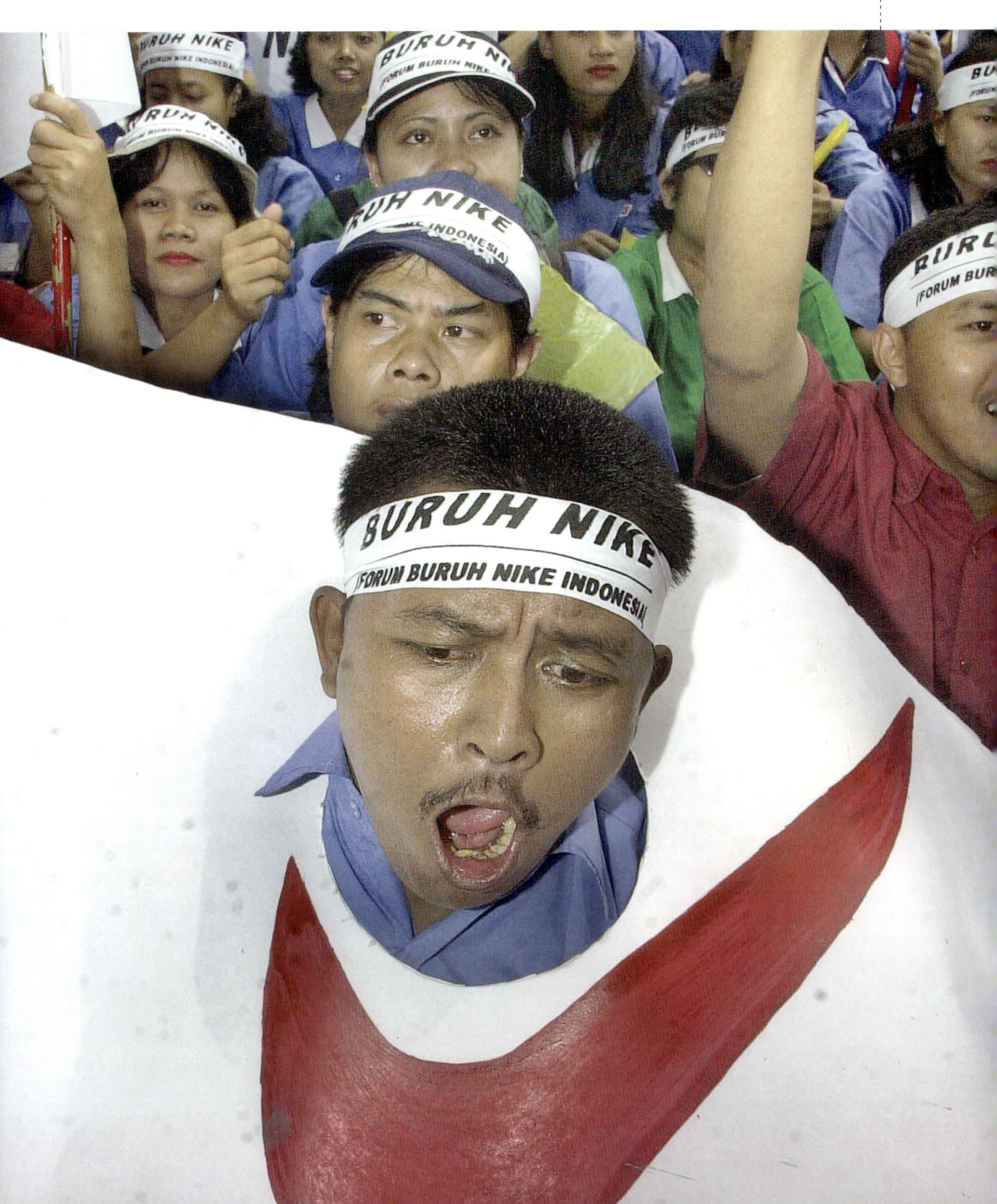
BURUH NIKE
(FORUM BURUH NIKE INDONESIA)
BURUH NIKE
(FORUM BURUH NIKE INDONESIA)
BURUH NIKE
INDONESIA
BURUH NIKE
(FORUM BURUH NIKE INDONESIA)
BURU
(FORUM BUR

"HELL OF A ROUND TIGER"

Amid mounting criticism over its labour practices, Nike made a bold move in 1996 by signing 20-year-old golf prodigy Tiger Woods. This decision would not only transform the trajectory of Woods' career but also redefine Nike's role in the world of golf.

By the time Woods turned professional, the world had already seen flashes of his extraordinary talent on the golf course. From the moment he announced his pro debut with Nike's iconic "Hello World" ad campaign, Woods and Nike became inseparable throughout his storied career.

Woods' partnership with Nike started modestly and was limited to clothing. Nike, a titan in sportswear but a relative newcomer to golf, saw in Woods an opportunity to reshape the sport's image and broaden its global appeal. They gambled on his star power, signing him to a $40 million deal—a bold move for a company not yet producing golf clubs or balls. But Nike's investment in Woods paid off faster than anyone anticipated. Less than a year later, Woods won the 1997 Masters. He won three more PGA Tour events in 1997 and in just his 42nd week as a professional, Woods was the No. 1 ranked golfer in the world. He would go on to hold on to that title for 683 weeks over his career.

By 2001, the relationship had evolved into something even more monumental. Woods signed a five-year, $105 million extension with Nike—the most lucrative endorsement deal in sports history at the time. The investment cemented their relationship and solidified Nike's dominance in golf. Woods was no longer just an athlete; he was a brand in his own right and Nike was his stage.

While their partnership drove tremendous business success for both parties, it was not without its challenges. In 2009, Tiger became embroiled in an infidelity scandal, with details of his extramarital affairs becoming public. Several sponsors severed ties with the gifted golfer, including Accenture, AT&T, Gatorade and General Motors. But not Nike. Phil Knight stood by Woods and the pair continued to work together. Knight commented on his decision to stay loyal to Woods, by saying "when his career is over, you'll look back on these indiscretions as a minor blip".

On January 6, 2024, Tiger Woods announced on social media that he is no longer a Nike brand ambassador, marking the end of one of the most iconic partnerships between an athlete and a brand. Over the course of his remarkable 27-year partnership with Nike, Tiger Woods earned an estimated $500 million from his deals with Nike. This staggering sum enabled Woods to become golf's first billionaire, helping to redefine the financial possibilities for professional golfers.

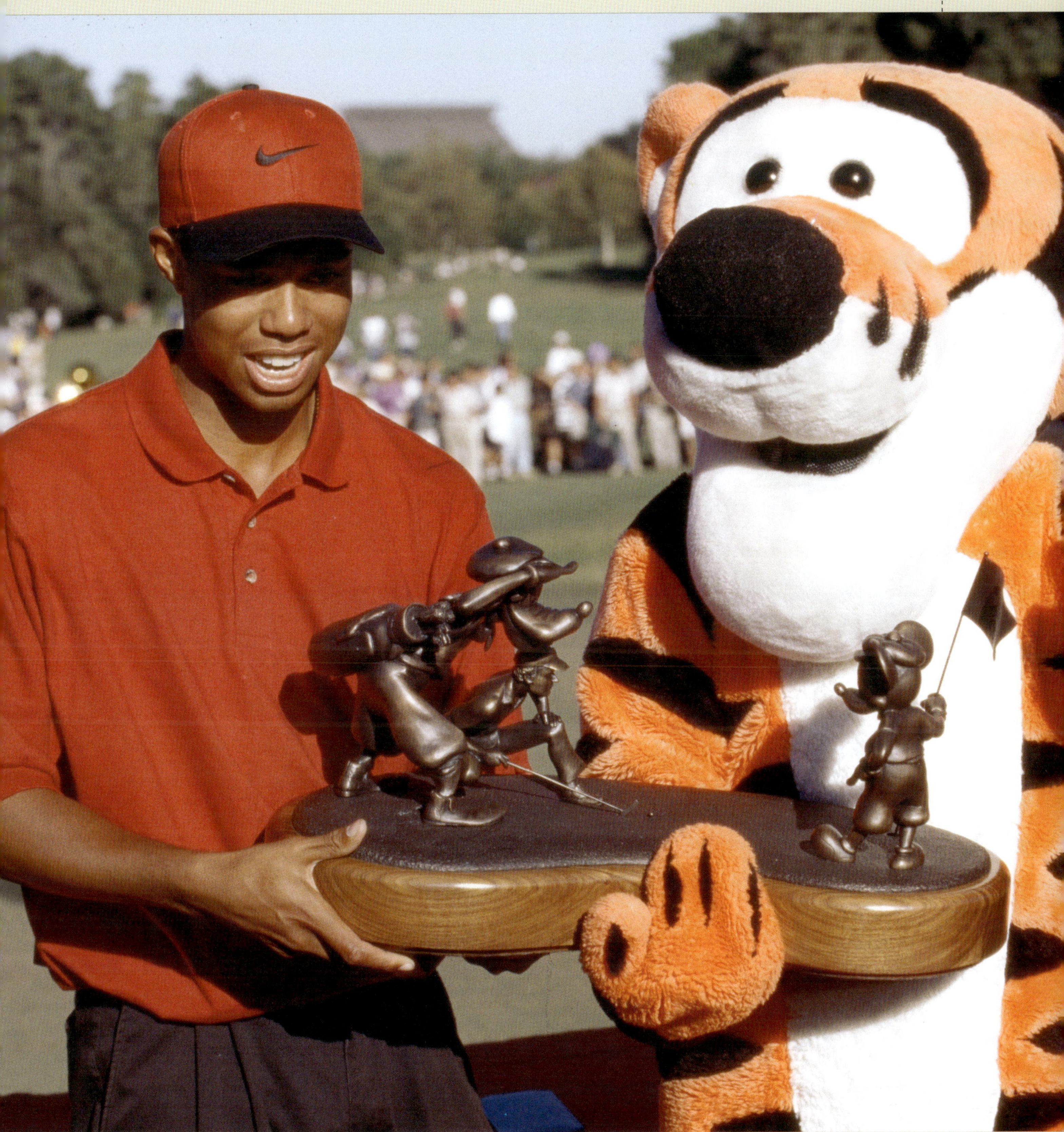

ABOVE: Tiger Woods wins the Walt Disney World/
Oldsmobile Classic in 1996

The company's celebration of the new partnership between Nike and Woods was quickly overshadowed by the wave of damning reports being published, reminding the world that success on the green didn't erase the growing controversies elsewhere.

Initially, Nike's leadership denied responsibility for the issues in its supply chain. Phil argued that the company contracted independent factories and therefore couldn't be held accountable for their practices, though this stance only fuelled further criticism, as it was seen as an attempt to deflect blame.

By the end of the 1990's, however, the mounting pressure forced Nike to take action. In 1998, Knight publicly admitted that the company had failed to live up to its responsibilities. Speaking at the National Press Club, he famously stated, "The Nike product has become synonymous with slave wages, forced overtime, and arbitrary abuse". Phil also

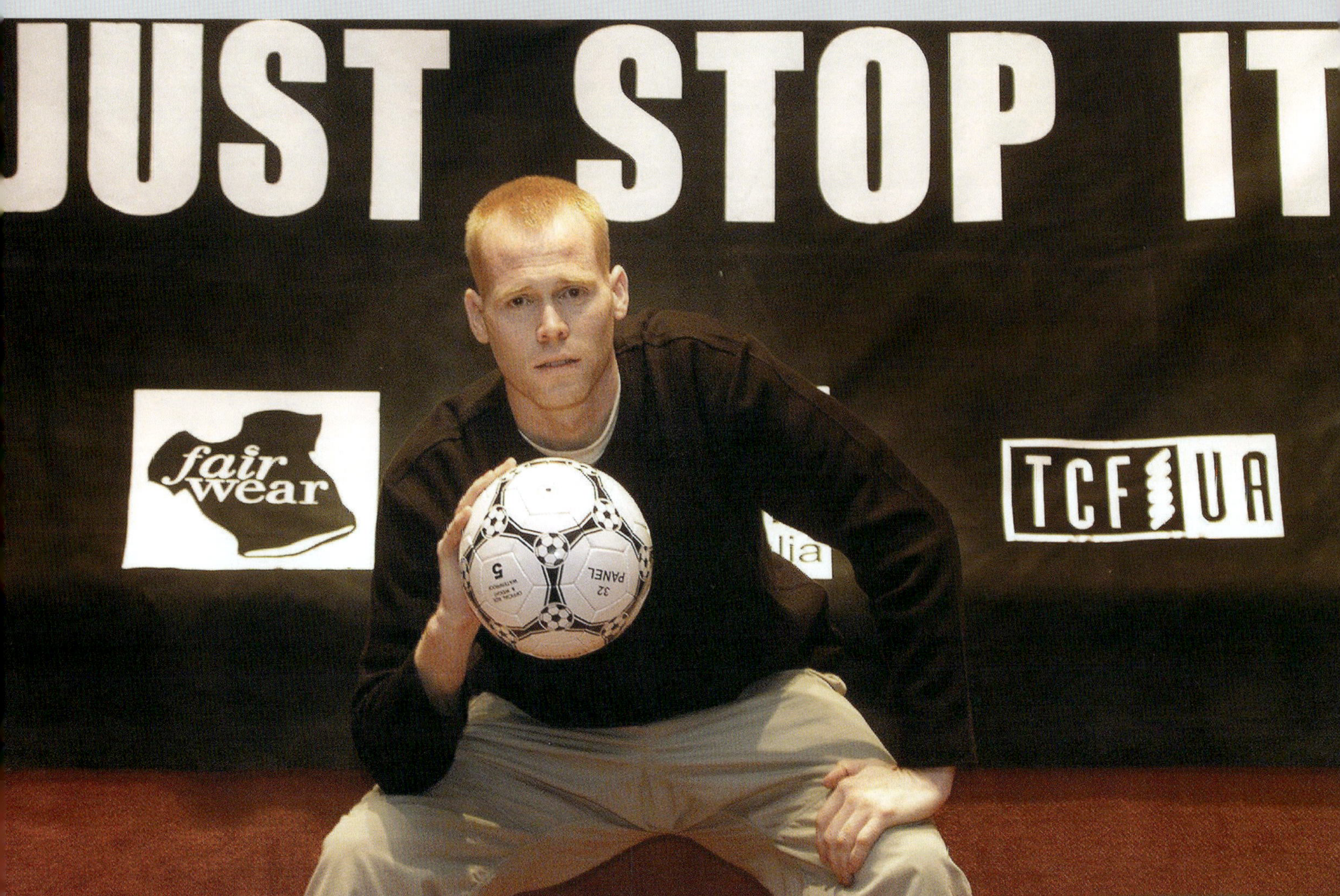

ABOVE: Former American soccer pro Jim Keady sits in front of a sign playing on Nike's 'Just Do It' slogan after a month living in Indonesia on the wage of a factory worker

OPP PAGE: Nike employee assisting customers

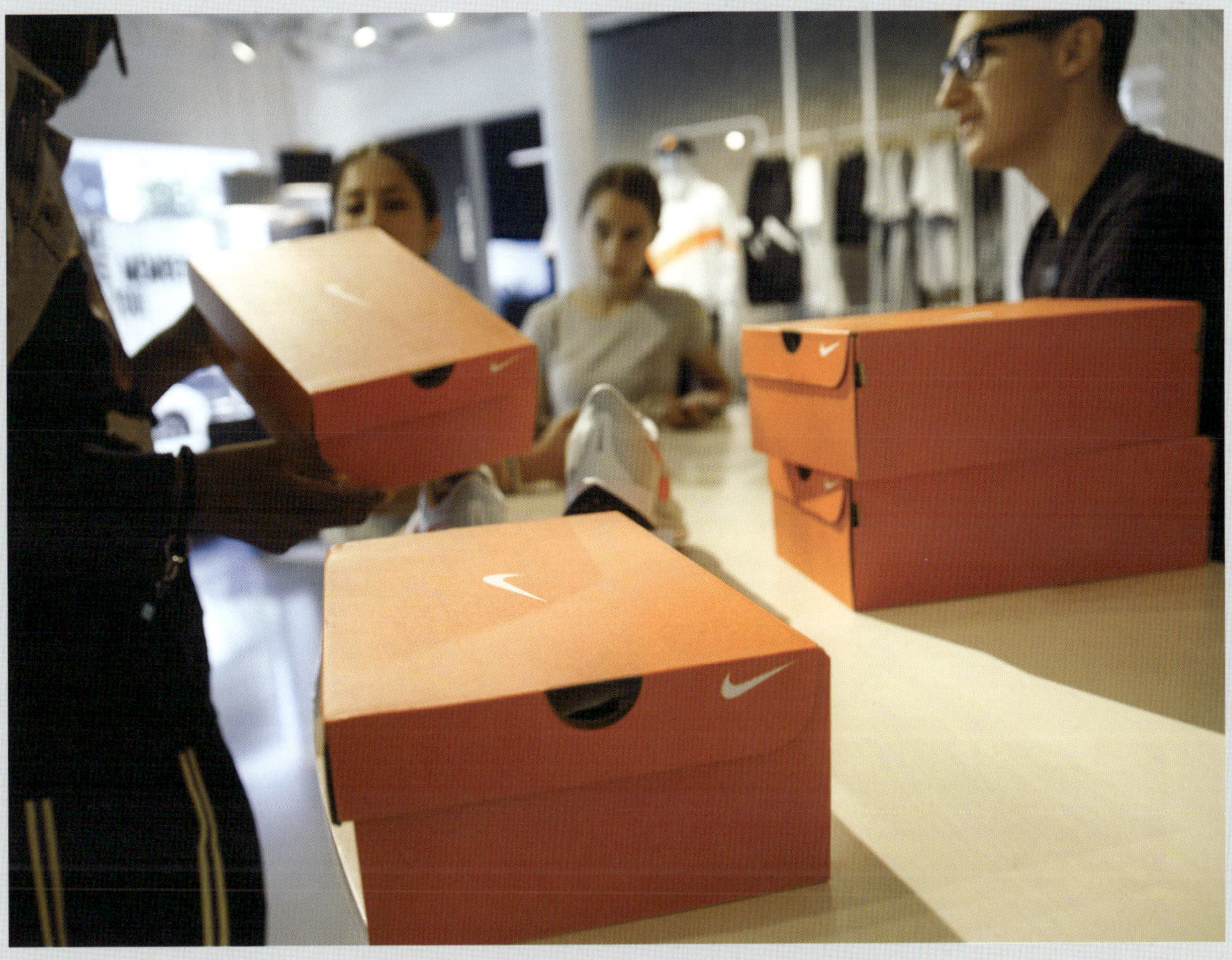

outlined a series of measures the company would implement going forward to address the issues at hand, including an increase in the minimum age of workers in Nike factories to 16 for apparel and 18 for footwear. He also stated that Nike would be adopting the U.S. Occupational Safety and Health Administration (OSHA) standards for air quality in factories as well as expanding monitoring efforts to include more frequent and independent inspections to increase transparency on their business practices. Additionally, Nike partnered with external organizations, including labour rights groups and the Fair Labor Association (FLA), to implement these reforms.

Nike's response to the scandals set the stage for broader changes within the industry, and in turn helped to rebuild the brand's image. Over time, Nike positioned itself as a leader in sustainability and ethical manufacturing, proving that willingness to adapt and change is not only a must, but a strength for any company, no matter the size.

A FATHER'S FAREWELL

1999-2004

"I didn't say I'm walking away. I said I was stepping down as chairman. I won't walk away. I'll be carried away"

Phil Knight

NIKE'S ORIGINAL INNOVATOR SAYS GOODBYE

The year 1999 marked a pivotal moment for both Nike and its co-founder, Phil Knight. In December of that year, Nike lost one of its founding fathers—Bill Bowerman, who passed away at the age of 88. Bowerman, a visionary track coach at the University of Oregon, had helped lay the foundation for what became one of the most recognizable brands in the world. His relentless drive for innovation, from the first "waffle" shoe design to his constant pursuit of bettering the performance of his athletes, had driven Nike's philosophy and its success from the very start.

Following his death, Phil wrote an essay where he tried to capture the legend that was his late business partner. "Bowerman was unique. He lived by a code: He would not be a bad father or husband; he would not have a beer with his athletes or even in front of them. He quoted scripture - usually incorrectly, but he made his point [...] He was an educated man capable of impressive use of the English language. I heard him give a lot of good talks to high schools and community gatherings. But he chose to educate me and others by making effective use of silence". Those silences eventually became permanent. Bill Bowerman's legacy as an original thinker and innovator will forever be linked with his many brilliant inventions, that in essence were so simple and intuitive, they resonated immediately and broadly with anyone who wore them.

But above being one of the most influential figures in Nike, Bowerman was Phil's coach, business partner, father figure, mentor and most importantly lifelong friend. Bowerman's passing would leave an indelible mark on sports history, but that was nothing in comparison to the void he left on the people who knew him.

OPP PAGE: Phil Knight, founder and CEO of Nike

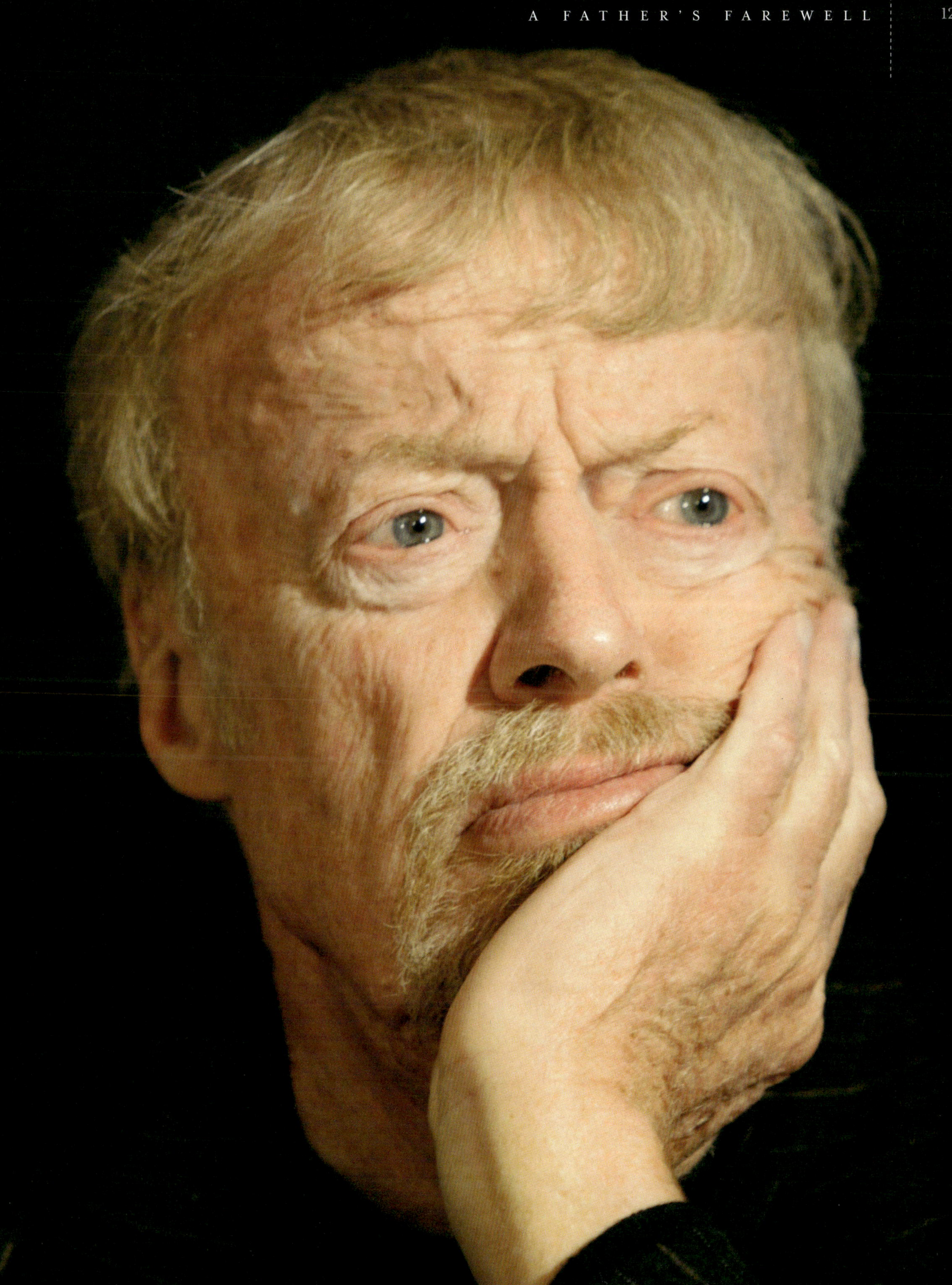

However, Nike would continue to forge ahead in the new millennium, carrying the weight of Bowerman's legacy while expanding into new territories. In 2002, Nike made a significant move to broaden its portfolio when it acquired the surf-apparel company Hurley for an undisclosed sum. Hurley, a leading brand in the surf and youth lifestyle market, provided Nike with a fresh angle into a different, more subcultural market, strengthening its foothold in the action sports world. This was part of Nike's broader strategy of diversification—an effort to move beyond its core athletics base and tap into the growing demand for youth-oriented and alternative sports products.

Nike continued to build new partnerships with up-and-coming athletes. In 2003, the company struck a massive endorsement deal with 18-year-old LeBron James, who was widely regarded as the future of basketball. That same year, Nike also locked in a long-term deal with the NBA's Kobe Bryant. Together, LeBron and Kobe represented the next generation of basketball superstars—both powerful figures who would carry Nike's banner far into the future. Nike's supremacy over the basketball market was made abundantly apparent when the company acquired Converse for $309 million in early 2004. Converse, the once-dominant basketball footwear brand, had lost its lustre and was brought back under Nike's umbrella. While Nike continued to evolve and reach unprecedented

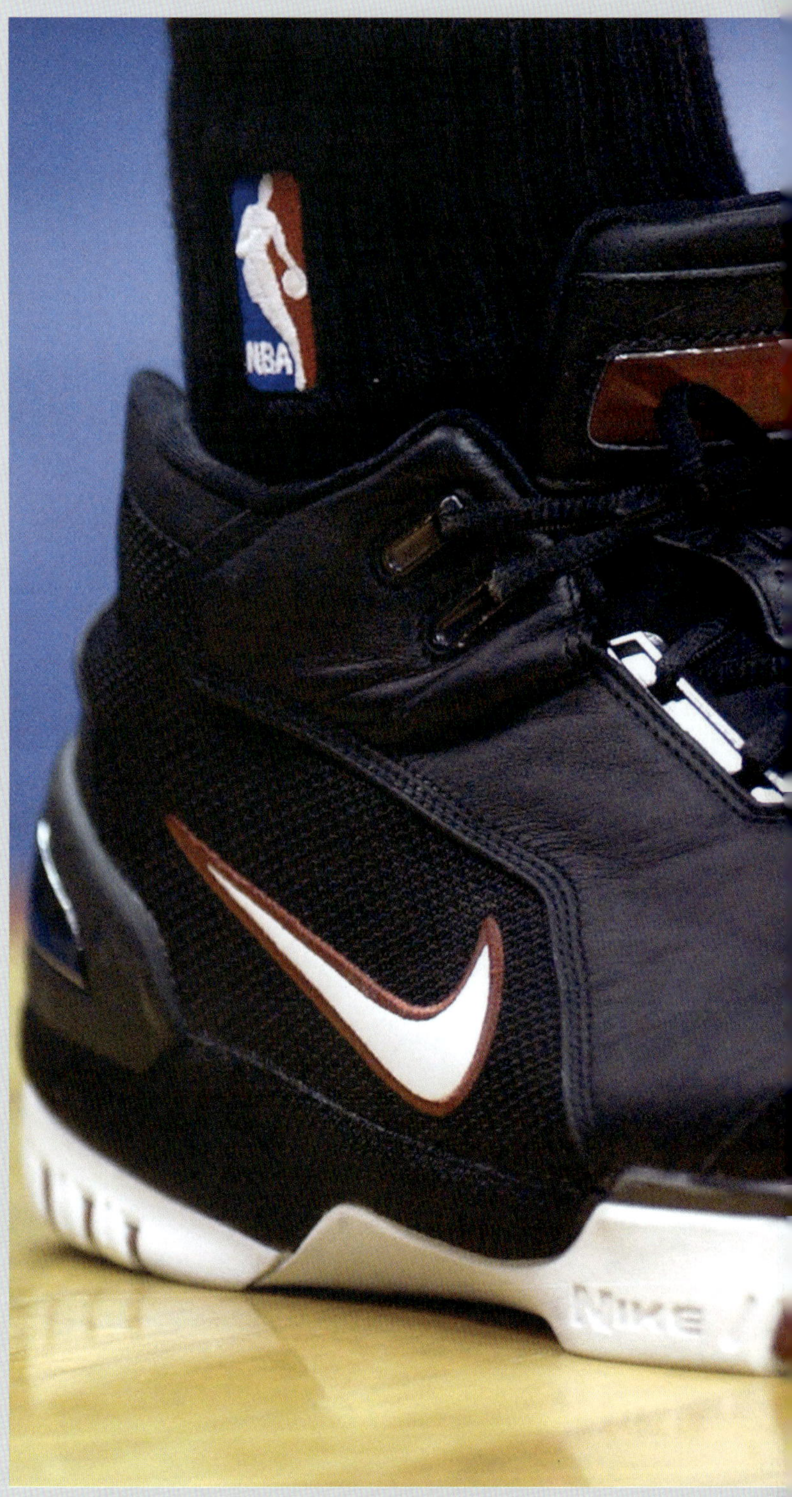

ABOVE: The Nike shoes worn on court by Cleveland Cavaliers forward LeBron James in 2003

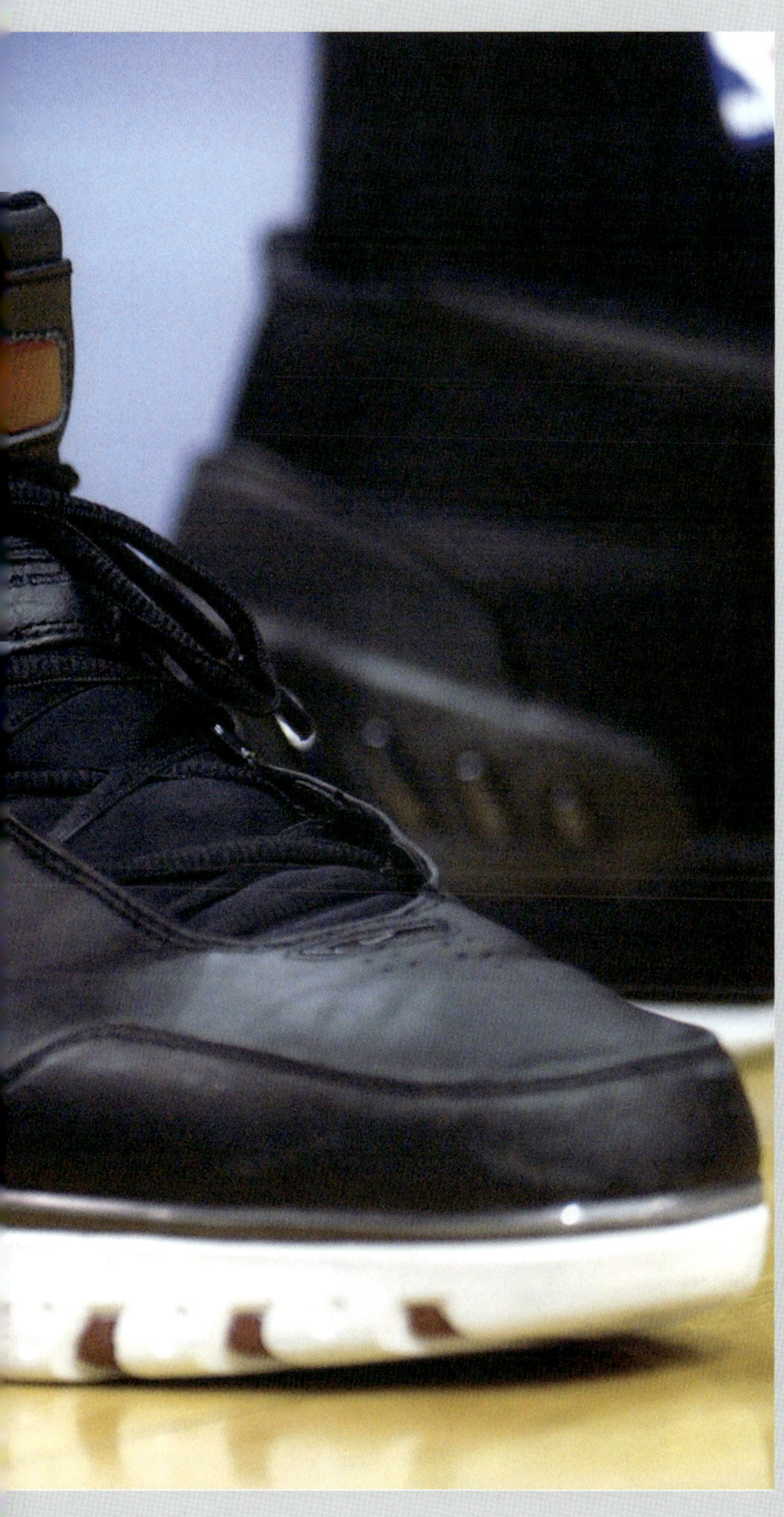

levels of success, Phil endured the worst tragedy of all. In May 2004, his eldest son, Matthew Knight, passed away in a scuba diving accident at the age of 34. Matthew's death was a devastating blow to the Knight family, one from which Phil admitted he struggled to recover. A talented filmmaker and artist, Matthew had often been described as a free spirit, deeply curious and endlessly creative. His loss left a void that no success, no accolade, could ever fill. "That's the thing no parent should have to face, a child dying before you," Knight said in an interview with Oprah, "It aged me much faster than anything you can imagine". For Phil Knight, Nike had always been more than just a business; it was a family, born from shared dreams and bound by collective ambition. But the loss of his eldest son forced him to reevaluate his priorities. By the end of 2004, after nearly four decades at the helm of Nike, Phil decided to step down as CEO. Although he remained actively involved as Chairman of the Board, his decision to relinquish the day-to-day responsibilities reflected a profound shift in his focus. He dedicated more of his time to his family and philanthropy, founding the Matthew Knight Foundation to honour his son's memory and supporting causes that aligned with Matthew's artistic passions. Phil Knight's farewell to his role as CEO was more than just the end of an era at Nike. It was the beginning of a new chapter for the company, one that continued to carry forward the legacy of both Bowerman and Knight.

PASSING THE TORCH
2004-2024

When Phil Knight stepped down as CEO in 2004, Nike faced a world already conquered in many respects. Yet the two decades that followed proved that Nike was nowhere near finished evolving. Even without Knight at the head of the company, the Swoosh continued to march steadily forward, as an emblem of individuality, in an age where individuality became rampant.

In 2006, the brand teamed up with Apple for the Nike+ platform, transforming a humble running shoe into a digital feedback device. Over time, this fusion of sport and technology would deepen, creating fitness apps,

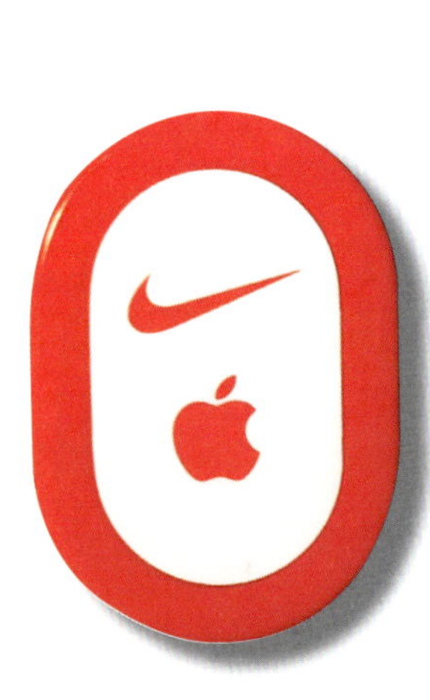

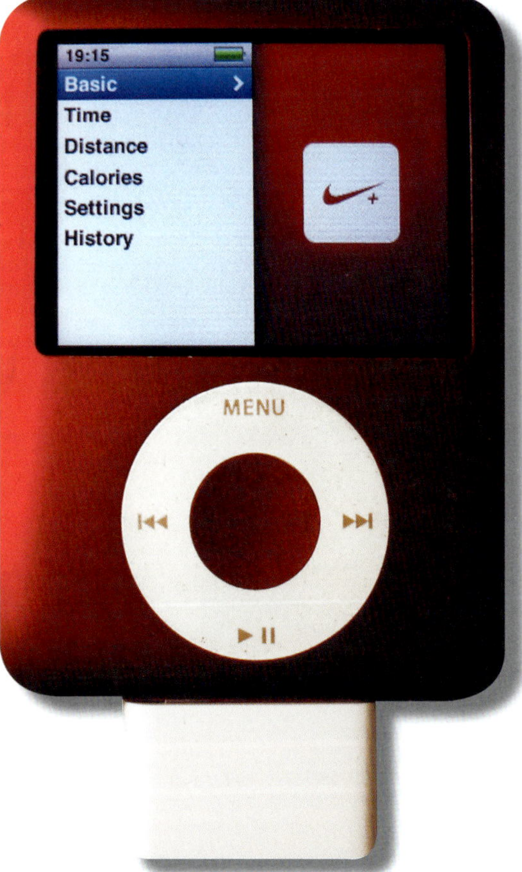

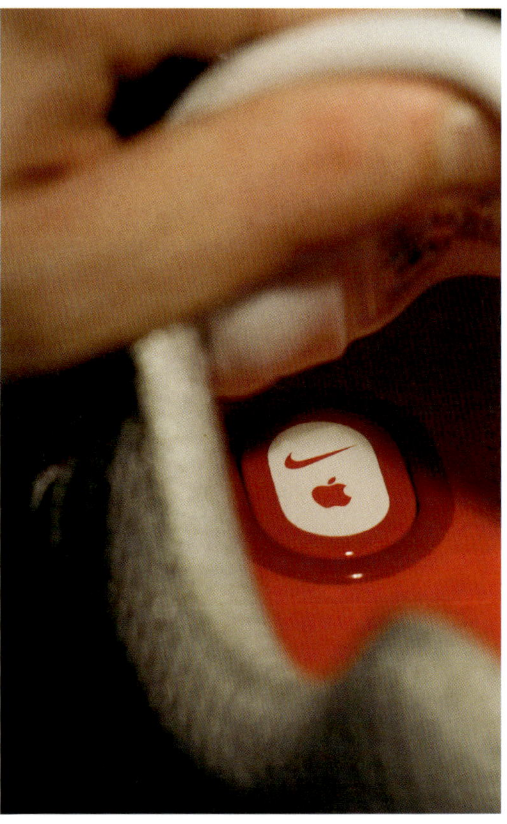

ABOVE: 3G iPod with Nike+ reciever attached, alongside the transmitter placed in a running shoe
OPP PAGE: The Louis Vuitton and Nike expression of the Air Force 1 by Virgil Abloh

smart devices, and wearable tech, providing Nike consumers with visionary tools to measure progress, share victories, and chase personal bests.

Signature collaborations with designers and cultural figures—like Virgil Abloh's Off-White line and partnerships with artists such as Travis Scott—turned Nike sneakers into covetable icons of style. The brand's embrace of high fashion and limited-edition drops sparked intense hype, making sneaker releases major cultural events rather than mere product launches. In a world saturated with trends, Nike consistently positioned itself at the centre of conversation, bridging the worlds of sport, art, music, and fashion.

The endorsement deals that defined Nike in the '80s and '90s took on new dimensions as well. While still honouring legends like Michael Jordan, Nike bet on a continuous pipeline of emerging athletes who would become ambassadors of performance and style. Women's sports grew increasingly central, as the company amplified the voices and accomplishments of Serena Williams, Megan Rapinoe, and many others, demonstrating that greatness in sport transcended gender, background, and the old definitions of athletic celebrity.

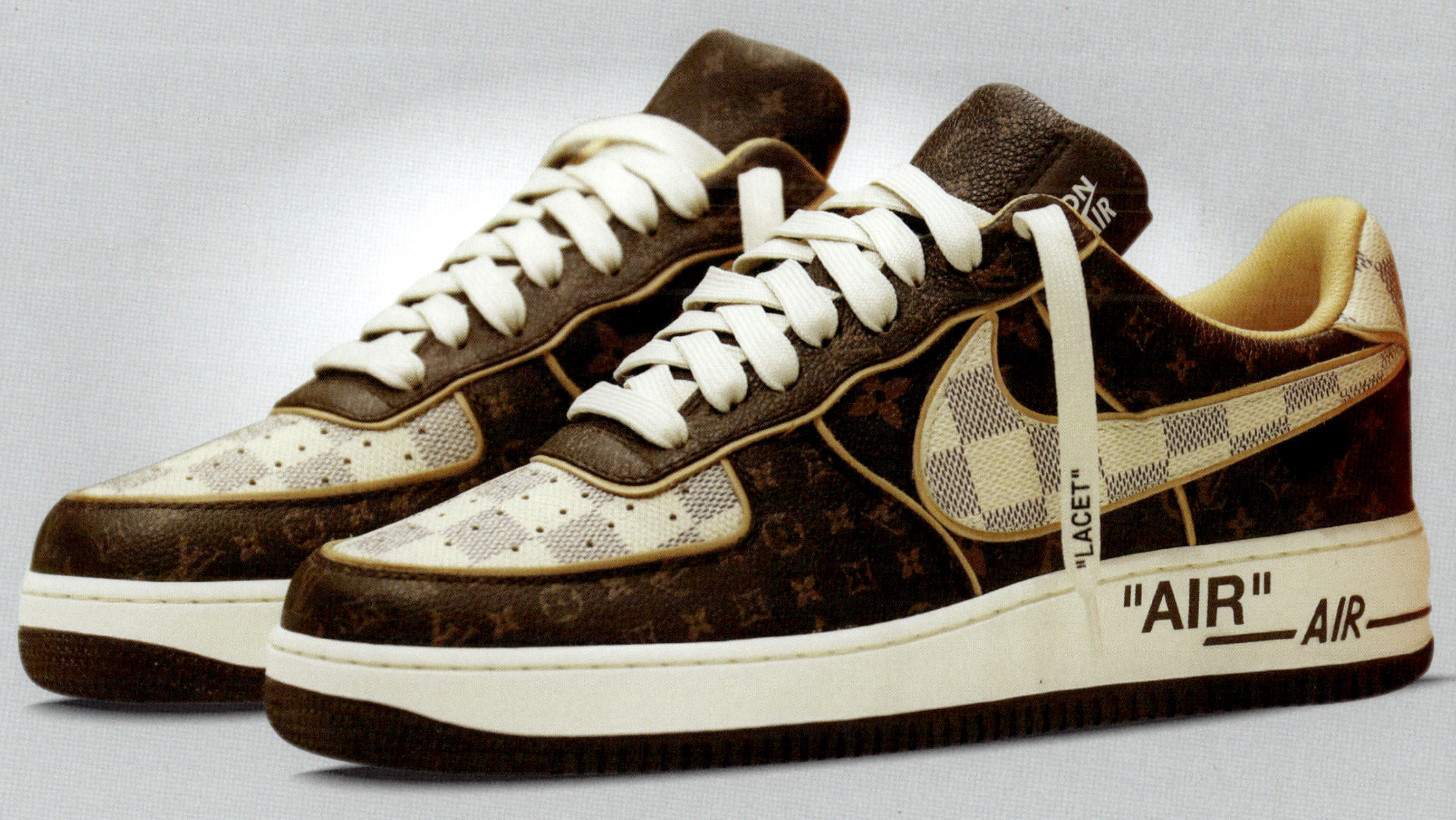

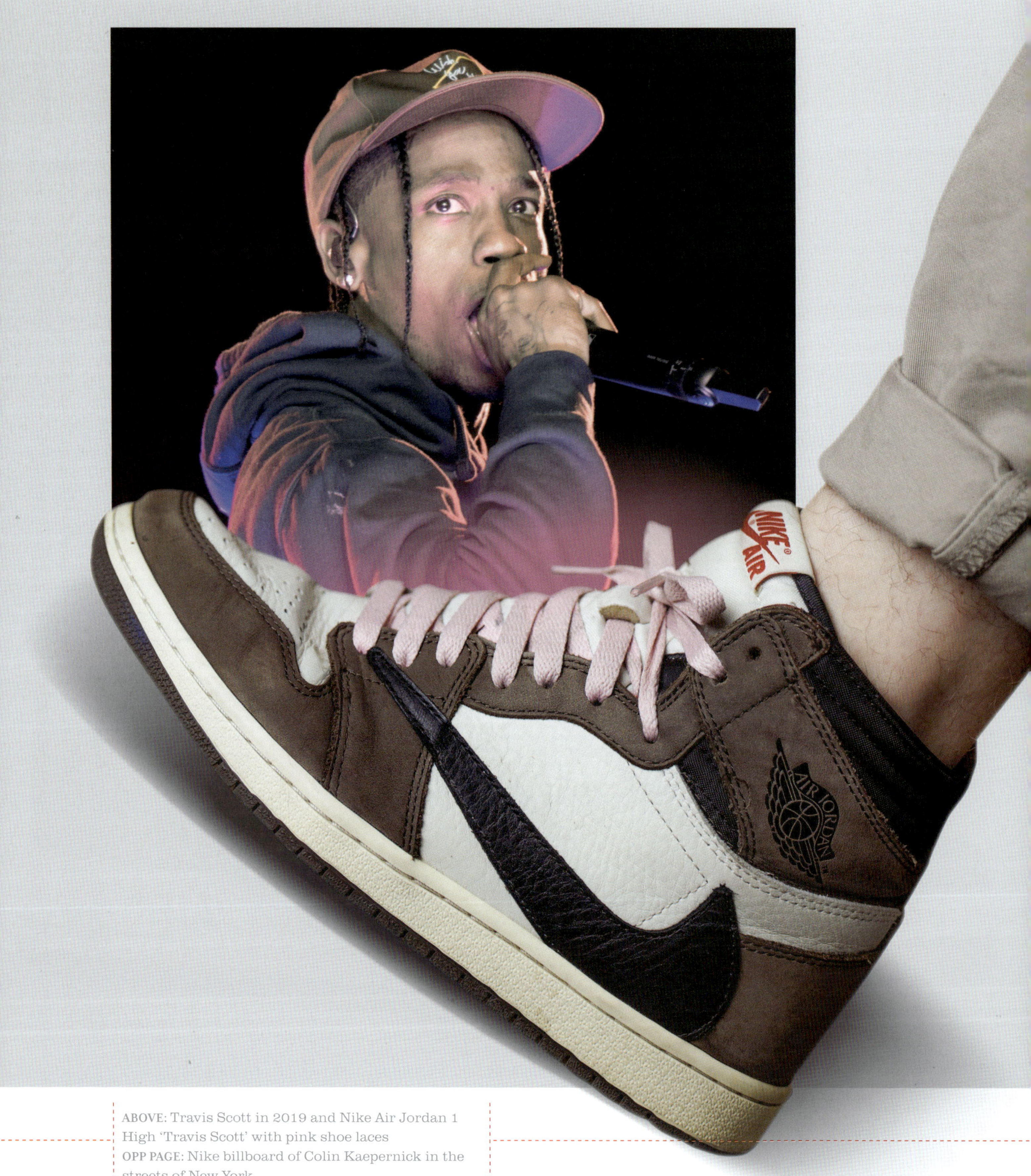

ABOVE: Travis Scott in 2019 and Nike Air Jordan 1 High 'Travis Scott' with pink shoe laces

OPP PAGE: Nike billboard of Colin Kaepernick in the streets of New York

DREAM CRAZY

Nike continued to champion its role as a platform for change. In 2018, the company sparked both controversy and admiration with its "Dream Crazy" campaign featuring Colin Kaepernick. This bold move underscored Nike's willingness to engage in critical social issues. In doing so, Nike reminded the world that its brand continues to be a megaphone for values, not just products.

Looking back at the journey, one thing is clear: Nike won its cultural marathon by refusing to stand still. It didn't rest on its laurels after Jordan and Tiger, nor did it crumble under controversies or market shifts. Instead, Nike pressed on, refining its voice, broadening its vision, and honouring its core values of inspiration and innovation. Long after Phil Knight handed over the reins, Nike proved that a brand born of athletic performance could mature into a beacon of creativity, community, and global dialogue.

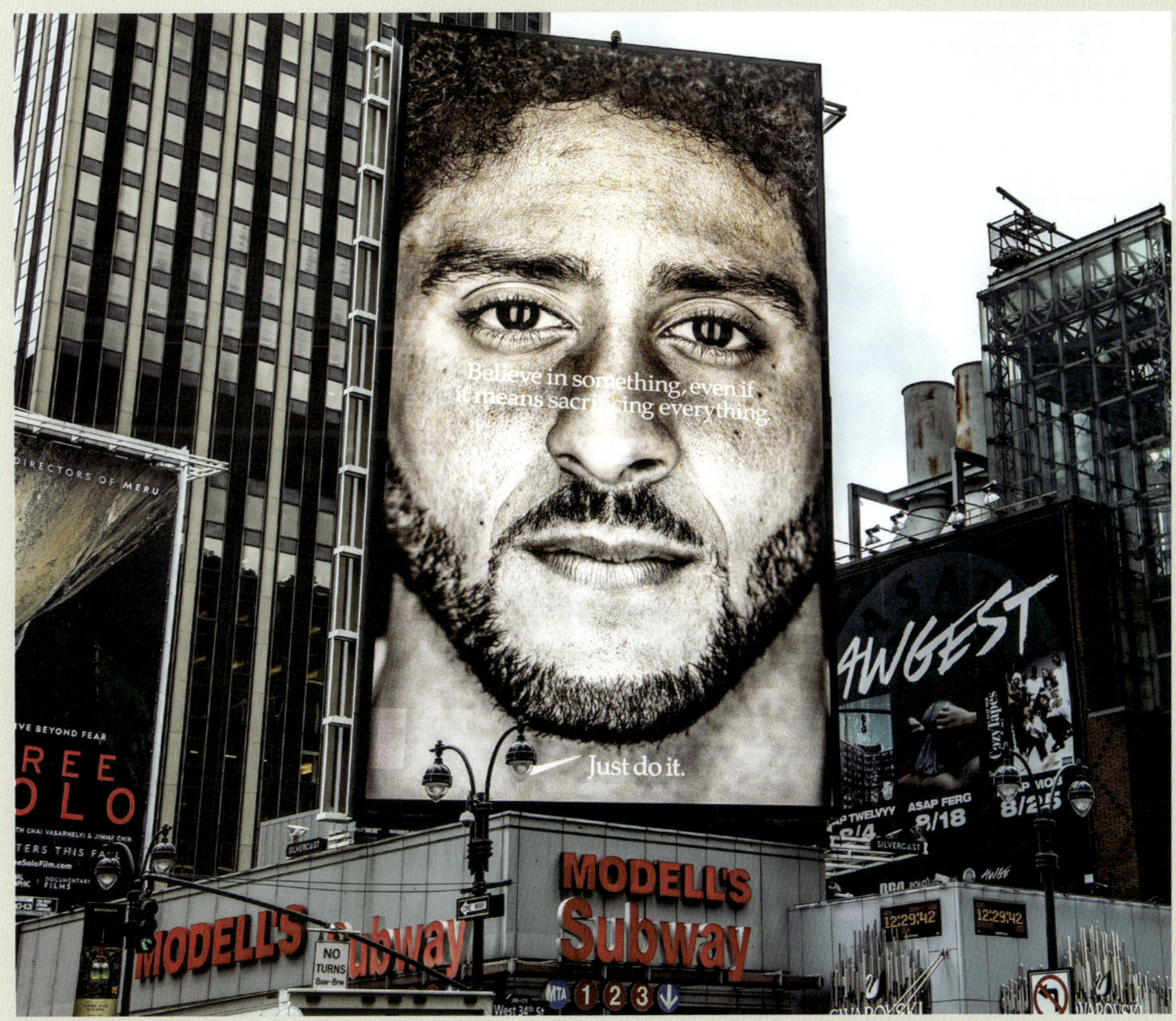

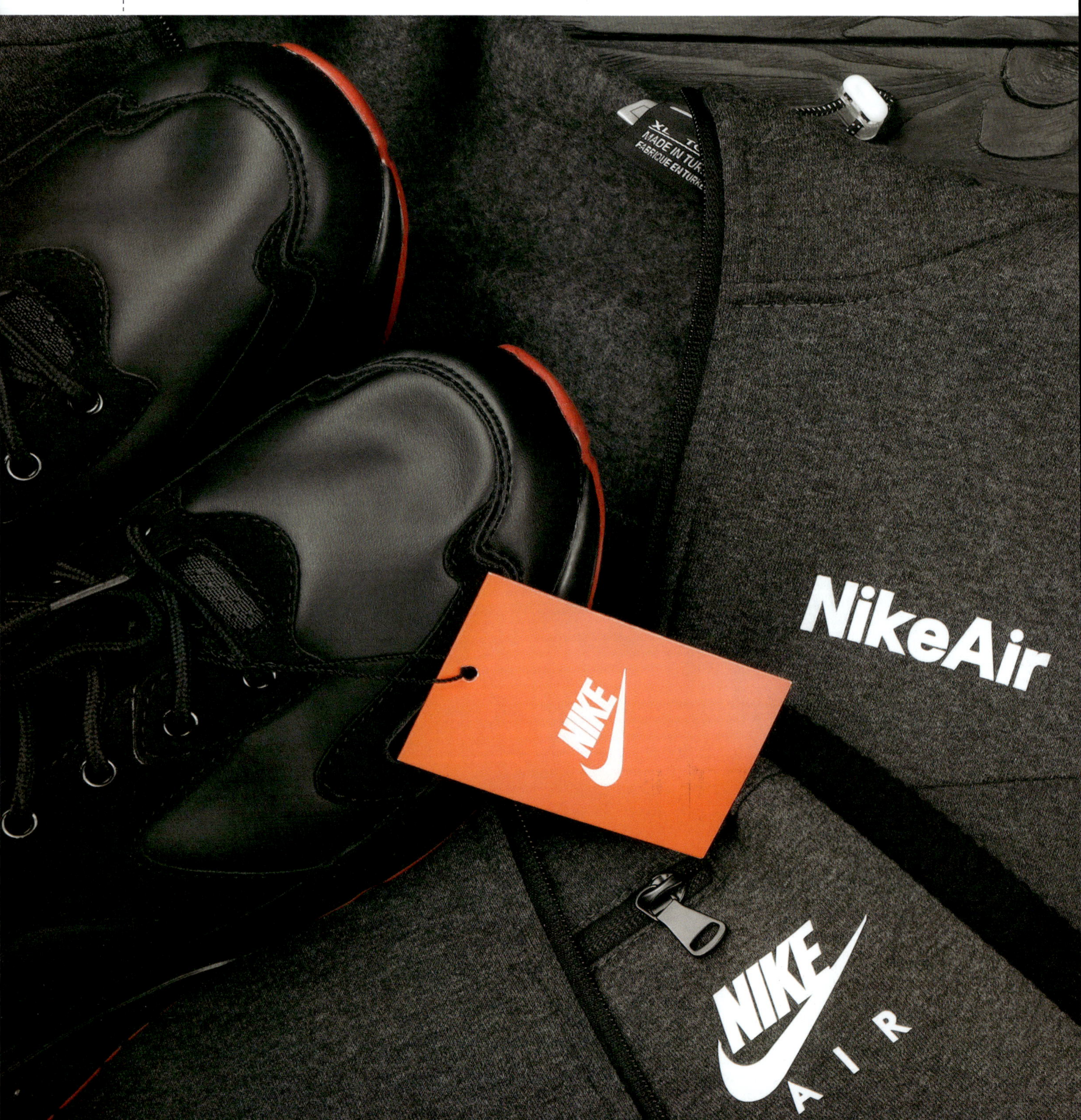
NikeAir
NIKE
NIKE
AIR

Nike's story is not just about shoes or sports, but about the guts to take an audacious idea and to turn it into something more. Nike's journey demonstrates that sustained success can only be achieved by embracing change—pushing boundaries, weathering controversies, and continually redefining what's possible.

Its legacy lies not simply in record sales or championship trophies, but in the millions of people it has empowered to DREAM BIGGER, MOVE FASTER, AND ALWAYS...

ABOVE: 'Just do it' sign in a Nike factory store
LEFT: Nike Air apparel

KEY MOMENTS IN NIKE'S HISTORY

1964

Phil Knight and **Bill Bowerman** establish **Blue Ribbon Sports** (BRS), initially distributing Japanese running shoes made by Onitsuka Tiger.

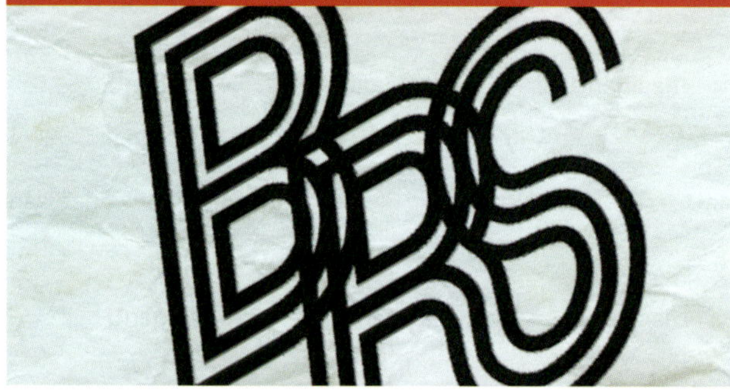

1971

Blue Ribbon Sports parts ways with Onitsuka Tiger and **officially rebrands as Nike, Inc.**

The iconic Swoosh logo, designed by Portland State University student Carolyn Davidson for $35, makes its debut.

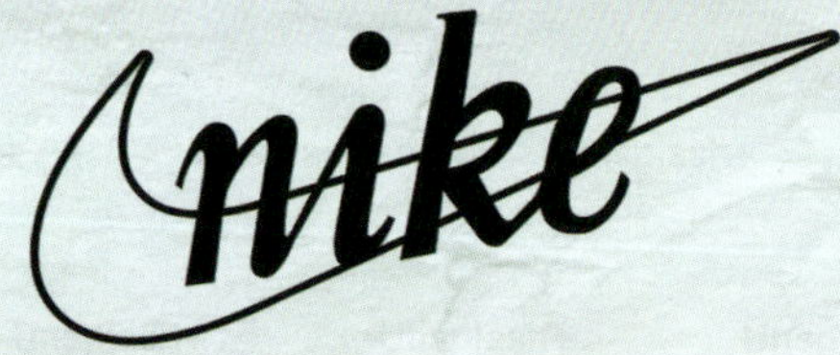

Bill Bowerman experiments with rubber in a waffle iron, creating the **Waffle Trainer's signature sole pattern.**

1972

Nike secures its **first athlete endorsement** deal with Romanian tennis star Ilie Năstase.

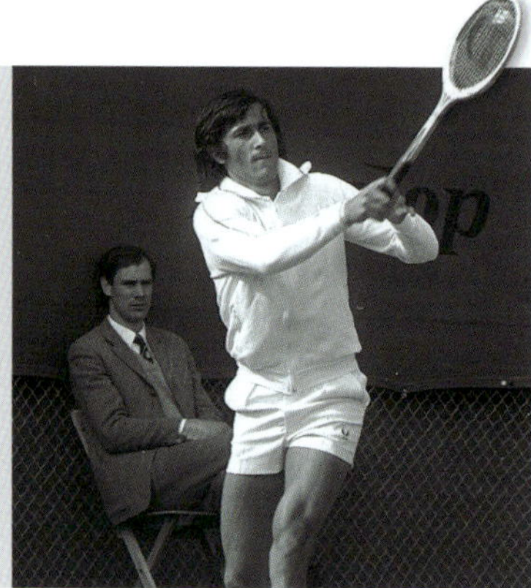

1979

Nike introduces its patented **"Air" cushioning technology** with the release of the Tailwind running shoes.

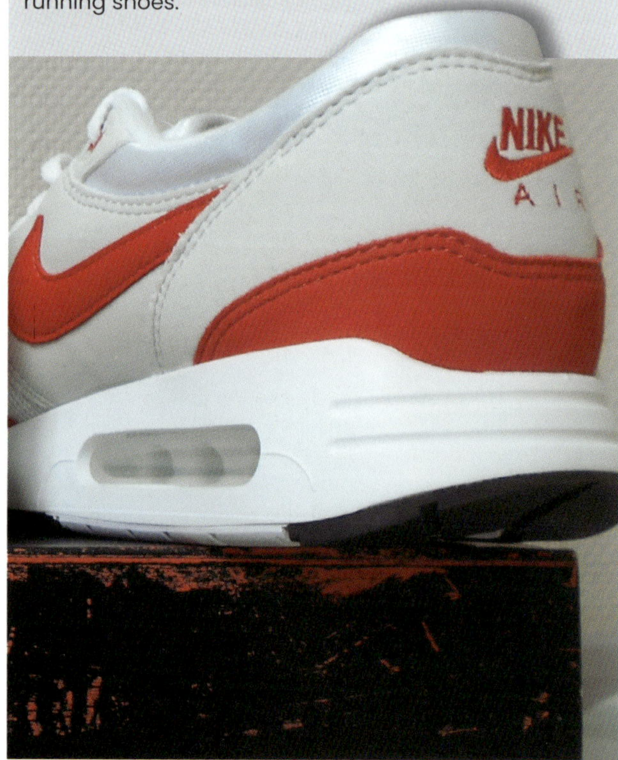

1980

Nike goes public, launching an IPO at 18 cents per share (adjusted for subsequent stock splits).

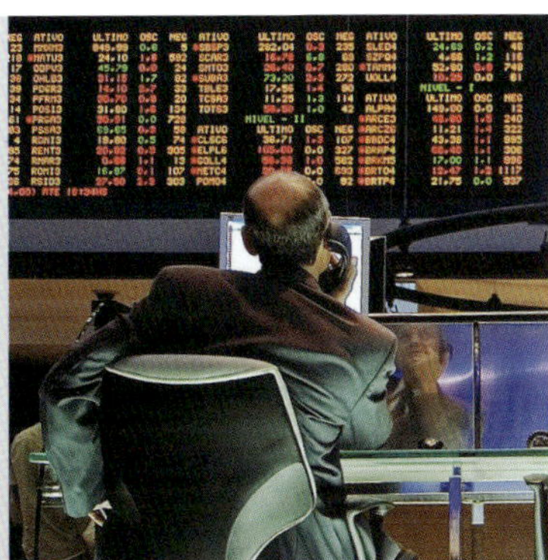

1984

Nike **signs basketball rookie Michael Jordan**, launching the **Air Jordan** series and reshaping sports marketing.

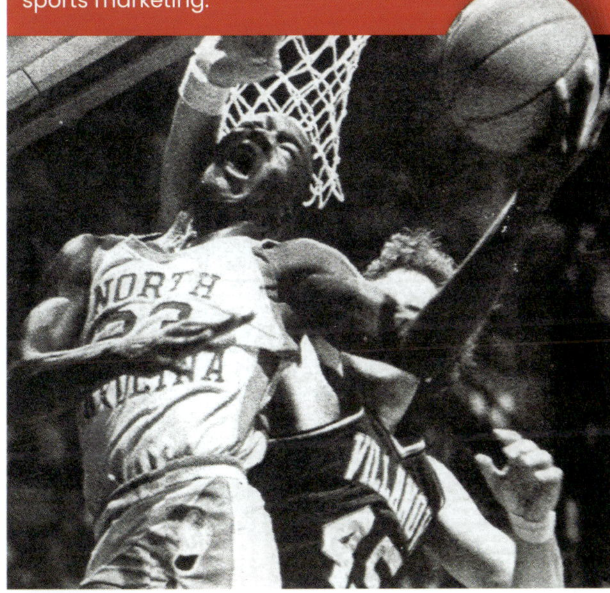

1987

Nike releases an **Air Max advertisement** featuring The Beatles' "Revolution," becoming the first ad to use the band's music.

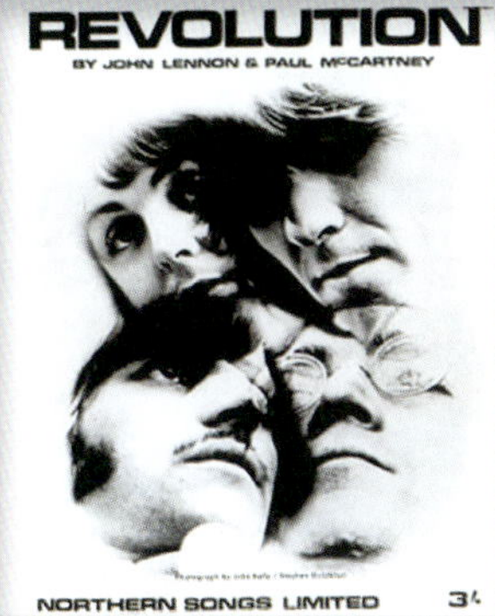

1988

The **"Just Do It" campaign launches**, kicking off with an ad featuring 80-year old runner Walt Stack crossing the Golden Gate Bridge.

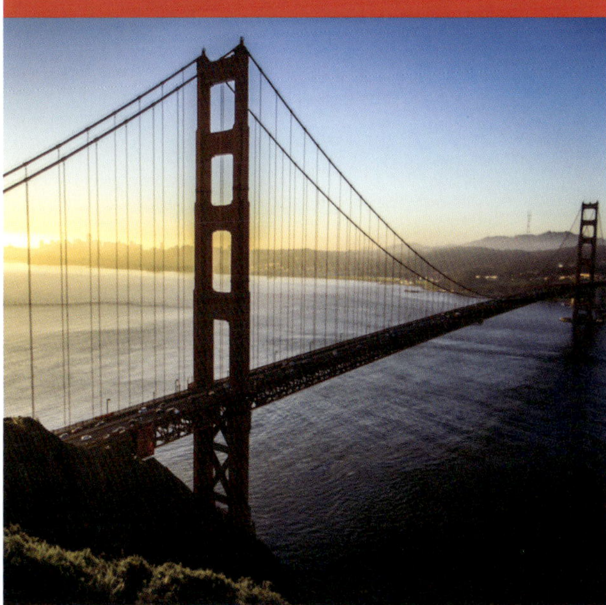

1990

Nike opens its first **Niketown retail store** in Portland, Oregon.

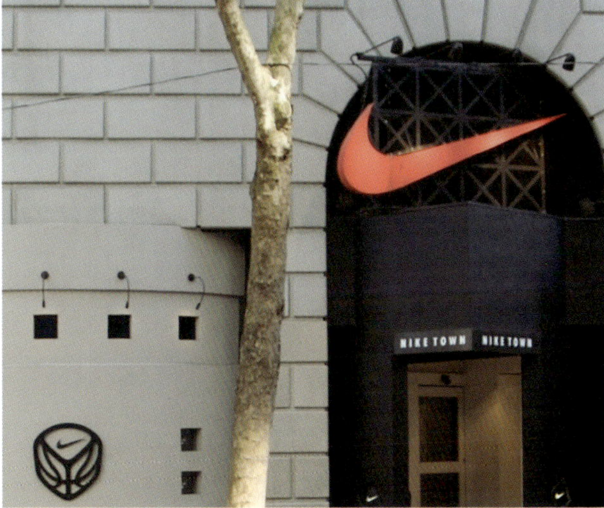

1991

Activist Jeff Ballinger's exposé on low wages and poor conditions in Indonesian Nike factories prompts Nike to issue its **first factory codes of conduct**.

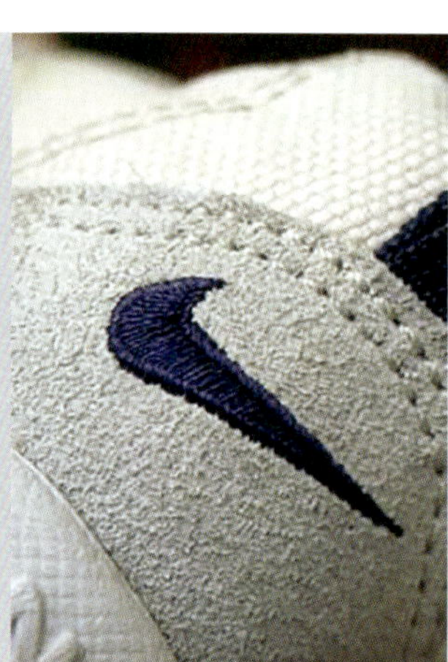

1996

Nike **signs golfer Tiger Woods**, further expanding its presence in high-profile professional sports.

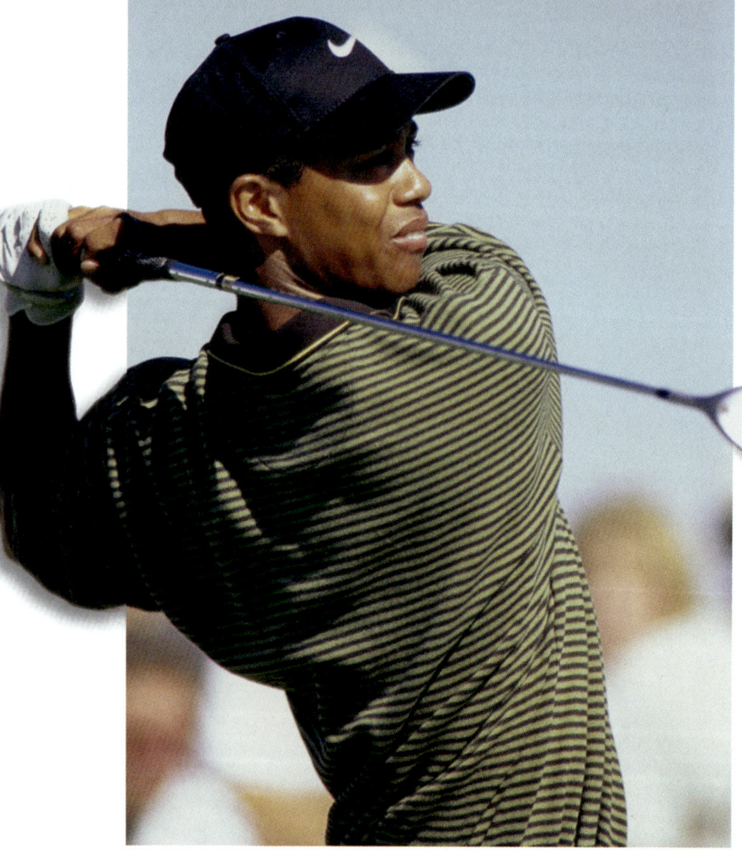

1998

Facing global criticism over labour practices, Nike **increases the minimum age of workers** in its factories, strengthens oversight, and adopts U.S. OSHA **clean-air standards** abroad.

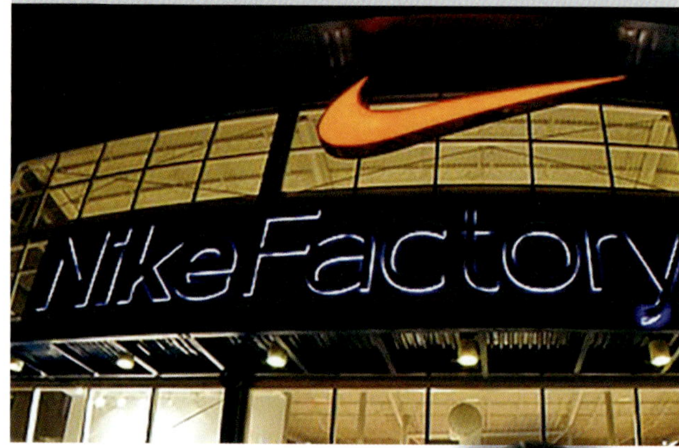

1999

Bill Bowerman, Nike's co-founder, **passes away** at age 88.

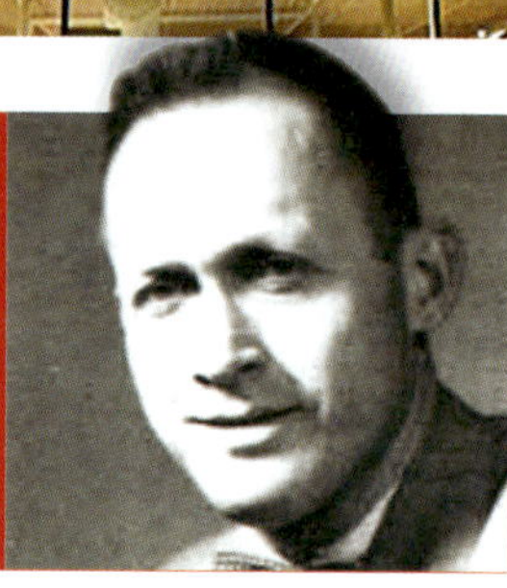

2002

Nike **acquires surf-apparel brand Hurley**, diversifying its portfolio.

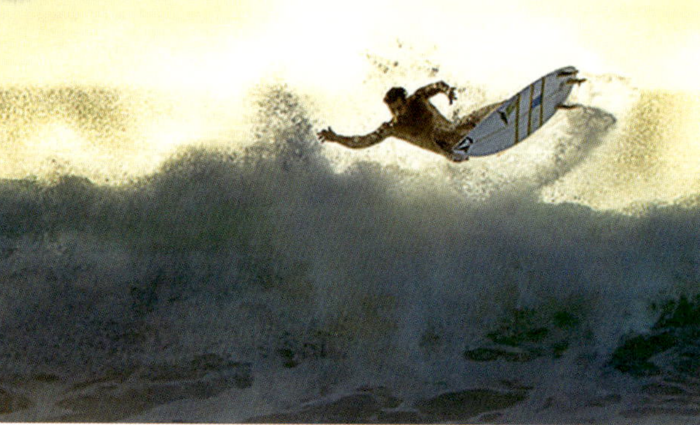

2003

Nike **signs basketball phenoms LeBron James and Kobe Bryant**, reinforcing its dominance in the NBA market.

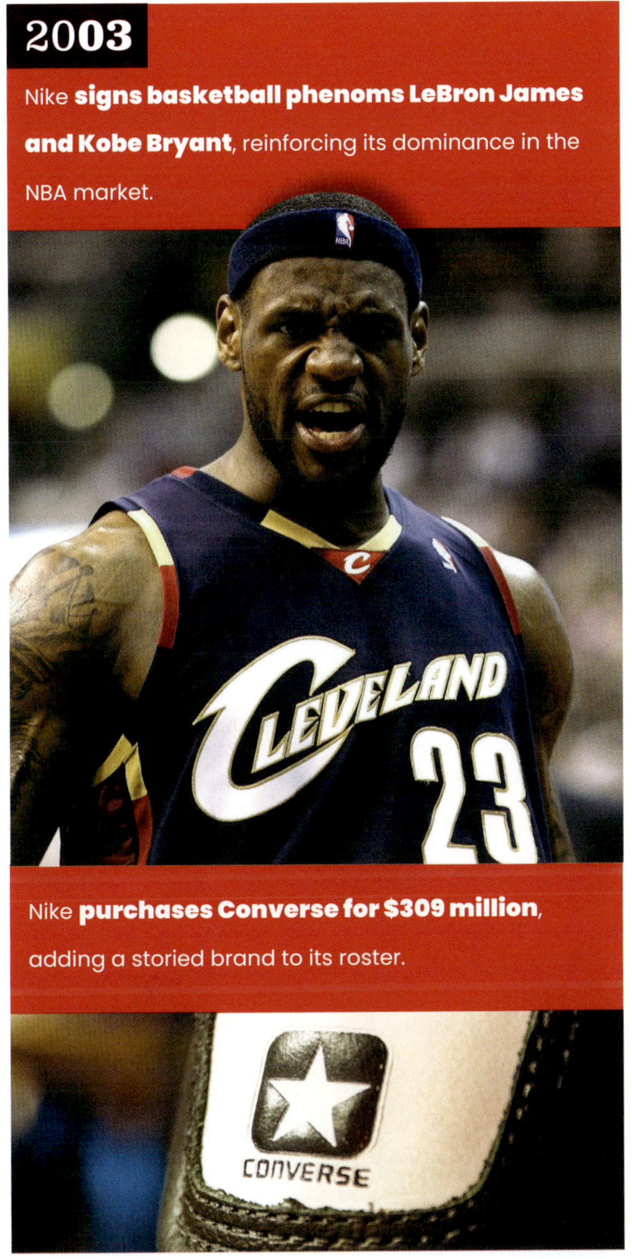

Nike **purchases Converse for $309 million**, adding a storied brand to its roster.

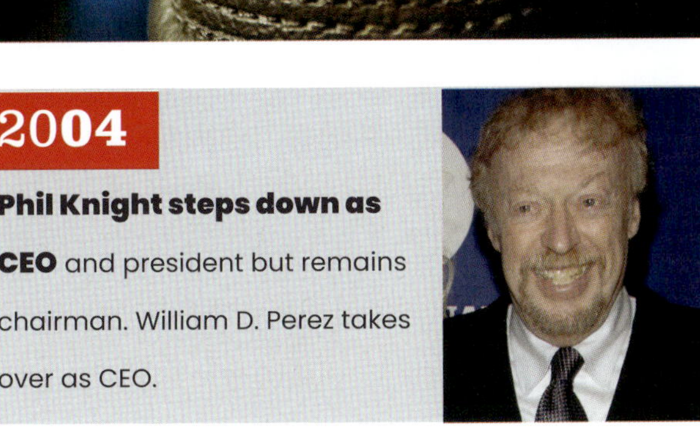

2004

Phil Knight steps down as CEO and president but remains chairman. William D. Perez takes over as CEO.

2008

Nike **signs baseball icon Derek Jeter**, expanding its stable of premier athletes.

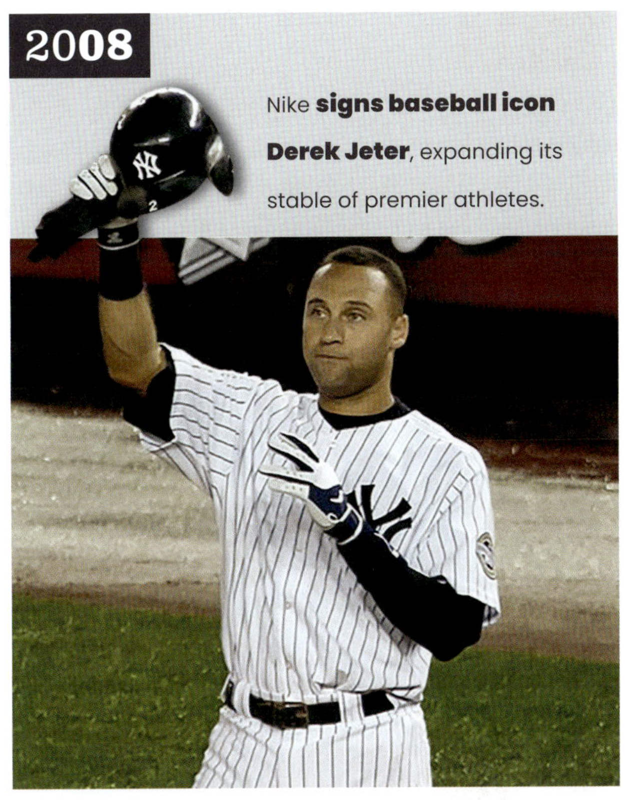

2012

Nike **becomes the official supplier of NFL apparel**, further cementing its position in American sports.

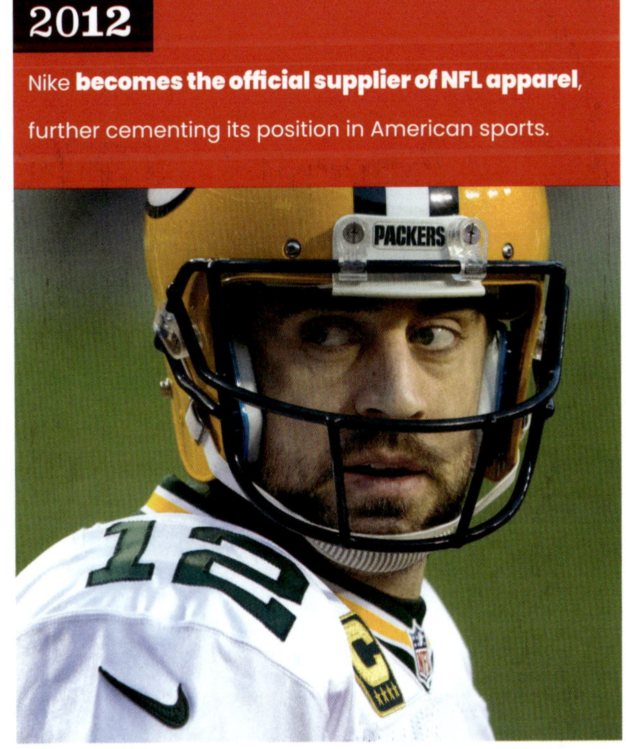

2015

Nike signs to become the **official supplier of NBA apparel**, outfitting the world's top basketball league from 2017.

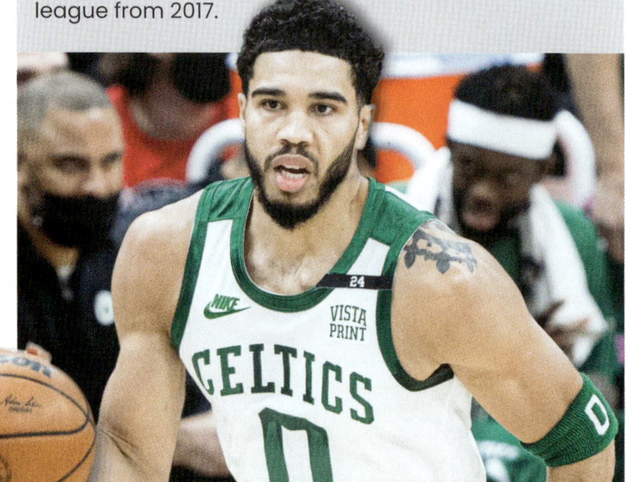

2018

A new **Nike ad campaign featuring Colin Kaepernick generates widespread debate**, blending sports, politics, and social justice.

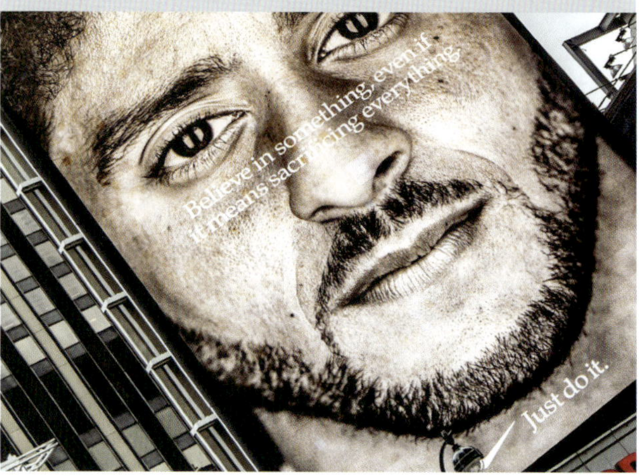

2017

Nike **launches its first plus-sized clothing line**, reflecting evolving consumer demands for inclusivity.

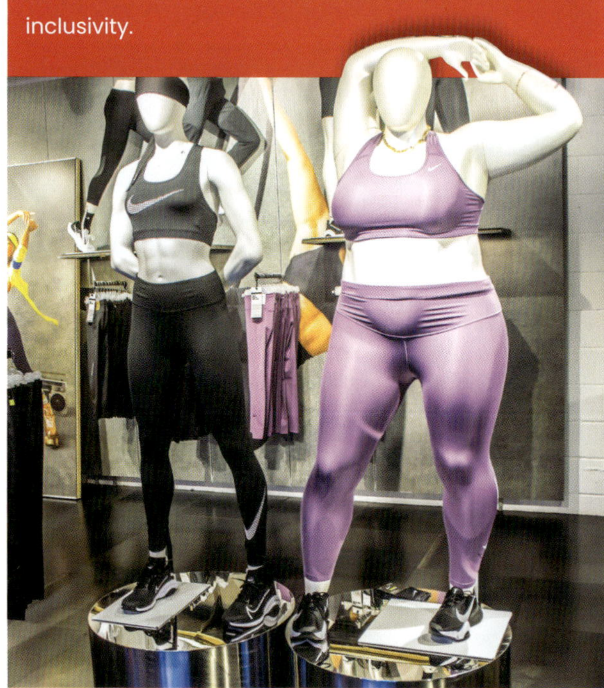

2019

Nike **pulls a planned sneaker featuring the 13-star Betsy Ross flag** after Colin Kaepernick raises concerns about its historical associations.

Nike announces it will **cease selling directly on Amazon**, refocusing on direct-to-consumer sales channels.

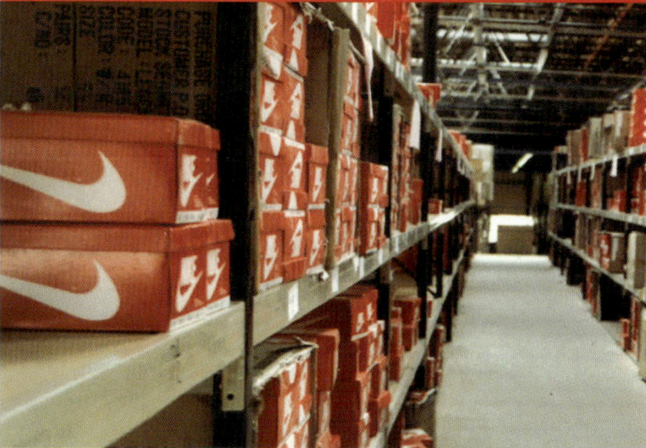

2020

Amid the COVID-19 pandemic, Nike reports a 5% drop in sales in China—its first decrease in six years—but sees a **surge in online sales to $5.5 billion**.

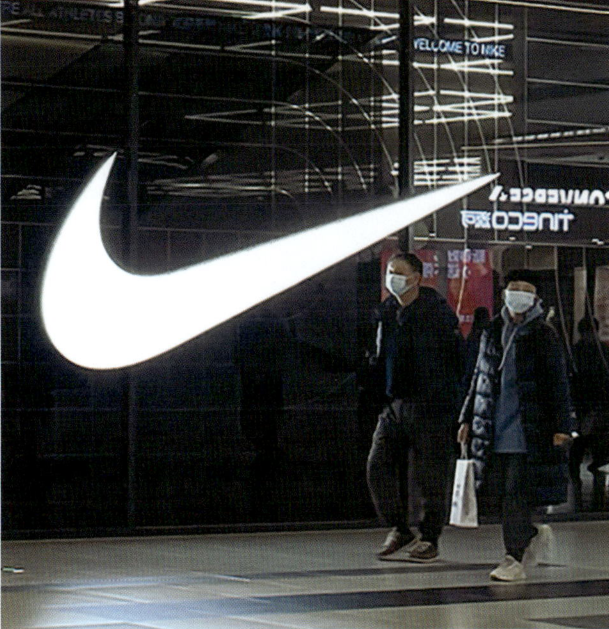

John Donahoe is appointed as CEO, guiding Nike through unprecedented global challenges.

2021

Nike **shares reach an all-time high** of $172.49 (November 5), propelled by successful direct-to-consumer strategies.

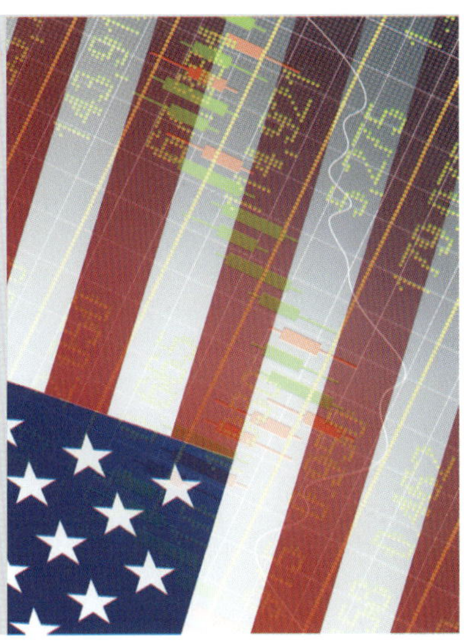

2024

Nike's **uniforms for female athletes at the Summer Olympics in Paris spark controversy**, criticized for being too revealing and highlighting ongoing issues of sexism in sports.

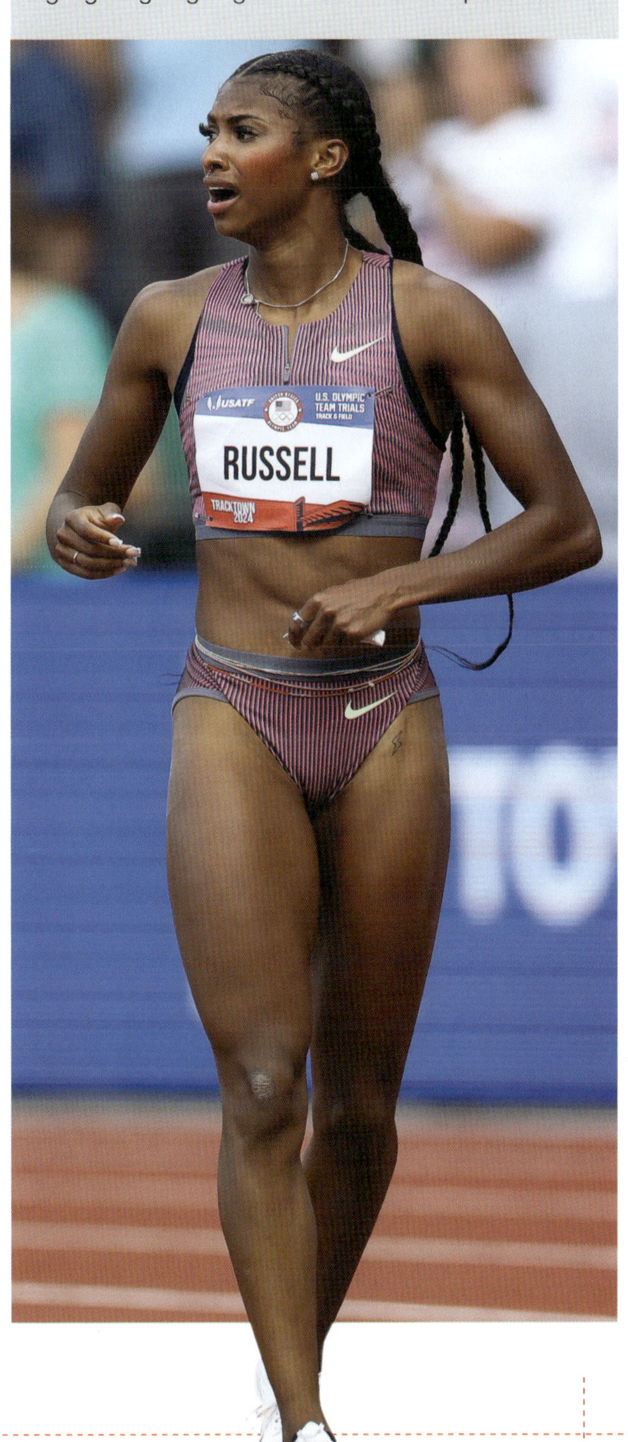

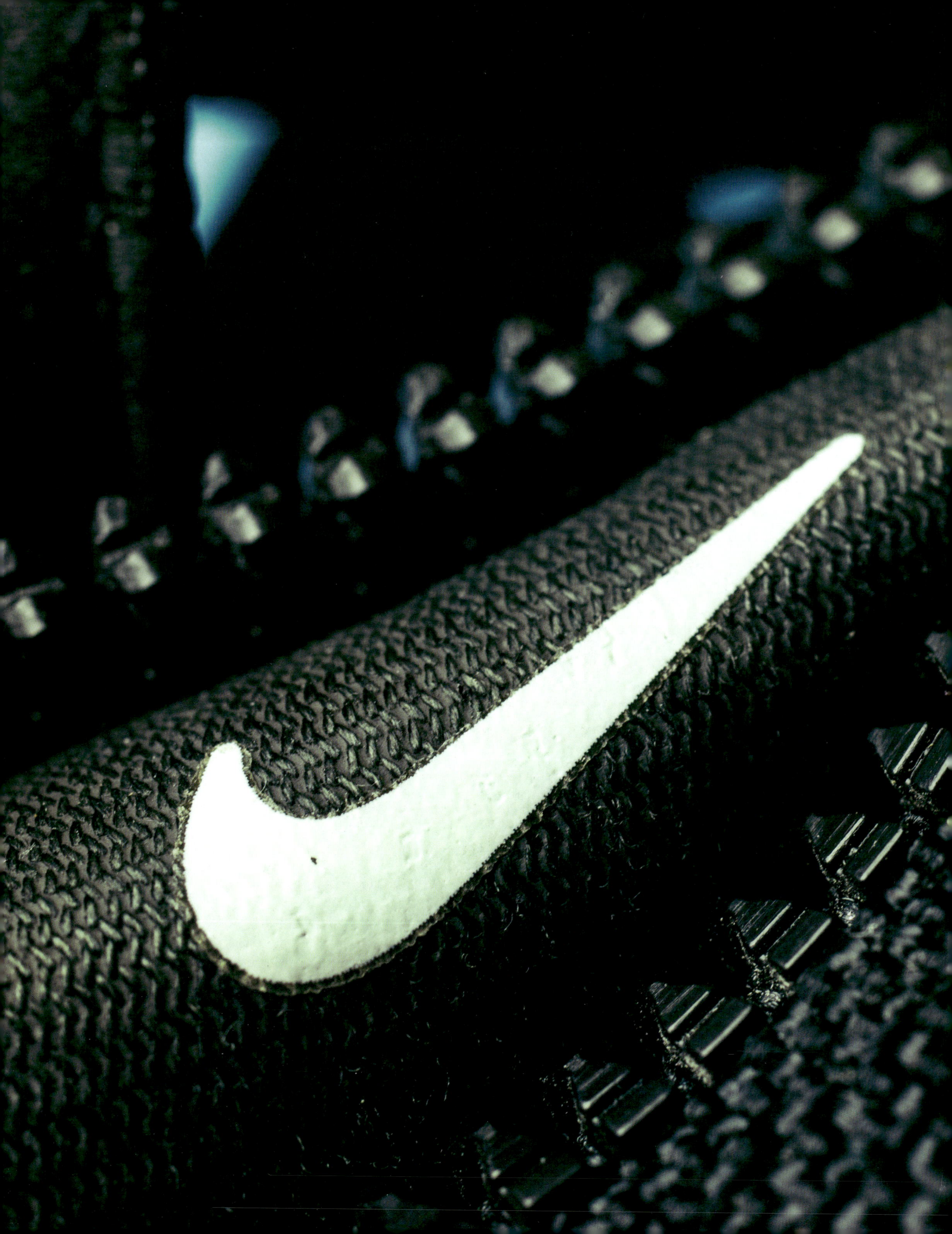